SOCIAL ISSUES, JUSTICE AND STATUS

MODELING SOCIAL BEHAVIOR AND ITS APPLICATIONS

SOCIAL ISSUES, JUSTICE AND STATUS

Additional books in this series can be found on Nova's website
under the Series tab.

Additional e-books in this series can be found on Nova's website
under the e-book tab.

SOCIAL ISSUES, JUSTICE AND STATUS

MODELING SOCIAL BEHAVIOR AND ITS APPLICATIONS

LUCAS A. JÓDAR SÁNCHEZ
ELENA DE LA POZA PLAZA
PALOMA MERELLO GIMÉNEZ
AND
LUIS ACEDO RODRÍGUEZ
EDITORS

nova
science publishers
New York

Library of Congress Cataloging-in-Publication Data

ISBN: 978-1-53613-666-1

Published by Nova Science Publishers, Inc. † New York

CONTENTS

PREFACE

In this book you will find a collection of human behaviour models combining two approaches the individual but also the social one in a multidisciplinary scenario including: sociology, public health, economics and finance, medicine, technology and engineering. Both approaches are linked throughout the social contagion because as humans, we imitate our peers in an attempt to socialize and integrate ourselves at organizations.

Topics contained in this book challenge the reader with sociological problems treated with quantitative analysis and techniques combined with empirical data.

The first chapters deal with applications to sociology and public health. In particular, L. Jódar et al., treat the happiness perception. E. de la Poza et al., study the propagation of bullying in Greece. Social inequality is considered by M. Staníčková et al. Female leadership is analysed by M. Caballer-Tarazona and C. Pardo-García while M. Molasy et al., models social behaviour in organizations. Finally F. Guijarro el al. proposes a ranking for Universities in Colombia.

Next chapters deal with economics and finance. So H.Ariza and E. de la Poza analyse country risk in Spain and Greece while C.Burgos et al., develop a method to determine speculative strategies based on spread derivatives. Implications of behavioural economics for monetary policy is treated by K. Dvoroková, M. Dolinová. The challenge of valuation of brands is studied by M. Alcaide González et al., while R. Selles et al. explores the business characteristics that affect their adoption of Twitter. In addition, C. Burgos et al., predict the number of users of e-commerce over the next few years. Also, F. Pardo et al. propose a capitalization model of leases operations. Finally, managing behaviour and accounting methodologies for the case of Italy is treated by M. A. Pérez et al.

Following in the book you will find two contributions in the medicine field, such as I. Barrachina and D. Vivas who analyse and interpret the present-day needs to train specialised doctors for a concrete area of Spain, and also J. Diaz-Carnicero et al., model the spatial variability of the type 2 diabetes mellitus medication and cost.

The books ends with three application to architecture, archaeology and engineering.

The Editorial team

In: Modeling Social Behavior and Its Applications   ISBN: 978-1-53613-666-1
Editors: L. A. Jódar Sánchez et al.   © 2018 Nova Science Publishers, Inc.

Chapter 1

MODELING PERCEIVED HAPPINESS WITH SOCIO-DEMOGRAPHIC AND ECONOMIC DIMENSIONS

Lucas A. Jódar Sánchez[1], Paloma Merello Giménez[2,]
and Elena de la Poza Plaza[3]*
[1]Instituto de Matemática Multidisciplinar,
Universitat Politècnica de València, Valencia, Spain
[2]Department of Accounting, Universitat de Valencia, Valencia, Spain
[3]Centro de Ingeniería Económica
Universitat Politècnica de València, Valencia, Spain

ABSTRACT

This chapter attempts to identify and quantify the drivers of happiness perceived by individuals, and measures the relevance that the socio-demographic condition of individuals has on the happiness they perceive. Multivariable statistics techniques are applied to propose three mathematical models that explain the happiness perceived by individuals according to their level of income (low, medium, high) with seven variables (personal character, economic income, leisure time, relationships, health, job, beliefs). Our results show that individuals seek to be happy and adapt to their circumstances by persuading themselves into the belief that they enjoy a satisfactory and happy life. Thus a low-income individual knows that achieving a successful, recognized and high-income job is difficult, so they convince themselves that their work does not condition their level of happiness, and confer it limited importance. These individuals find their happiness in other variables that are within their reach, such as relationships.

* Corresponding Author's address: Email: Paloma.merello@uv.es.

Keywords: happiness, multivariate regression analysis, income, health, religion, job, relationships

INTRODUCTION

The study of happiness and its quantification has been the object of numerous studies in recent years (Boorks, 2012; Pasricha, 2016). Understanding what satisfies individuals and how they improve their well-being status is relevant for the advertising campaigns of products and services, but also for policymakers to better orientate their actions and to understand citizenship. In fact previous studies have developed questionaires to meaure levels of happiness, such as the Oxford Happiness Questionnaire (Hills & Argyle, 2002).

It is important to remark that individuals' well-being depends on both internal and external factors. Internal factors, such as emotional stability, extroversion or any personality trait, affect individuals' perception of happiness (Goldsmith, 2016). Following this line of thought, Nikolaev and McGee, (2016) have shown how verbal intelligence has a strong effect on happiness; people with greater verbal proficiency than their peers are more likely to perceive a higher level of happiness. Their study was based on Christakis and Fowler (2009), who found that social networks play an important role in influencing people's thoughts, feelings, and also happiness. In the same vein, Lane concluded his study in 2017, and reporting that happiness results from pro-social behavior and that it negatively correlates with selfishness, but positively with trust.

External factors condition the happiness perceived by an individual; when analyzing the external factors that affect the perception of well-being, we think of climatological conditions; e.g., solar activity can be thought to be a predictor of happiness. However in his study, Kristoufek showed that solar activity does not positively correlate with individuals' happiness, (Kristoufek, 2018).

An external factor, such as culture, affects individuals' subjective well-being; that is, the perception of happiness is directly connected to our social context (Conzo et. al., 2016). In fact the socio-political, but also the economic, environment actually matter and directly impact both our well-being and our perception of happiness. Hence the study by Coupe and Obrizan (2016) quantified how the average level of happiness declined substantially in areas that directly experience war, with the drop in happiness being roughly comparable to the loss of happiness that a relatively well-off person would experience if they were to suddenly become poor.

These issues may lead one to expect that happiness is difficult to achieve, and even if it is achieved, it will not last long. Recently, fragility of happiness has been the object of analysis by Joshanloo (2018), who concluded that aversion to happiness could be based on insecure attachment and subjective well-being.

This study attempts to identify and quantify the drivers of the happiness perceived by individuals, and measures the relevance of the socio-demographic individual condition on the self-perception of happiness.

MATERIALS AND METHODS

Statistical Analyses

In this paper we apply exploratory statistical techniques, as well as a Factor Analysis, a Multiple Linear Regression (MLR), a Cluster Analysis, a Correspondence Analysis and a Chi-Square Test.

The purpose of the Factorial Analysis is to explain a set of observed variables with a small number of latent or unobserved variables. It is an interdependence technique in which all the variables are simultaneously considered. Each one relates to all the others so that factors are formed to maximize their explanation of the series of variables. The Principal Components Method is applied to identify the underlying dimensions.

From a set of explanatory variables, MLR identifies those that significantly influence the dependent variable. The starting hypothesis is that the dependent variable values have been generated by a linear combination of the values of one explanatory variable, or more, and a residual. Coefficients are chosen so that the difference between the sum of squares of the observed and predicted values (residual variance) is minimized. The Least Squares Estimation Method produces optimal estimators so that estimated parameters are centered and are of minimum variance if the linearity, homoscedasticity, independence and normality assumptions are satisfied by the data.

A Cluster Analysis in its non hierarchical modality (k-means method) is used by grouping objects based on the characteristics that they possess by maximizing the homogeneity of the objects within clusters, while maximizing the heterogeneity between aggregates at the same time (Hair et al., 1999). Ward's hierarchical method is applied as a confirmatory tool.

The Correspondence Analysis is an exploratory method whose objective is to summarize a large amount of data in a small number of dimensions. This analysis is implemented to analyse, from a graphical point of view, the dependency relations of a set of categorical variables from contingency table data. The qualitative character of the variables means that using a different distance to the Euclidean is necessary.

The Questionnaire

The individuals answered a questionnaire that contained socio-demographic information and an evaluation of the different happiness variables.

The socio-demographic variables considered in the questionnaire were: age, sex, marital status (single, in a relationship, divorced, married), Spanish Autonomous Community of residence, level of education (primary, secondary, higher education), level of education of parents (primary, secondary, higher education), family level of income (low, medium, high), employment status (full-time, part-time, self-employed, unemployed, student) and number of children.

From 0 to 100 points, where 100 points is the maximum value, individuals scored how relevant all the following variables meant for their perception of happiness: level of income, health, relationships (family, friendship, love relationship), leisure time, type of job, personality traits (optimism, dynamism, resilence), human values and/or religious beliefs.

Finally, individuals were asked to provide details of any variable/s that contributed to their level of perceived happiness, but was not included in the survey, and to then score it/them from 0 to 100.

Pearson's Correlation Analysis was performed for each pair of variables to identify their linear relation. Although all the pairs of variables significantly correlated, the highest Pearson correlation coefficient was 0.35. Therefore, it seemed reasonable to keep all the variables initially considered in the study, thus none was eliminated.

The Sample

The sample was collected in 2011 following a stratified procedure. In order to make the sample representative of the Spanish population, a random resampling of the original sample was performed by applying the sex and age proportions of the Spanish population in 2011 (INE: the Spanish Statistics Institute). The final sample comprised 475 Spanish individuals older than 17 years of age.

The individuals in the sample had 1.33 children on average.

The sample's socio-demographic characteristics are shown in Table 1.

An Exploratory Analysis of the happiness variables was performed. The descriptive statistics are shown in Table 2.

The variables "Health" and "Relationships" obtained the highest mean value and positive asymmetry. A study of the histograms of each variable reflected a strong asymmetry toward high values in the sample. This tendency extended to other factors, albeit less markedly.

No abnormal cases were identified to be removed from the sample.

Table 1. The descriptive statistics of the sample

	Frequency	Percentage %	Cummulated percentage %
Sex			
Man	248	52.2	52.2
Woman	227	47.8	100
Marital status			
Married	200	42.1	42.1
Divorced	38	8.0	50.1
In a relationship	92	19.4	69.5
Single	145	30.5	100.0
Studies			
Primary	71	14.9	14.9
Secondary	207	43.6	58.5
Tertiary	197	41.5	100.0
Level of Income			
Low	55	11.6	11.6
Medium	349	73.5	85.1
High	71	14.9	100.0

Source: The authors.

Table 2. Descriptive statistics of the happiness variables

	Mean	Standard deviation	Asymmetry	Curtosis
Level of Income	69.31	21.26	-0.792	0.461
Health	89.49	15.69	-2.258	5.915
Relationships	84.33	18.03	-1.654	2.890
Leisure time	70.82	21.82	-0.700	-0.002
Type of Job	71.88	22.53	-1.172	1.210
Character	78.67	19.23	-1.447	2.357
Beliefs	65.71	27.98	-0.761	-0.388

Source: The authors.

RESULTS

Dimensions of Happiness: Factorial Analysis

A Factorial Analysis was performed to determine if the questionnaire results indicated that a data structure underlay the seven considered variables.

The measure of KMO adequacy (Kaiser-Meyer-Olkin) was 0.703. Moreover in the Bartlett sphericity test, the null hypothesis (absence of a significant correlation between determinants of happiness) was rejected (p-value < 0.05). Therefore, both tested the adequancy of using a Factorial Analysis.

A solution with four components was selected, which explained 73.93% of data variability. Although the fourth component had an eighenvalue < 1, it was selected because it increased explained variance by 10%. As seen in Table 3, this last component encompassed information about the "Leisure Time" variable and seemed to have significant importance to the level of perceived happiness (mean = 70.82).

The results in Table 3 allowed us to provide a name and a brief description of each identified dimension.

Factor 1 could be named "Professional situation." It contained information about level of income and type of job. Factor 2 could be named the "Resilience" factor. It contained information on personal character and religious values. Factor 3 could be named the "Personal situation" Factor, and it contained health information and sentimental relationships. Factor 4 contained leisure time information.

Table 3. Matrix of the rotated components

	Component			
	1	2	3	4
Level of Income	0.784	-0.207	0.261	0.070
Health	0.235	0.007	0.838	0.047
Relationships	-0.059	0.388	0.706	0.090
Leisure time	0.169	0.074	0.096	0.966
Type of Job	0.763	0.324	-0.053	0.187
Character	0.343	0.640	0.254	-0.044
Beliefs	-0.109	0.835	0.078	0.115

Source: The authors.

All the variables were explained by the factors by more than 50% (commonality > 0.5). The worst represented were Relationships (0.66) and Personal character (0.594), and the best represented was Leisure time (0.977).

The Role of Socio-Economic Characteristics on
the Happiness Variables

The Multiple Regression (MLR) analyses were performed separately for each happiness variable (dependent variable) according to each socio-economic variable (independent variables), whose categories were included as dummy variables in the regression analysis.

The socio-economic variables categories that were significant, along with their coefficient, are shown for each happiness variable (Table 4).

Table 4. The MLR analysis results: significant independent variables

Dependent variable	Independent variable	B	Statistical t	p-value
Level of Income				
	Medium	8.68	2.865	0.004
	High	16.35	4.36	0.000
Health				
	Age > 60	-10.57	-2.75	0.006
	Medium income	6.759	3.00	0.003
Type of Job				
	Unemployed	-7.23	-2.69	0.007
	Medium income	6.67	2.041	0.042
	High income	12.94	3.198	0.001
Relationships				
	Divorced	-6.78	-2.15	0.032
	Single	-6.25	-2.99	0.003
	Medium income	6.45	2.47	0.014
Leisure time				
	Age 45-49	-13.05	-3.595	0.000
	Age 50-54	-7.939	-2.14	0.032
	Age 55-59	-11.28	-2.341	0.020
	Age >60	-12.17	-2.089	0.037
Beliefs				
	Age>60	14.57	2.100	0.036
	Single	-10.85	-3.59	0.000
Personal character				
	Medium income	6.45	2.32	0.021
	High income	7.347	2.135	0.033

Source: the authors.

Next the data in Table 4 were interpreted. Aged more than 60 and medium level of income were significant for the "Health" happiness variable. Therefore, those individuals aged over 60 years old attached an average importance of 10.57 points less to that variable as a contibutor to their happiness than the other age group did. People with a medium level of income gave an average of 6.76 points for more importance to health than the people with the other levels of income did.

In Table 4 we can see that the socio-demographic variable that best discriminated the relative importance of the happiness variables was Level of Income because it was significant for five of the seven happiness variables. Age was the second most significant demographic variable (for three of the seven happiness variables).

Note that the higher the level of income, the higher the value that individuals gave to type of job. Students were more concerned than average about type of job (more important for their perceived happiness), while the unemployed were much less concerned than average. The elderly or those about to retire were less concerned about type of job.

Young people (20-35 years) attached more importance to leisure time. Older people (> 60 years) attached much more importance to religious beliefs and values for their happiness.

Note that the interest of these analyses did not lie in finding the optimal estimation of the parameters, but to identify their significance so that the strict satisfaction of the linearity, homoscedasticity, independence and normality hypotheses of the data was not required.

Defining Profiles of Individuals According to Their Perceived Happiness: A Cluster Analysis

A Cluster Analysis was performed by considering the happiness variables. We chose a solution with three groups because we were interested in relating these profiles to the demographic variable Level of Income. Cluster 1 had 300 members (63.16%), Cluster 2 had 77 (16.21%) and Cluster 3 had 98 (20.63%).

A Chi-square Test was performed as proof of independence, and consisted in checking if two qualitative characteristics (level of income and the happiness cluster) were related to one another. This test verified two hypotheses, a null hypothesis of independence of the variables (H0) and an alternative hypothesis of the association of the variables (H1).

The test resulted in a Pearson Chi-square value of 14,310, with 4 degrees of freedom and an asymptotic bilateral significance (p-value) of 0.006. The results were significant (p-value < 0.05), so there was enough evidence to reject H0 and to confirm the association between the Happiness Profile and Level of Income variables.

A perceptual map was devised (Figure 1) with a Correspondence Analysis, which allowed us to observe the relationship between both categorical variables.

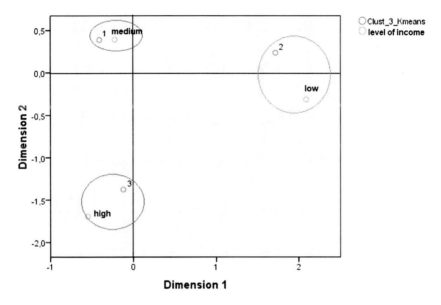

Figure 1. Perceptual map.

Each cluster can be associated with a level of income as follows: Cluster 1 to a medium level of income, Cluster 2 to a low level of income and Cluster 3 to a high level of income.

Table 5. Cluster Analysis centroids

	Medium level of income (C1)	Low level of income (C2)	High level of income (C3)
Personal character	86.2833	65.2597	65.9388
Level ofIncome	73.0067	45.5325	76.7041
Leisure time	76.3767	53.6234	67.3469
Relationships	91.3167	73.2987	71.6429
Health	94.1433	69.4416	91.0204
Type of Job	79.7267	43.8571	69.8878
Beliefs	77.5067	63.4935	31.3367

Source: The Authors.

The Cluster Analysis centroids (Table 5) show the absolute weight of the happiness variables for each profile (cluster).

The individuals in Cluster 1 (Medium Level of Income) gave a higher average score for all the items. They attached special importance to relationships and health, and also more importance to personal character and beliefs.

The individuals in Cluster 2 (Low Level of Income) attached the least importance to their level of income and type of job. What they valued the most were relationships, but they attributed a lower average score than the medium-income individuals.

The individuals of Cluster 3 (High Level of Income) attached the most importance to level of income and health. Note the slight importance they attached to beliefs for their perceived happiness.

Modeling Happiness by Levels of Income

By considering the proven relationship of the importance of each happiness variable depending on an individual's level of income level, we propose three mathematical models of happiness, one per level of income.

Thus the centroid of each cluster was taken as an estimator of the average importance of the happiness variables for each level of income. The equation parameters represent the relative importance of each happiness variable and are calculated as the original score of each variable (centroid) divided by the total sum of the centroids. The proposed model of happiness is presented as follows:

$$H = \alpha_1 \text{ character} + \alpha_2 \text{ income} + \alpha_3 \text{ leisure} + \alpha_4 \text{ relationships} + \alpha_5 \text{ health} + \alpha_6 \text{ job} + \alpha_7 \text{ beliefs} \tag{1}$$

where the value of each parameter depends on the level of income (Table 6), and each individual scored their level of satisfaction from 1 to 10 according to their current situation in each happiness variable. The result (H) would be the level of subjective happiness (from 1 to 10) of an individual according to his/her personal scale.

Table 6 shows that individuals' happiness is provided by those variables that they perceive to have within their reach. Individuals seek being happy and adapt to their circumstances by convincing themselves that their level of happiness is satisfactory.

A low-income individual knows that having a successful, recognized and high-income job is difficult to achieve. So they choose to consider that type of job is not going to condition their happiness and they attach very little importance to it. These individuals find their happiness in other variables that are within their reach, such as relationships.

High-income individuals attach more relative importance to health (they can invest more money in it with care, practicing sports, etc.) and to level of income than medium- and low-income individuals.

Table 6. Parameter values of the happiness models
by level of income

	Low income (C2)	Medium income (C1)	High income (C3)
Personal character (α_1)	0.16	0.15	0.14
Level of income (α_2)	0.11	0.13	0.16
Leisure time (α_3)	0.13	0.13	0.14
Relationships (α_4)	0.18	0.16	0.15
Health (α_5)	0.17	0.16	0.19
Type of Job (α_6)	0.11	0.14	0.15
Beliefs (α_7)	0.15	0.13	0.07
TOTAL	1	1	1

Source: the Authors.

Note that the parameters in Table 6 were calculated in such a way that the result of H would lie between 0 and 10 by weighting the original scores of each variable. However, the total sum of the original weights substantially differed among levels of income (414.5, 578.36 and 473.87 for low, medium and high, respectively).

We found that medium-income people were more optimistic because their total weight was 578, unlike 414 or 473. They valued on average 23 points more per variable than low-income individuals and 15 points more than high-income individuals.

Therefore, the reflection that arose was whether the result of the happiness model being comparable for two people with a different level of income level would be comparable. Note that we are talking about the stable, but subjective and personal "perception" of how happy an individual is, which can substantially differ from how happy someone else thinks that this individual should be in his/her current situation.

CONCLUSION

This study attempts to identify and quantify the drivers of the happiness perceived by individuals, and measures the relevance of their socio-demographic individual condition according to their perceived happiness. For this purpose, a questionnaire was passed to individuals to ask them to score from 0 to 100 to what degree seven determined variables contributed to their perceived happiness. Then a factorial analysis was performed and obtained four factors to group the seven happiness variables, which explained 73.93% of data variability. Clustering individuals according to their level of income allowed us to note differences among happiness perceptions; low-income individuals (Cluster 2) poorly valued their level of economic and type of job as contributors to their perceived happiness. Thus their perception of happiness was independent of both variables, while happiness was promoted by their relationships.

In contrast, high-income individuals (Cluster 3) considered their health and level of incometo be the key drivers of their happiness, while they considered beliefs/religion values to be the least important ones.

Finally, three mathetical models were proposed, one per level of income. Our results seem to indicate that people seek happiness in their living context. When setting objectives, they prefer to be rational by setting reachable ones. This means that, to a greater extent they tend to value those aspects of their lifes in which they perceive they have strength. Finally, our results are not conclusive, but suggest that individuals have a predisposition to be happy.

REFERENCES

Brooks, D. (2012). *The Social Animal*. Short Books, London, United Kingdom.

Christakis, N. A., & Fowler, J. H. (2009). Connected: *The surprising power of our social net- works and how they shape our lives*. Little, Brown.

Conzo, P., Aassve, A., Fuochi, G., Mencarini, L. (2016). The cultural foundations of happiness. *Journal of Economic Psychology* 62 (2017) 268–283.

Coupe, T., Obrizan, M. (2016). The impact of war on happiness: The case of Ukraine. *Journal of Economic Behavior & Organization* 132 (2016) 228–242.

Goldsmith, R. E., Flynn, L. R., Clark, R. A., 2011. Materialism and brand engagement as shopping motivations. *Journal of Retailing and Consumer Services* 31 (2016) 52–61.

Hills, P., & Argyle, M. (2002). The Oxford happiness questionnaire: a compact scale for the measurement of psychological well-being. *Personality and Individual Differences*, 33: 1073-1082.

Joshanloo, M. (2018). Fear and fragility of happiness as mediators of the relationship between insecure attachment and subjective well-being. *Personality and Individual Differences* 123 (2018) 115–118.

Kristoufek, L., (2018). Does solar activity affect human happiness? *Physica A* 493 (2018) 47–53.

Lane, T. (2017). How does happiness relate to economic behaviour? A review of the literature. *Journal of Behavioral and Experimental Economics* 68 (2017) 62–78.

Nikolaev, B., McGee, J. J. Relative verbal intelligence and happiness. *Intelligence* 59 (2016) 1–7.

Pasricha, N. (2016). *The Happiness Equation: want nothing + do anything = have everything*. Putnam's Sons, New York, United States.

Spanish Institute of Statistics, (2018). www.ine.es.

In: Modeling Social Behavior and Its Applications   ISBN: 978-1-53613-666-1
Editors: L. A. Jódar Sánchez et al.   © 2018 Nova Science Publishers, Inc.

Chapter 2

MODELING BULLYING PROPAGATION IN GREECE

Elena de la Poza Plaza[1,], Lucas A. Jódar Sánchez[2]*
and Konstantina Marga[2]
[1]Centro de Ingeniería Económica
[2]Instituto de Matemática Multidisciplinar,
Universitat Politècnica de València, Valencia, Spain

ABSTRACT

Bullying can be defined as an unwanted, aggressive behavior among school aged children that involves a real or perceived power imbalance. The behavior is repeated, or has the potential to be repeated, over time. Both kids who is bullied and who bullies others may have serious, lasting problems. The aim of this chapter is to forecast and quantify the propagation of bullying in the Greek school population aged [12, 18] during the period July 2015- January 2020. Finally, the results obtained are compared with the situation in Spain.

Keywords: bullying, Greece, propagation, forecast, victim, aggressor, outsider, defender

INTRODUCTION

Bullying is a social phenomenon in a universal range. A large number of studies conducted in different countries indicate that bullying at school occurs all over the world

* Corresponding Author address: Email: elpopla@esp.upv.es.

and is not confined to any geographical region, socioeconomic or cultural group. The involvement in bullying and victimization can affect on children concerning their psychology, behavior, emotions, academic career, and social consequences, as well as their mental and physical healh, [1].

Literature shows scarce researchers trying to analyze this phenomenon in Greece. According to a recent research about bullying behavior in Greek schools [2], approximately one in five students is involved in incidents related to bullying at least once a month. The percentage decreases to four students in one hundred, referring to a weekly basis of involvement.

Moreover, it has been observed a strong cross-sectional association between frequent victimization and suicidal ideation in late adolescence [3]. Victims of bullying behavior, especially those who where bullied on a weekly basis, were apt to express suicidal ideation. On the other hand, the perpetrators were not as much sensitive to express similar behavior as the aforementioned team.

A recent research in 2016 [4] provides a quantitative and qualitive aspect on bullying propagation in Greek schools, taking into consideration the family's socioeconomic situation, the reason of the victimization, the gender of the participants, and their feelings and reactions on these occasions. Also, the reaction of the teachers is necessary because the students come to them for mentioning bullying behaviors and policies to deal with this phenomenon. According to the results obtained, approximately one in three students has become a victim and, likewise, a perparator during the years of education. As far as the gender, males participate more often in bullying in comparison with females. Moreover, only two in ten students choose to express their feelings and mention possible events to their teachers. On the contrary, they prefer to talk to their parents, friends or not at all. Finally, but importantly, the results show that the main reason for victimization is the ancestry of the victim. This fact is highly important if someone considers the present situation of the country (financial-economic crisis; inmigration from Middle East countries; Greek emigration; etc.).

This chapter focuses on applying a population dynamics model [5] to forecast the propagation of bullying in a Greek school population aged (12, 18) over the period from July 2015 to January 2020, by taking into account qualitative and quantitative factors. Additionally, one of the main aims of this chapter is to provide a comparison between the number of victims in Greek schools and the number of victims in Spanish schools over the same period of study following [5]. Following [5], we replicate the same model for the particular case of Greece. Thus, we present the study population; then, the transition coefficients are modelled and the mathematical model applied is shown. Afterwards, results are presented and a sensitivity analysis is performed. To conclude the study, the bullying propagation in Greece is compared with the situation in Spain and conclusions are detailed.

STUDY POPULATION

The target study (S) population embraces all Greek schoolchildren whose ages fall within the interval (12, 18) during the study period, which went from July 2015 to January 2020.

The first hypothesis of the model construction consists in splitting the population into five categories, as in [5-7], and by paying attention to the active, passive or neutral role adopted by students in the event of bullying:

- Victims (V)
- Defenders (D)
- Outsiders (O)
- Cooperators (C)
- Aggressors (A)

The study period from July 2015 to July 2020 was split into semesters, where n = 0 is the initial study time and corresponds to July 2015.

The vector of subpopulations (1) represents the amounts of subpopulations after n semesters.

$$X(n) = [V(n), D(n), O(n), C(n), A(n)]^T \qquad (1)$$

Then the study population (S) quantifies the total of subpopulations at the beginning of our study period (July 2015).

Thus S(0) = 723,404 is the population aged (12,18) in July 2015 in Greece, [8]. Next, we obtained the initial subpopulations in July 2015 by collecting and managing data from [4]. Below we provide the numbers of scholars and the percentage that each subpopulation represents:

- V(0) = 261,149, victims represent 36.1% of S(0)
- D(0) = 44,489, defenders represent 6.15% of S(0)
- O(0) = 116,034, outsiders represent 16.04% of S(0)
- C(0) = 67,494, cooperators represent 9.33% of S(0)
- A(0) = 234,238, aggressors represent 32.38% of S(0)

Following [5] both V(n) and A(n) are cumulative categories that grow continuously during the study period because the condition of being a victim or aggressor remained with time. This implies that those who became victims in the first semester (July 2015) would still be considered victims in July 2020, V(10).

MODELING TRANSITION COEFFICIENTS

In this section we explain very briefly the trasit coefficients. Since this study is an application of the model proposed by [5].

Thus, we assumed that the net balance of the demographic change was equally distributed according to the initial proportions of each subpopulation at the initial time, n = 0, which corresponded to July 2015. We denote the demographic net balance by the notation*. This coefficient was assumed constant for the study period.

We denoted the vector of the net demographic balance by:

$$P^* = [V^*, D^*, O^*, C^*, A^*]^T \tag{2}$$

The net demographic balance provides an amont of incomers, expressed as follows following [5]:

$$P^* = \begin{bmatrix} V^* \\ D^* \\ O^* \\ C^* \\ A^* \end{bmatrix} = \frac{(Z-H)}{2} \cdot r = \frac{(Z-H)}{2} \cdot \begin{bmatrix} 0.361 \\ 0.0615 \\ 0.1604 \\ 0.0933 \\ 0.3238 \end{bmatrix} \tag{3}$$

where Z=107,661 represents the new incomers into the system; H=115,074 is the sum of those who left the system as they had reached the age of 19, along with the annual rate of mortality and the net migration amount, [8].

Then r is the vector that contains the original proportion of each subpopulation.

Following [5], the coefficients $\beta(DV)$, $\beta(OV)$, $\beta(OD)$, $\beta(CO)$, $\alpha(DO)$ were assumed constant for the study period. (see Table 2).

On the contrary, the coefficients $\alpha_n(OC)$ and $\alpha_n(CA)$ are depending on the rate of unemployment in Greece, so they were computed as follows:

$$\alpha_n (OC) = 0.06 - \frac{1}{2} \cdot 0.01 \cdot dn$$
$$\alpha_n (CA) = 0.05 - \frac{1}{2} \cdot 0.01 \cdot dn \tag{4}$$

where dn is the employ recovery rate per semester.

Table 1. The Greek unemployment rates for the period 2016-2020

Year	Unemployment rate (%)
01/2016	24.3
07/2016	23.3
01/2017	23.2
07/2017	22.2
01/2018	21.7
07/2018	21.3
01/2019	20.9
07/2019	20.5
01/2020	20.1
07/2020	19.8

Source: OECD, Hellenic Statistical Authority and tradingeconomics.com.

Mathematical Model and Simulations

The mathematical formulation of the model is as expressed as follows according to [5]:

$$V(n+1) = V(n) + \beta(DV) \cdot D(n) + \beta(OV) \cdot O(n) + V^*$$
$$D(n+1) = \beta(OD) \cdot O(n) + (1 - \beta(DV) - \alpha(DO)) \cdot D(n) + D^*$$
$$O(n+1) = \alpha(DO) \cdot D(n) + \beta(CO) \cdot C(n) + (1 - \beta(OV) - \beta(OD) -$$
$$\alpha n(OC)) \cdot O(n) + O^*$$
$$C(n+1) = \alpha n(OC) \cdot O(n) + (1 - \beta(CO) - \alpha n(CA)) \cdot C(n) + C^*$$
$$A(n+1) = A(n) + \alpha n(CA) \cdot C(n) + A^* \tag{5}$$

Then by computing the difference system of model equations and subpopulations $V(n)$, $D(n)$, $O(n)$, $C(n)$ and $A(n)$ for each semester, we forecasted the subpopulations expected at the end of semester n and, in particular, at the end of the study period (July 2020).

RESULTS

In this section we firstly show each subpopulation size according to the assumed hypotheses (see Table 4), along with the relative proportion of each subpopulation at the initial time, $n = 0$ and $n = 10$ (see Table 3).

As the category of victims and aggressors was cumulative, we considered interesting to estimate the semester variation of both categories (see Table 5). The increase in victims was higher than 1% per semester. This observation indicated that measures should be implemented to break this pattern.

Table 2. The transition coefficients of the subpopulations

	$\beta(DV)$	$\beta(OV)$	$\beta(OD)$	$\beta(CO)$	$\alpha(DO)$	$\alpha_n(OC)$	$\alpha_n(CA)$
Jan 2016	0.06	0.02	0.08	0.125	0.2	0.0565	0.0465
July 2016	0.06	0.02	0.08	0.125	0.2	0.055	0.045
Jan 2017	0.06	0.02	0.08	0.125	0.2	0.0595	0.0495
July 2017	0.06	0.02	0.08	0.125	0.2	0.055	0.045
Jan 2018	0.06	0.02	0.08	0.125	0.2	0.0575	0.0475
July 2018	0.06	0.02	0.08	0.125	0.2	0.058	0.048
Jan 2019	0.06	0.02	0.08	0.125	0.2	0.058	0.048
July 2019	0.06	0.02	0.08	0.125	0.2	0.058	0.048
Jan 2020	0.06	0.02	0.08	0.125	0.2	0.058	0.048
July 2020	0.06	0.02	0.08	0.125	0.2	0.0585	0.0485

Source: Own performance.

Table 3. Subpopulations expressed as percentage

	V (%)	D (%)	O (%)	C (%)	A (%)
July 2015 (n = 0)	36.1%	6.15%	16.04%	9.33%	32.38%
July 2020 (n = 10)	42.33%	4.29%	12.2%	5.30%	35.83%

Source: Own performance.

Table 4. The forecasted subpopulations per semester

	V	D	O	C	A
July 2015	261,149	44,489	116,034	67,494	234,238
Jan 2016	264,801	41,977	114,615	62,129	236,176
July 2016	268,274	40,004	112,416	57,525	237,772
Jan 2017	271,584	38,368	109,083	53,829	239,161
July 2017	274,730	36,891	105,983	50,332	240,383
Jan 2018	277,725	35,550	102,366	47,398	241,574
July 2018	280,567	34,268	98,632	44,789	242,649
Jan 2019	283,258	33,021	94,906	42,416	243,599
July 2019	285,799	31,800	91,222	40,237	244,435
Jan 2020	288,193	30,602	87,604	38,221	245,166
July 2020	290,443	29,425	84,022	36,369	245,820

Source: Own performance.

**Table 5. Forecast growth of victims and aggressors per semester
for the period 2016-2020**

	V(n + 1) – V(n)	A(n + 1) – A(n)
n = 1 (January 2016)	3,652	1,938
n = 2 (July 2016)	3,473	1,596
n = 3 (January 2017)	3,310	1,389
n = 4 (July 2017)	3,146	1,222
n = 5 (January 2018)	2,995	1,191
n = 6 (July 2018)	2,842	1,075
n = 7 (January 2019)	2,691	950
n = 8 (July 2019)	2,541	836
n = 9 (Janurary 2020)	2,394	731
n = 10 (July 2020)	2,250	654

Source: Own performance.

Sensitivity Analysis

The transit coefficient β(DV) was built based on the hypotheses of the random meetings occurring between defenders and victims according to [5]. Then, it was assumed a probability about 0.1 due to the approximate amount of victims (36.1%) obtained from the data at the beginning of the study (July 2015). However due to the uncertainty about the value adopted by the parameter, a sensitivity analysis was performed by changing this probability.

As the results in Table 6 show, when the β(DV) value doubles, the percentage of victims grows. Figure 2 draws the amount of victims' trend when modifying the β(DV) value at n = 10 (July 2020).

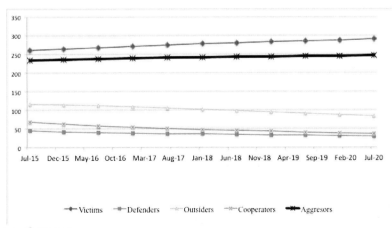

Source: Own performance.

Figure 1. Trend of the subpopulations for the study period (×10000).

Table 6. Sensitivity analysis β(DV)

	V (%)	D (%)	O (%)	C (%)	A (%)
β(DV) = 0.06	42.33	4.29	12.25	5.30	35.83
β(DV) = 0.03	40.74	5.01	12.95	5.39	35.91
β(DV) = 0.015	40.09	5.42	13.18	5.44	35.87

Source: Own performance.

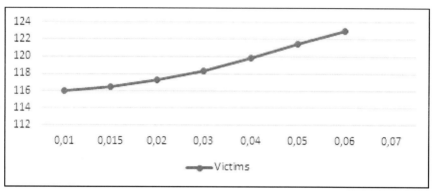

Source: Own performance.

Figure 2. Sensitivity analysis of the victim subpopulations to the β(DV) values at n = 10 (×1000).

Comparison between Greece and Spain

Following, we compared the subpopulations of victims and aggressors of Greek and Spanish [3] populations (Tables 7 and 8). As we can observe, at the beginning of the research (n = 0) (see Table 7), there was a great difference between the two countries according to the number of victims and aggressors. More extensively, the difference of number of the victims is 26.8% and of the number of the aggressors is 22.48%.

As time goes by, the amount of the populations of each country are getting closer. Specifically, at the end of the research (n = 10) (see Table 8), the difference of number of the victims is 17.74% and of the number of the aggressors is 14.54% Figures 3 and 4 draw both populations in Spain and Greece during the study period.

Table 7. Populations of victims and aggressors share, expressed as a percentage at the beginning of the research (n = 0)

	Victims	Aggressors
Spain	9.30%	9.90%
Greece	36.1%	32.38%

Source: Own performance.

Table 8. Populations of victims and aggressors share, expressed as a percentage at the end of the research (n = 10)

	Victims	Aggressors
Spain	24.59%	21.29%
Greece	42.33%	35.83%

Source: Own performance.

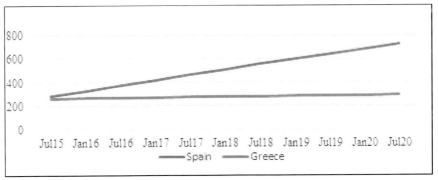

Source: Own performance.

Figure 3. Trend of the victim population of each country ($\times 1000$).

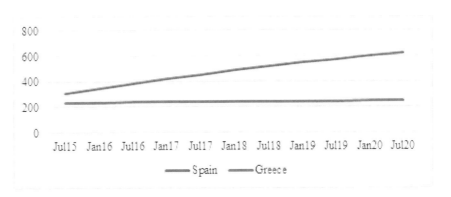

Source: Own performance.

Figure 4. Trend of the aggressors subpopulations of each country ($\times 1000$).

CONCLUSION

In this chapter, we applied a dynamic population model developed by [5] that reckons with sociological factors, such as demography, economy, culture, consumption of drugs, alcohol and social contagion. The proposed model quantifies the amount of victims and aggressors of school bullying in Greece by assuming that the policy does not change over a short study period. During this research, we follow two assumptions: at first, the victims and aggressors categories are cumulative. Furthermore, there is no recovery about the category of aggressors. They can potentially express themselves in other violent ways, for example, against their partners or the members of their families.

We quantifed the measure of this phenomenon in Greece and according to the results, the trend of the victims, as much the aggressors, are quite high. That means that the victimization of a child in the school area is much more common than we may think. Society as a whole needs to pay attention to this phenomenon. Initially, the goverment must apply the appropriate measurements in schools. Moreover, the teachers should remain watchful for possible cases and, finally, the family members have to listen to and take care of their children.

REFERENCES

[1] Salmivalli, C. (2010). Bullying and the peer group: A review. *Aggression and Violent Behavior* 15,112–120.

[2] Magklara, K., Skapinakis, P., Gkatsa, T., Bellos, S., Araya, R., Stylianidis, S., and Mavreas, V. Bullying behaviour in schools, socioeconomic position and psychiatric morbidity: a cross-sectional study in late adolescents in Greece. (2012). *Child Adolesc Psychiatry Ment Health*, 2012, 6: 8.

[3] Skapinakis, P., Bellos, S., Gkatsa, T., Magklara, K., Lewis, G., Araya, R., Stylianidis, S., and Mavreas, V. (2011). The association between bullying and early stages of suicidal ideation in late adolescents in Greece. (2011). *BMC Psychiatry.* 2011 Feb 8; 11:22.

[4] Greek Ministry of Education, Research and Religious Affairs, V. Artinopoulou, T. Babalis, B. I. Nikolopoulos: *Panhellenic research on bullying in Primary and Secondary Education.* (2016).

[5] De la Poza, E., Jódar, L., Ramírez, L. (2017). *Modelling bullying propagation in Spain: a quantitative and qualitative approach.* Qual. Quant. (2017). https://doi.org/10.1007/s11135-017-0541-4.

[6] Musalem, B., R., Castro, O. P. (2015). Qué se sabe de bullying. [What is known about bullying.] *Revista Médica Clínica Las Condes*, 26(1), 14-23.

[7] Salmivalli, C., Lagerspetz, K., Björkqvist, K., Österman, K. and Kaukiainen, A. (1996), Bullying as a group process: Participant roles and their relations to social status within the group. *Aggr. Behav.* 22: 1–15.

[8] *Hellenic Statistical Authority* (2011). http://www.statistics.gr/en/home/.

In: Modeling Social Behavior and Its Applications   ISBN: 978-1-53613-666-1
Editors: L. A. Jódar Sánchez et al.   © 2018 Nova Science Publishers, Inc.

Chapter 3

THE APPLICATION OF SOCIAL INEQUALITY MODELS ON SELECTED REGIONS OF THE EUROPEAN UNION

*Michaela Staníčková, Lukáš Melecký and Lenka Fojtíková**

Department of European Integration, Faculty of Economics
VŠB - Technical University of Ostrava, Ostrava, Czech Republic

ABSTRACT

Regional disparities – economic, social and territorial – among countries and especially regions is an important topic in the frame of the enlarged European Union. Not only the EU enlargement by the Central and Eastern European Countries, but also the economic crisis hit all the EU Member States hard, though the impact of the crisis varied considerably. The low growth performance in the EU has increased concerns regarding an increasing wage dispersion, income inequality at large, and social exclusion in line with poverty. Inequality should be seen as a cornerstone of both sustainable and inclusive growth. Social inequality in the EU is a very real problem which hampers sustainable economic growth. The purpose of this chapter is to introduce the evaluation of the social development convergence and divergence trend among selected regions of the EU in the context of the cohesion concept, or social cohesion. The concept of cohesion can be distinguished in several dimensions – economic, social and territorial. It also corresponds to the dimensions of disparities. We can identify several approaches and methods of the measurement and evaluation of disparities among states and regions at the European level. The methods differ in the structure of using the indicators of disparities and the ways of their processing. The aim of the chapter is to apply a specific integrated approach in the form of a Weighted Aggregated Index of Regional Disparities in the social dimension, and thus evaluate social inequalities in the case of selected EU regions. The chosen approach of regional disparities measurement based on selected multivariate mathematical and statistical methods leads to the construction of a three-layer model of a Weighted Aggregate Index of Social Disparities. The theoretical part of the paper defines

---

* Corresponding author: Sokolská třída 33, 702 00 Ostrava 1, Czech Republic. Email: lenka.fojtikova@vsb.cz.

the concept of regional disparities in the EU context with special attention paid to the dimension of social inequalities, and the methodological background of a convenient statistical approach for the evaluation of disparities. The empirical part of the chapter deals with the measurement, evaluation and comparison of disparities in the Visegrad Four (V4) countries at the level of NUTS 2 regions during the reference period 2000–2016 through the computed values of a Weighted Aggegated Index of Social Disparities.

Keywords: cohesion, disparities, composite index, entropy method, NUTS 2 regions, social inequalities, Visegrad Four countries, weights

INTRODUCTION

The European Union (EU) faces many challenges. On the global stage, the EU has to speak with one voice to counter a plethora of political, military and economic crises. Internally, it needs to foster cohesion in spite of the many events that threaten the EU at its core, create challenges and threaten the whole territory, especially in the form of disparities not only among countries, but especially at the regional level. Disparities in the frame of regional development are a major obstacle to the balanced and harmonious development of the regions, but also of the whole territory. The analysis of disparities brings important information about the key problematic issues in the region (and thus in the country) on the one hand, and its development potential on the other hand. The main goal of the chapter is the verification of the composite indices approach through the evaluation of social disparities reflecting the level of social cohesion in the evaluated examples of selected regions in the reference period. In this chapter, the measuring and evaluation of disparities is based on linkage between disparities and cohesion at the territorial level as defined by Willem Molle (2007), which has become a generally accepted concept. There are different approaches to the definition of regional disparities in the EU and therefore disparities are usually considered a multidimensional problem. According to the horizontal classification of disparities, in EU we usually define three basic types of regional disparities: economic, social and territorial. In the European concept, the level of disparities is usually regarded as the measure of cohesion. Cohesion can be expressed by the level of differences between countries, regions or groups that are politically and socially tolerable (Molle, 2007). Based on the discussed typology of disparities, three dimensions of cohesion are recognised on an economic, social and territorial level.

In view of the current debate and the literature review, the objectives of this chapter focus on the following key issues: 1) to describe the recent evolution of disparities using different definitions of social inequality measures; and 2) to apply a specific integrated approach in the form of a Weighted Aggregated Index of Regional Disparities in the social dimension, and thus to evaluate social inequalities in the case of selected EU regions. The purpose of this chapter is to assess the social dimension and inequality problems in the regions of the Visegrad Four (V4) countries by applying the integrated approach in the form of constructing a Weighted Aggregated Index of Social Disparities. This chapter contains the changes of key social equality indicators related to the cohesion concept based on the EU Cohesion reports approach and compares the regional progress in the reference period 2000-2016. Development challenges are discussed for the improvement of the socio-economic well-being and to avoid social disparities.

THEORETICAL BACKGROUND OF INEQUALITIES

The term disparity is a very frequent term in the last decades. It comes from the Latin word disparitas, which means divided. There exist a lot of definitions of the terms disparity and regional disparity in theoretical literature but also in encyclopaedias and explanatory dictionaries. In encyclopaedias we can mostly find nearly the same general characteristics of this term, while in technical literature disparity is usually of a territorial dimension or is objectively applied according to the needs of the given branch, i.e., in the case of this chapter – understanding disparities in the field of social quality, or better to say inequality. According to the dictionary, disparity is an inequality or difference. Usually it concerns inequality or difference as a result of a society development tendency and it is exactly the high level of their variability that results in development inequality. Thus, the social subjects and their parts, or the phenomena and processes running within them, are unequally developed and this results in their inequality or difference, i.e., among these subjects or their parts disparities are developing. To take disparities as a manifestation of complicated social subjects demands leaving single approaches and seeing the problems of disparities as a complicated problem demanding that the multidimensional approach is accepted in its research. Such an approach means, above all, a holistic (system) view on the research subject. That is why it is needed to expand the research to other dimensions as well.

The multidimensional nature of quality and inequality issues and the disparate social policy priorities of nations and other regions in addressing these calls for a reconciliatory performance evaluation framework. The competitiveness and welfare level of the people of any country is clearly related to the performance of its potential economic growth. A keen interest in economic growth or productivity growth is the objective of economic policies. Therefore, the economic performance of countries and the world as a whole has formed the subject matter of numerous studies over the last decades. Academics and policy makers are concerned with the evolution of inequality and its negative effect on development; see Rajan (2010), Stiglitz (2009) or Krugman (2008). This is also the case of the EU. For the EU, the deepening social inequalities represent a very real threat to the well-being of many EU citizens, with so many being left behind as the overall European prosperity increases. Nevertheless, the differences between the EU Member States are enormous, as mentioned above. Small rich countries, such as Luxembourg, contrast sharply with big poor ones, such as Romania. Despite this, many indicators are published which refer to the EU as a whole, including the measures of socio-economic inequalities in time. The recent economic crisis revealed many of the weaknesses of the current European economic policy, not least at the level of its fiscal policy, monetary policy, industrial policy and social policy, and its inability to address problems related to inequality. Inequality is a key problem which the EU is facing, and it has significant impacts not only on human well-being, but also on economic performance. In order to address this problem properly, there is a need for substantial changes in economic theory, and in the empirical measurement of inequality. The effectiveness of the European convergence policy can also be improved by a clever choice of country-specific social activities and significant economic growth. Inequality can have many dimensions. Economists are concerned specifically with the economic or monetarily measurable dimension related to individual or household income and consumption. However, this is just one perspective, as inequality can also be linked to inequality in skills, education, opportunities, happiness, health, life expectancy, welfare, assets and social mobility. Inequality can be defined and measured as a specific resource distributed across the whole society; while economic inequality means primarily differences in earnings and incomes, social inequality relates to differences in access to social commodities including education and healthcare, but also social and institutional networks. While the EU has a clear role and competences in reducing inequality, reducing inequality at the national level within the EU countries is still a precondition for reducing inequality at the multinational level of the EU as a whole.

In this context, Staníčková (2017) also raised the question about influencing the aspects of social quality and inequality – do social issues matter at all? If we look at the EU evolution over the past decades, substantial progress has been made in terms of building an internal market and an economic and monetary union, albeit not without problems, as the 2008 crisis has shown. In fact, it looks as if the EU and its Member States were mostly thinking in economic terms, hoping that economic solutions will fix all social problems at once. To negate the importance of social issues is to undermine the EU foundations (Allmendinger and Driesch, 2014). Many politicians and economists believe that economic growth replaces or diminishes the need for social policies. However, the EU growth over the last decades has been accompanied by an increase in inequalities in many countries. Inequalities threaten social cohesion and growth.

If such concerns are correct, it is essential not only to build institutional structures for the European social union but also to map social inequalities in the EU. The low growth performance in the EU over the recent decades has increased concerns regarding an increasing economic dispersion, income inequality at large, and social exclusion. Recent research works have stimulated fierce debate on inequality among academics and policy makers. The recent economic crisis has revealed many of the weaknesses of the current European economic policy, not least at the level of its fiscal policy, monetary policy, industrial policy and social policy, and its inability to address problems related to inequality. Inequalities in the EU have been the object of extensive research over the last decade. Several factors can explain this widespread interest; especially the revival of the growth theory (Romer, 1990; Aghion and Howitt, 1998) was contemporaneous with the growing empirical literature on economic convergence (Sala-i-Martin, 2006; Quah, 1997; Barro and Sala-i-Martin, 1995), as also stated by Staníčková (2017).

The level of social inequalities ranks among important indicators influencing the socio-economic development and other processes taking place in the social and economic realm. Facilitating rational income distribution and reducing poverty is mentioned as one of the main goals of the public policy. It should be mentioned that such multidimensional phenomena such as income disparity and poverty might be analysed from many different perspectives, including national and international, also within the EU. Striving for fairness in economic development is crucial in order for societies to be stable and citizens not to feel disenchanted. The economic crisis has put inequalities high on the political agenda, and made this an issue of serious public concern. There is an increasing recognition that social policy can reduce inequality and poverty while simultaneously improving the economic functioning of the country with references to a high-employment economy delivering economic, social, and territorial cohesion in which the benefits of growth and jobs are shared.

METHODOLOGICAL BACKGROUND: MATERIALS AND METHODS

Multidimensionality and the holistic character of searching for regional differentiation problems concern namely the identification of their factors and determinants and diagnosing their content and scope, as also stated by Fojtíková et al. (2014, 2017). The above-mentioned system based on the form of multidimensionality or multidisciplinarity results in the necessity to use plural research methodologies by using different research methods and techniques. There are two basic reasons why we want to identify the relevant characters of subjects as the bearers of given properties, to compare them and to examine them as the subject of our knowledge, our activity or our interest, as stated by Kutscherauer et al. (2010). The first reason is the need to identify and to examine the differences in the subjects' relevant characters; generally it is finding what the different subjects are, within a defined (given) set of states, countries, regions, municipalities, enterprises, etc. and what the impact is on their changes, namely the system changes in structure and behaviour. Generally this is such adominant approach that finding the negative characters is often said to be a disparity approach. The second, less frequent reason up to now is examining the difference of the subjects (their relevant characters), leading to understanding their uniqueness and capability to differ specifically and efficiently from the other subjects under examination and also e.g., to put their comparative advantages to efficient use. This means that capability plays a certain positive role. However, this must be measured in some way and some manner. The present regional practice assesses regional disparities or uses methods based on interregional comparison, under which selected regions are compared based on experience and knowledge, or based on statistical methods, the practical use of which, at the level of different institutions dealing with the problem of territorial differences, is nevertheless very limited. The identification and measurement of regional disparities is the basic condition for taking space-oriented economic-political measures with which it would be possible to minimise these disparities or to eliminate them (Wishlade and Yuill, 1997). Discussion relating to regional disparities is usually concentrated on the following questions (Wishlade and Yuill, 1997, p. 4):

- what type of disparity it concerns,
- what indicator can be used for identified disparity measuring,
- what factors determine this disparity,
- if there are any wider relationships of disparities in the national or international context?

Based on answering the above–mentioned question Wishlade and Yuill (1997) structured disparities into three dimensions including social ones, i.e., disparity decomposition in the social sphere. The quality of life in regions is affected by many factors conditioned on one another, as also Sucháček (2013) discussed. It is very complicated to separate economic and social factors not only in theory but also in practice. Each event usually includes both dimensions and it depends on the point of view which of them will be predominant for the given purpose. The social sphere co-generates conditions for guaranteed incomes that are reflected in the population's standard of living and affect the total social climate of the society.

The recent interest in inequality is simply the recognition of the centrality of the topic to economic theory, policy and performance. The recent return of the topic of inequality has been triggered by important contributions to the empirical analysis of inequality (Galbraith, 2009), but these empirical analyses must be combined with an economic theory that is adequate to address the macroeconomic and microeconomic effects of inequality on social welfare. These problems are not always well diagnosed because the empirical measurement of inequality is often unable to take into account the geographical dimension of inequality, which is particularly complex in Europe. As Galbraith (2009) notes, if we take into account inequality in Europe as a whole, rather than focusing on inequalities within specific countries, we find that inequality in Europe is a much more serious problem than is usually believed. To study inequality in Europe as a whole, one needs adequate statistical tools which can be used in the geographical and political context faced by Europe. Economic analysis is in need not only of an economic theory that focuses on the macroeconomic and microeconomic impact of inequality, but also of economic measurement that takes into account the several dimensions of inequality across individuals in Europe, including the geographical dimension (Martins et al., 2015).

There is ongoing and increasing interest in measuring and understanding the level, causes and development of inequality. European inequality, however, has been explicitly covered less often and only by Brandolini (2007) and Franzini (2009). Disparity measurement and evaluation at any level of territorial development is associated with a lack of integrated approaches and methodology in most cases. A relatively independent and in recent years frequently used approach to the measurement and evaluation of disparities in socioeconomic development is the construction of comprehensive integrated indicators and composite indices (CI) that represent a useful tool in policy analysis and public communication. The number of CIs in existence around the world is growing year byyear (for a recent review see e.g., the author' own approaches to the CI issue (Melecký, 2016; Melecký and Staníčková, 2015) or Bandura (2006). CIs can be better to describe rather than to examine several independent indicators separately. On the other hand, they can send misleading messages to policy makers if they are poorly constructed or interpreted as evidenced by Nardo et al. (2005). Composite indicators are much like mathematical or computational models. As such, their construction falls under universally accepted scientific rules for encoding. The European Commission adopts a definition type of composite indicator developed in this chapter, i.e., a composite indicator based on sub-indicators that have no common meaningful unit of measurement and there is no obvious way of weighting them (Saisana and Tarantola, 2002, p. 5).

Table 1. Basic Scheme of the Empirical Analysis

Input data analysis » A collection of convenient selected indicators of regional disparities for 35 NUTS 2 regions of the V4 countries » » Data normalisation (Z-score transformation method) » » Dataset of normalised variables for selected V4 35 NUTS 2 regions »
Calculation of synthetic indices of disparities » Calculation of distance (Euclidean Distance Method) » » Calculation of synthetic indices of disparities » » Calculation of relative weight for each dimension of disparities» » Calculation of a Weighted Synthetic Index of Social Disparities » » Descriptive characteristics of synthetic index variability »
Results and discussion » Comparison of regional disparities across the social dimension of disparities » » Derivation of the cohesion level in explored NUTS 2 regions » » Interpretation of results and discussion »

Source: authors` proposal and elaboration, 2017.

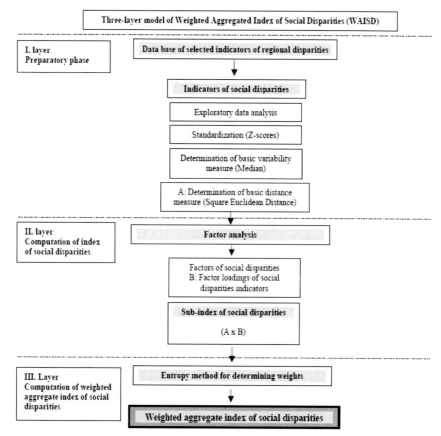

Source: authors' proposal and elaboration, 2017.

Figure 1. Construction of the Weighted Aggregated Index of Social Disparities (WAISD).

The chapter contribution to regional disparities in social inequality measurement is represented by the construction of the Index of Social Disparities (ISD) and the Weighted Aggregated Index of Social Disparities (WAISD) respectively, as presented in Figure 1. The procedure of ISD and WAISD is based on a combination of selected multivariate mathematical and statistical methods that lead to a unique model that includes an index of social disparities that can summarise a view of regional disparities in social inequality and more easily interpret than a set of many separate indicators, as presented in Table 1. ISD and WAISD respectively reduce the visible size of a selected set of regional social indicators without dropping the underlying information base.

Based on Figure 1, in the first layer of the model, the method of a standardised variable (Z-score transformation) and method of distance from an imaginary point, presented as the square Euclidean distance from the median, is used. In the second layer, the exploratory factor analysis for a partial calculation of factor loadings (saturation) is used. Factor loadings present the correlation coefficients between the original variable and the extracted factor from the Principal Component Analysis and show how much of the variability of the factor is explained. Factor loadings therefore represent a full explanation of the role of each character (variable) in the definition of the factor. Factor loadings obtained from the factor analysis play a key role in the second layer of the construction of the composite index. They are used as normalised weights of standardised individual indicators of social disparities. The normalised factor loadings for each indicator within the social dimension of disparities are therefore included in the calculation of the Index of Social Disparities (ISD). This procedure is recommended e.g., by Nardo et al. (2005) or OECD (2008). The Synthetic Index of Social Disparities is, from a statistical point of view, designed as a modified weighted squared Euclidean distance, defined by formula (1):

$$ISD_{r,t} = \sum_{d=1}^{j} \sum_{i=1}^{k} zw_{i_s} D_{ES}^{*}(zx_{i,r,t}, z\tilde{x}_{i,r}), \qquad (1)$$

where:

$ISD_{r,t}$ index of social disparities for dimension *d-th* and region *r-th* in time *t*;

zw_{i_s} normalised weight based on factor loadings for dimension *d-th* (social) and indicator *i-th*;

$D_{ES}^{*}(zx_{i,r,t}, z\tilde{x}_{i,r})$ modified square Euclidean distance of indicator *i-th* for region *r-th* in time *t*;

$zx_{i,r,t}$ standardised value of indicator *i-th* for region *r-th* in time *t*;

$z\tilde{x}_{i,r}$ median of indicator *i-th* for region *r-th* in the whole time period;

R region; r = {1 = CZ01, ... , 8 = CZ08, 9 = HU10, ..., 15 = HU33, ... , 16 = PL11, ..., 31 = PL63, 32 = SK01, ..., 35 = SK04};

d dimension of disparities; d = {social};

i indicator of disparities; i = {1= ER15to64, ..., 8 = AAP};

t time; t = {2000;...,2016}.

Weighting and aggregation systems have a crucial effect on the outcome of each composite index. There is not only one proper method. That is why this part of constructing the composite index is the most discussed and criticised by the opponents of composite indices. Although various functional forms for the underlying aggregation rules of a composite indicator have been developed in literature, in standard practice, the composite indicator as well as WAISD can be considered as a weighted linear aggregation rule applied to a set of variables as shown in Figure 1. The evaluation of the criteria weights may be subjective, objective and integrated. The list of the most common weighting methods is summarised, for instance, in OECD (2008). In the concept of WAISD we used the objective approach based on the entropy method to determine the entropy weight (*ewi*) for the Index of Regional Disparities. Finally, the calculation of

WAISD in *the third layer* is based on a weighted linear aggregation defined by formula (2):

$$WAISD_{r,t} = ISD_{r,t} ew_{i_s} \qquad (2)$$

where:

$WAISD_{r,t}$ weighted aggregated index of social disparities for region
             r-th in time *t*;

$ISD_{r,t}$ index of social disparities for region *r-th* in time *t*;

ew_{i_s} normalised entropy weight for the social dimension of
             disparities;

r region; r = {1 = CZ01, … , 8 = CZ08, 9 = HU10, …, 15 =
             HU33, … , 16 = PL11, …, 31 = PL63, 32 = SK01, …,
             35 = SK04};

t time; t = {2000 …, 2016}.

The case study of regional disparities measurement and evaluation is based on 8 selected indicators of social inequalities. The selection of adequate indicators of social disparities observed at the level of NUTS 2 regions has been identified within the Reports on Economic, Social and Territorial Cohesion, i.e., the EU Cohesion reports that evaluate the trends of disparities and cohesion in the EU Member States and their NUTS 2 regions (see European Commission, 2007, 2010, 2014, 2017). The reference period 2000-2016 is determined by the selection of all indicators and their data availability for 35 NUTS 2 regions of V4 countries. The used selected indicators are social disparities as follows in Table 2.

Table 2. Selected Indicators of Regional Disparities for V4 NUTS 2 Regions

Indicator of social disparities	Abbreviation	Criterion	Source
Employment rate	ER15to64	Maximum	Eurostat
Employment rate of women	ERw15to64	Maximum	Eurostat
Employment rate of older workers	ER55to64	Maximum	Eurostat
Unemployment rate	UR15to64	Minimum	Eurostat
Unemployment rate of youth	URy15to24	Minimum	Eurostat
Long-term unemployment	LtUR	Minimum	Eurostat
Population aged 25-34 with tertiary education attainment	PATE	Maximum	Eurostat
Annual average population change	AAP	Maximum	Eurostat

Source: European Commission, 2007, 2010, 2014, 2017; Eurostat, 2017;
authors' proposal and elaboration, 2017.

EMPIRICAL ANALYSIS: RESULTS AND DISCUSSION

Most individual results obtained from the computed synthetic index based on the dataset of 8 selected disparities indicators revealed that the development in 35 NUTS 2 Visegrad Four regions indicates a positive trend of social disparities recorded in the reference period 2000-2016. The results in the social dimension of disparities indicate that most computed standardised values of the synthetic index converge to the optimal value (i.e., to 0) more at the end of the reference period (2016) than at the beginning of the reference period (2000).

The following graphical apparatus shows the graphical results of computed median values of the index of social disparities in the form of a Weighted Aggregate Index of Social Disparities (WAISD) within 35 V4 NUTS 2 regions for the whole reference period (Figure 2), but also the results of years within the whole reference period (Figure 3). The average values of the computed indices define the area of two polygons. The optimal form of illustrated polygons will be such a point that would correspond with zero modified square Euclidean distances in the social dimension. The smaller area of the polygon marks the lower rate of disparities and therefore the higher level of cohesion and derived socioeconomic development in selected V4 NUTS 2 region. The bigger area of the polygon marks the higher rate of disparities in the social dimension and therefore the smaller level of cohesion and derived socioeconomic development in selected V4 NUTS 2 regions. The average values of the synthetic index for the whole reference period, as well as the individual values for each year of the period, show that the rate of regional disparities in NUTS 2 regions with the agglomeration of capital cities (CZ01, HU10, PL12 and SK01) is rather smaller than in the rest of V4 NUTS 2 regions of each country. Based on the results of the Synthetic Index of Social Disparities, the smallest value of ISD is represented by Czech NUTS 2 regions CZ01 (Praha, 1st position), CZ02 (StředníČechy, 3rd position) and CZ03 (Jihozápad, 4th position). There is also the Slovak region SK01 (Bratislavskýkraj, 2nd position) and Hungarian HU10 (Közép-Magyarország, 7th position), and Polish PL12 (Mazowieckie, 12th position) with the smallest value of social disparities. Based on the analysis of the results, the initial presumption of the chapter, that in NUTS 2 regions of the V4 countries which will be evaluated as the areas with the lowest level of disparities and highest derived level of development potential, the agglomeration of capital cities will be located, has been confirmed. Table 3 illustrates the WAISD scores division among the individual 35 NUTS 2 regions of V4 as median values, and sorts regions based on their scores into ranks. Table 3 illustrates WAISD scores based on colour range – the highest and higher index score, the darker green colour shade; the lowest and lower index score, the darkred colour shade.

Table 3. WAISD Results for V4 NUTS 2 Regions – Rank and Scores

Rank of regions by the median of WAISD		
1.	CZ01	0.024
2.	SK01	0.138
3.	CZ02	0.524
4.	CZ03	0.628
5.	CZ06	1.101
6.	CZ05	1.122
7.	PL12	1.426
8.	CZ07	1.609
9.	HU10	2.041
10.	HU22	2.308
11.	CZ04	2.493
12.	CZ08	2.545
13.	PL21	2.782
14.	SK02	2.924
15.	PL31	2.938
16.	PL11	2.966
17.	PL34	2.981
18.	HU21	3.057
19.	PL63	3.126
20.	PL41	3.207
21.	PL33	3.744
22.	PL32	3.771
23.	PL51	3.895
24.	PL52	4.006
25.	PL43	4.224
26.	PL22	4.485
27.	HU33	4.768
28.	PL61	4.831
29.	PL62	4.985
30.	PL42	5.516
31.	HU23	5.714
32.	SK03	5.830
33.	HU32	7.524
34.	SK04	7.727
35.	HU31	7.953

Source: authors' calculation and elaboration, 2017.

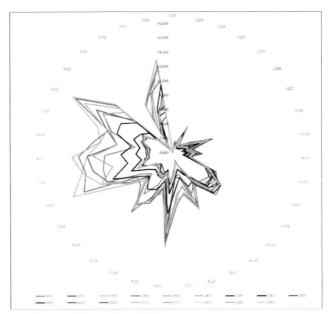

Source: authors' calculation and elaboration, 2017.

Figure 2. WAISD Results for V4 NUTS 2 Regions in the Reference Years 2000-2016.

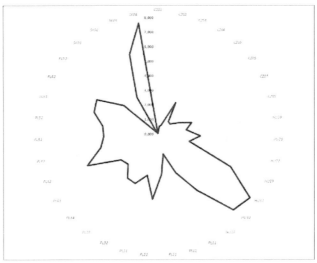

Source: authors' calculation and elaboration, 2017.

Figure 3. WAISD Results for V4 NUTS 2 Regionsin the Reference Period 2000-2016.

For a better illustration of the differences among NUTS 2 regions in the sample of the V4 countries within the individual years and within the whole reference period, Figure 2 and Figure 3 show the WAISD results in the form of polygons.

The calculated values of ISD can be analysed through selected descriptive characteristics of the central tendency and variability that is provided in Table 2 with a record of the maximum, minimum, mean and median value of the synthetic index for the whole reference period. The smallest range is presented in social disparities where the indices scores differ from a minimum of 0.005 in region CZ01 (Praha) to a maximum of 16.403 in region PL62 (Warmińsko-Mazurskie). Other selected descriptive characteristics of the absolute and relative variability of the synthetic index are presented in Table 4. The scores represent mainly the arithmetic mean, i.e., the sum of all values divided by their number and standard deviation as an arithmetic mean of the absolute deviations of each set of values from the mean value. Statistics presented as Range is the difference between the biggest (maximum) and the smallest (minimum) computed value of synthetic indices and provides an indicative characteristic of absolute variability in the dataset. The minimum (lowest) value of this statistics indicates the existence of a minimal modified square Euclidean distance, i.e., the minimal differences of calculated values from the median value of the synthetic index in the social dimension of disparities among all 35 V4 NUTS 2 regions, and the maximum (highest) value presents the highest achieved modified square Euclidean distance, i.e., the maximal differences of calculated values from the median value of the synthetic index in the social dimension of disparities in indicators across all 35 V4 NUTS 2 regions. The coefficient of variation indicates the relative variability related to the median and is calculated as the ratio of standard deviation and arithmetic mean. The coefficient of variation is used to compare the variability of characters having different units or varying levels of position. It is stated as an index or in a percentage and usually helps to detect outliers. If the coefficient of variation exceeds 0.5 (50%), it means that the dataset of results is highly heterogeneous (containing outliers), as is seen in the case of the scores of ISD in the following Table 4.

Table 4. Descriptive Statistics of the Index of Social Disparities

Range	Min	Max	Mean	Median	Std. Deviation	Variance	Variation Coefficient	Skewness	Kurtosis
16.397	0.005	16.403	4.859	4.225	3.523	12.411	0.725	0.817	0.119

Source: authors' calculation and elaboration, 2017.

CONCLUSION

The measurement and evaluation of regional disparities in the social dimension within this chapter has been performed through the construction of a weighted synthetic index as an example of composite indicators calculated from standardised values of social disparities by the modified square Euclidean distance and Exploratory Factor analysis. The main advantage of the used approach lies namely in the ability to summarise the different units of measure under one synthetic characteristic (index), which is a dimension less figure. The analysis showed that, for the most part, there was a consensus in the trends of V4 countries NUTS 2 regions in terms of the attainment level of disparities and development potential, depending on the level of existing social disparities. The construction of the synthetic index and calculation of social disparities showed that since the year 2000 positive social development has been monitored in NUTS 2 regions of the Visegrad Four countries and thus the level of social cohesion recorded an increasing trend thanks to a mostly decreasing volume of regional disparities. In spite of the narrowing rate of social disparities and convergence process in the level of cohesion, significant regional disparities between the V4 countries remain. In relative terms, the Index of Social Disparities in the V4 countries reached a higher rate of relative variability presented by the coefficient of variation.

Inequality is a key problem faced by the EU, which has significant impacts not only on human well-being, but also on economic performance. This chapter has tried to show that inequalities in the EU are not a recent phenomenon and that they have, in general, increased over the recent years in most of the EU countries. As a general principle, it is important to note that many differences among people in the EU are created by society and systematically linked to life opportunities. The only way for the EU to meet these challenges is to not only strengthen economic growth policies through broad-based economic programmes promoting marketisation but also to resolutely push for the expansion of the social aspects of the EU model (Allmendinger and Driesch, 2014). The future design of the European economic policy must then provide a framework in which the policy instruments essential for a monetary, fiscal, industrial, sectorial and social policy consistent with full employment and a reduction in inequality play a more prominent role. Europe 2020 is a credible strategy of industrial policy for the future of Europe and has the merits of presenting clear actions, clear targets and a detailed measurement strategy to monitor implementation. Combatting inequality should be considered as an instrumental target for both sustainable and inclusive growth. European policymakers have a long to-do list to foster inclusive growth in Europe (Darvas and Wolff, 2016). In all countries of the EU, the welfare state has come under intense scrutiny as a result of budgetary pressures and wider societal developments. The European social policy responses need national and regional contextualisation. Simultaneously, the EU needs a sense of common purpose and a common policy framework in support of national social policies, i.e., the creation of a virtuous circle whereby both pan-European cohesion and national cohesion are enhanced. Its aim should be to create a virtuous circle whereby both pan-European cohesion and national cohesion are enhanced. Cohesion is about income and employment, but also about other dimensions of well-being. The convergence processes of V4 to other EU countries must be based on the strong socio-economic growth of GDP, investment flows, new technologies and productivity. The recent trends of the EU economic development show a moderate GDP growth and require social legislation improvement, income level, labour market and education system development. Future social development investigations and governmental decisions need a pragmatic approach in order to create employment, and reduce poverty and social disparities in the national economy.

Acknowledgment

The chapter is supported by the SGS project SP2017/111 of Faculty of Economics, VŠB-TUO and the grant No. 17-23411Y of the Czech Science Agency.

References

Aghion, P. & Howitt, P. (1998). *Endogenous growth theory*. Cambridge: MIT Press.

Allmendinger, J. & Driesch, E. (2014). Social Inequalities in Europe: Facing the challenge. *Discussion Paper P 2014-005*. Berlin: Social Science Center.

Bandura, R. (2006). *A Survey of Composite Indices Measuring Country Performance* [online]. Available at: http://www. thenewpublicfinance.org/background/ Measuring%20country%20performance_nov2006%20update.pdf.

Barro, R. & Sala-i-Martin, X. (1995). *Economic growth*. New-York: McGraw Hill.

Brandolini, A. (2007). Measurement of Income Distribution in Supranational Entities: The Case of the European Union. *Temi di discussione, No. 623*. Rome: Bank of Italy.

Darvas, Z. & Wolff, G. B. (2016). *An anatomy of inclusive growth in Europe*. Brussels: Bruegel.

European Commission (2007). *Growing Regions, Growing Europe. Forth Report on Economic and Social Cohesion*. Luxembourg: Office for Official Publications of the European Communities.

European Commission, (2010). *Investing in Europe's future. Fifth report on economic, social and territorial cohesion*. Luxembourg: Office for Official Publications of the European Communities.

European Commission, (2014). *Investment for jobs and growth. Sixth Report on Economic, Social and Territorial Cohesion*. Luxembourg: Office for Official Publications of the European Communities.

European Commission, (2017). *New Cohesion report fuels the discussion on EU funds after 2020. Seventh Report on Economic, Social and Territorial Cohesion*. Luxembourg: Office for Official Publications of the European Communities.

Eurostat (2017). *General and regional statistics* [online]. Available at: http://ec.europa.eu/eurostat/web/regions/overview.

Fojtíková, L., et al. (2014). *Postavení Evropské unie v podmínkách globalizované světové ekonomiky*. [*The EU's Position in Terms of the Globalized World Economy*]. Ostrava: VŠB-TU Ostrava.

Fojtíková, L., Staníčková, M. & Melecký, L. (2017). Modeling of Human Capital and Impact on EU Regional Competitiveness. In: Sanchéz, L. J., de la Poza Plaza, E. and Rodriguez, L. A. (eds.). *Modeling Human Behavior: Individuals and Organizations*. New York: NOVA Science Publishers, pp. 133-163.

Franzini, M. (2009). Why Europe Needs a Policy on Inequality. *Intereconomics, 44*(6).

Galbraith, J. K. (2009). Inequality, unemployment and growth: new measures for old controversies. *Journal of Economic Inequality, 7*(2), 189-206.

Krugman, P. (2008). *The return of depression economics and the crisis of 2008.* London: Penguin.

Kutscherauer, A., et al. (2010). *Regional Disparities. Disparities in the Regional Development, their Concept, Identification and Assessment.* Ostrava: VŠB-TU Ostrava.

Martins, N. O., Costa, L., Leitão, A., Marcelo, G., Oliveira, F. G. & Tavares, M. (2015). *The implications of inequality for European economic policy* [online]. Available at: http://www.progressiveeconomy.eu/content/implications-inequality-european-economic- policy-0.

Melecký, L. (2016). Application of Composite Weighted Indices Approach in Regional Disparities Measurement. In: *Proceedings of the 19th International Colloquium on Regional Sciences 2016.* Brno: Masaryk University, Faculty of Economics and Administration, pp. 98-106.

Melecký, L. & Staníčková, M. (2015). Contribution to Regional Disparities Measurement: Evidence of Composite Weighted Aggregate Index Based on EU Cohesion Concept. In: *Great transformation: recasting regional policy: conference procedings of The Regional Studies Association Winter Conference.* Seaford: Regional Studies Association, pp. 130-135.

Molle, W. (2007). *European Cohesion Policy.* London: Routledge.

Nardo, M., Saisana, M., Saltelli, A. & Tarantola, S. (2005). *Tools for Composite Indicator Building* [online]. Available at: http://publications.jrc.ec.europa.eu/repository/bitstream/111111111/936/1/EUR%2021682%20EN.pdf.

OECD, (2008). *Handbook on Construction Composite Indicators. Methodology and User Guide.* Paris: OECD Publishing.

Quah, D. (1997). Empirics for growth and distribution stratification, polarization and convergence clubs. *Journal of Economic Growth, 2*(1), 27-59.

Rajan, R. (2010). *Fault Lines: How hidden fractures still threaten the world economy.* New Jersey: Princeton University Press.

Romer, P. (1990). Endogenous technological change. *Journal of Political Economy, 98*(5), 71-102.

Saisana, M. & Tarantola, S. (2002). State-of-the-Art Report on Current Methodologies and Practices for Composite Indicator Development. *Working paper EUR 20408 EN.* Ispra: Joint Research Centre of the European Commission.

Sala-i-Martin, X. (2006). The world distribution of income: Falling poverty and... Convergence, Period. *The Quarterly Journal of Economics, 121*(2), 351-397.

Staníčková, M. (2017). Can the implementation of the Europe 2020 Strategy goals be efficient? The challenge for achieving social equality in the European Union. *Equilibrium. Quarterly Journal of Economics and Economic Policy*, *12*(3), 383-398.

Stiglitz, J. (2009). The global crisis, social protection and jobs. *International Labour Review*, *148*(1-2), 1-13.

Sucháček, J. (2013). Investment location from the perspective of urban and regional activities in the Czech Republic. In: *Proceedings of the 9th International Scientific Conference on Financial Management of Firms and Financial Institutions*. Ostrava: VŠB-TU Ostrava, pp. 851-857.

Wishlade, F. & Youill, D. (1997). Measuring Disparities for Area Designation Purposes: Issues for the European Union. *Regional and Industrial Policy Research Paper Number 24*. Glasgow: University of Strathclyde.

In: Modeling Social Behavior and Its Applications   ISBN: 978-1-53613-666-1
Editors: L. A. Jódar Sánchez et al.   © 2018 Nova Science Publishers, Inc.

Chapter 4

FEMALE LEADERSHIP: HIGHLIGHTING WOMEN'S STRENGTH IN A NEW LEADERSHIP MODEL

*Maria Caballer-Tarazona**
and Cristina Pardo-Garcia
Department of Applied Economics,
Universitat de València, Valencia, Spain

ABSTRACT

Should female characteristics be seen as a weakness or a strength for leadership in new business models? Traditional styles of leadership based on command and control approaches are now being called into question Consequently, today's firms need softer leadership skills such as empathy, communication or cooperative teamwork, typically regarded as female strong points. So, are women potentially better endowed for leadership? Transformational and transactional leadership styles are studied in the current context of lifelong learning. The characteristics of a successful leader are described, focusing on the advantages and disadvantages of women in leadership roles. At present, the role of women within society is in a state of change, and as we approach the gender equality paradigm, leadership models inevitably will adapt further to include those characteristics that have traditionally been more closely associated with women.

Keywords: female leadership, leadership styles, transformational leadership, transactional leadership, work and life balance

---
* Corresponding Author Email: maria.caballer@uv.es.

INTRODUCTION

Leadership is one of the most studied aspects of human behaviour. Moreover, leadership qualities are among the most sought after skills employers look for when recruiting new workers. Furthermore, employers seek workers who have the ability to work well in a team, which is seen as essential to reach the desired common goal of the firm. Therefore, many papers and business books have studied the causes and ways to improve leadership performance from a variety of approaches, each underlying different components of the issue. Even if providing a general definition of leadership is far from easy, we propose the following one:

> A leader is someone who knows how to guide a group of people (called followers) and guides them to achieve a specific goal or objective. The leader also has a clear idea of the aim to be achieved and works with his/her group to reach it.

According to this definition, leaders are not only managers of an important company or the principal researcher in research groups. A leader could also be a housewife at home, or a fireman in an emergency situation. All these people decide what to do and how to do it in order to achieve the fixed aim, namely involving others and engaging them to do their best. Being a leader does not depend on the position or the profession. Leaders know how to motivate a team to achieve a common objective, a concept that depends on what has to be done, and how it should be done. Therefore, everyone can be a leader in different fields of life. However, not everybody has so-called leadership skills. The most important skills for a leader today are the following (Martin et al. 2006):

1. Interpersonal Openness/Relationship Building
2. Commitment
3. Demonstrated Knowledge (Technical Skill)
4. Organization Skills (Project and Time Management).
5. Persuasion/Negotiation
6. Patience
7. Confidence
8. Decisiveness
9. Ethics/Integrity
10. Positive Attitude/Optimism

In the last two decades, the evolution and rapid transformation of the economy and the emergence of new business models have highlighted the problems and difficulties posed by more traditional styles of leadership, based principally on the ability to command and control.

Nowadays, some of the features that stereotypically were attributed to women (such as a tendency to emotionally engage, the ability to listen or the ability to focus on issues) have become desirable leadership qualities. Indeed these female characteristics are regarded as fundamental leadership qualities that are needed to drive organizations to new management models, which are more flexible and consistent with the modern economy and current social trends.

Both in large and medium enterprises there is a tendency towards constant innovation and dynamism, which requires new leadership styles and refreshed organization of working life.

This new context can transform the so-called female characteristics, seen traditionally as weaknesses, but now recognised as elements of strength. Within this context, the aim of this chapter is to highlight the current trends in leadership styles in general and then to analyze the particular strengths and weaknesses of women in this field.

STYLES OF LEADERSHIP

There are several ways to classify leadership styles. It is possible to distinguish between transformational and transactional leadership styles.

According to Eagly and Johannesen-Schmidt (2001) and Cancedda (2002), we could define these two leadership styles in the following ways:

- *Transformational leadership.* This style appeals to subordinates' self-interest by establishing exchange relationships with them. A transformational leader is future-oriented rather than present-oriented and inspires both commitment and creativity in his/her followers. Such leaders enable greater awareness and greater interest within the organization in order to create a shared vision.
- *Transactional leadership.* This style involves managing in the conventional sense of clarifying subordinates' responsibilities, rewarding them for achieved objectives, and reprimanding them for failing to meet objectives. The transactional leadership style is based on the allocation of rewards.

Alternatively, Eagly and Johannesen-Schmidt (2001) and Cancedda (2002) differentiate between task-oriented and interpersonal styles.

- *Task-oriented leadership style.* This style concerns accomplishing the assigned task by organizing task-relevant activities. The task-oriented style has a tendency to focus on carrying out tasks, and then guiding followers on the achievement of the objectives.

- *Interpersonal oriented leadership style*. This style is defined as a concern with maintaining interpersonal relationships by attending to morale and welfare of others. Thus, it tends to focus on interpersonal relationships and on the creation of a climate of mutual trust and aims to create harmony within the interactions of the group.

In the same line, Duffy (2004) classifies leadership styles as follows:

- *Directive leadership*. The leader gives instructions about the task including expectations, regarding how it should be done, and the timeline for completion. The leader also provides clear standards for performance, as well as rules of behaviour. Directive leaders thus clarify, often with one-way communication, what is to be done, how it is to be done, and who is responsible for doing it.
- *Supportive leadership*. Supportive leaders are friendly and approachable as they attend to the well-being and human needs of employees. They treat subordinates as equals and give them respect for their status. A supportive leader helps group members to feel comfortable about themselves, their co-workers and the situation of the organization. Figure 1 shows four different tendencies within the supportive leadership style and Table 1 describes their characteristics.
- *Participative leadership*. The participative leader invites subordinates to share in decision-making. Leaders consult with subordinates to obtain ideas and opinions, and then integrate suggestions into decisions regarding how to proceed.

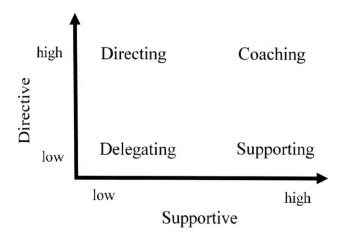

Figure 1. *Supportive leadership*: Different styles depending on the degree of support or direction offered.

Table 1. Supportive leadership: Key characteristics

Leadership style	Characteristics
Delegating	The leader offers less task input and less support facilitating employees' confidence in relation to the task. After agreeing on the final objective, the leader lets the employee take responsibility for completing the task.
Directing	Communication is focused on goal achievement. The leader gives instructions and supervises carefully.
Supporting	The leader does not focus exclusively on goals but uses supportive behaviours that bring out the employees' skills around tasks to be accomplished. Leader listens, asks for input, and gives feedback.
Coaching	Communication is focused on goal achievement and employees' socio-emotional needs. The leader gives encouragement and solicits input.

A more recent work by Guillén (2006), also distinguishes between two leadership styles: traditional and relational. Traditional styles are focused on what characteristics a leader has, how they behave or when and where the leadership appears. A more modern approach is applied in the relational styles, in which a mutual influence is detected between the leader and the follower, and the focus is more on the reason, i.e., what exactly he/she is a leader for. Within the relational leadership style, Guillén (2006) distinguish three types:

- *Transactional leadership*. Here, the influence relationship is seen as an exchange. The follower follows the leader expecting to get something in return.
- *Transformational leadership*. In this style the influence relationship sees the leader persuading followers to change their beliefs and attitudes in order to obtain commitment and engagement.
- *Service leadership*. Here the influence relationship sees the leader engage with his/her followers because of the service the leader is offering, even involuntarily. Leadership stems from the level of confidence generated.

It is important to emphasize that leadership is a multidimensional phenomenon, resulting from the dynamic influence relationship between both leader and follower, in which the follower freely follows the leader because of the confidence generated and consequently there is a clear ethical dimension (Guillén, 2006). This definition implies some practical applications:

1. Leadership skills can be acquired and improved, as long as the person is willing to use his/her abilities for the common good in the organization and improve them.
2. Leadership skills are possible for everyone with regard to their ethical dimension. It is based on his/her willingness to be a leader and the attitude of service to others.
3. The transcendent motivation (to act for the good of others and not only for one's own sake) is present in the behaviour of the ethically good leader.

CHARACTERISTICS OF A SUCCESSFUL LEADER IN THE FUTURE

Globalization and the use of new technologies are two of the main characteristics of the contemporary socio-economic paradigm which have considerably transformed organizations and the concept of time. The new way of organizing time has deleted the long run concept, because the market is too dynamic to allow enterprises to do the same thing in the same way for a long time. Our current *liquid society* (Bauman, 2007) forces us to constantly update our skills and knowledge, ready to adapt to a changing context. In essence, this consant renewal becomes long life learning. The short run path sets limits on the development of informal trust and usually makes relationships within the organizations weak and characterized by a short duration. Nowadays, within modern enterprises, instability and uncertainty are conceived as normal. Thus, creating strong engagement among employees becomes considerably more difficult.

Thanks to new telecommunications technologies, information exchange spreads very quickly. Therefore, it is necessary to accelerate the decision-making process. This kind of mechanism is only really possible within small work teams, whose members are flexible and engaged. For old style enterprises, with a strong hierarchy based on a bureaucratic pyramid, it is difficult to react in this new dynamic context (Sennett 2001).

Within this context and according to Kouzes et al. (2001), a good and effective leader should aspire to the following objectives:

- Challenge the process by looking for new ways of doing things.
- Inspire a shared vision by looking into the future and communicating the organization's goals to the rest of the group.
- Enable others to act by listening and encouraging others to participate.
- Model the way by first knowing the philosophy, goals and plan of the organization.

- A synergistic model of leadership would probably be most efficient, one that balances both male and female strengths.
- The fundamentals of leadership are integrating followers and helping them achieve the organization's common goals.

Soto Pineda and Cárdenas Marroquín (2007) propose the following list of desirable characteristics for a successful leader who wishes to reach the above objectives:

1. The leader is in charge of finding the most capable workers to develop a specific activity.
2. The leader anticipates and foresees what will happen tomorrow and communicates this to his/her employees.
3. The leader faces any situation, always has answers, options that no one considers.
4. The leader understands, assumes and internalizes people's feelings.
5. The leader is honest with his/her organization. He/she looks for the common good of the organization.
6. The leader believes in the objectives of the organization and is able to convince all the employees.
7. The leader acknowledges his/her own mistakes.
8. The leader has a higher strength than other people.
9. The leader knows how to order and accept principles beyond his/her order rights.
10. The leader has a special power of attraction that encouarges other people to follow him/her.

Thus, we could summarize those skills that a successful leader should develop as the following : Collaboration, change in leadership, building effective teams, influence without authority, driving innovation, coaching, building and mending relationships, adaptability, paying attention (seeing things from different angles).

A STUDY CASE: RESULTS FROM FEPIC PROJECT

Societal sensitivity regarding the need to define new models of leadership has increased considerably during the last decade. In particular, the role of women in high responsibility positions and in general as leaders, has raised interest among scholars due to their underrepresentation. An example of these concerns is the work carried out by the FEPIC project.

The FEPIC project, Female Engineers Pushing Innovation in Companies, has been funded within the E.U's "Lifelong Learning Programme." Led by the University of Bologna (Italy), seven partners from seven European countries participated. The project started in October 2008 and ended in November 2010, with the aim of emphasizing creativity and leadership to tackle the persistent underrepresentation of women in senior positions. The project aims to concentrate on the gender dimension of training and professional processes, by empowering those female engineers with high potential. The overall objective is to overcome the barriers that too often stop women from achieving senior positions.

Within this project, in February 2009 a survey was carried out among 63 female leaders with a scientific background from seven European countries (Estonia, Hungary, Italy, Malta, Poland, Sweden and United Kingdom). The aim of the survey was, among others, to identify those skills that female leaders consider to be the most important for successful leadership both in the current changing context, as well as for the future.

Respondents had to rank from 1 to 5 the importance of various key leadership characteristics. Figure 2 summarizes those characteristics that women leaders ranked with the highest score.

This research clearly highlights that certain soft skills are considered more important than more tradtional leadership skills such as vision or technical and professional ability. In line with these results Martin et al. (2006) quote the Key Leadership Skills in the Future as: 1) Interpersonal Openness/Relationship Building; 2) Organization Skills (Project and Time Management); 3) Persuasion/Negotiation; 4) Communication/Feedback; 5) Demonstrated Knowledge (Technical Skill); 6) Delegation; 7) Vision; 8) Patience; 9) Decisiveness and 10) Confidence. This ranking shows that soft skills such as communication, relationship building or time management are more valued than hard skills such as technical skills.

Contemporary approaches to good leadership models not only recommend a reduction in hierarchy but also place the leader in the role of coach or teacher, unlike more traditional styles of leadership. This new style of leadership is more transformational in the sense that it strengthens organizations by inspiring followers' commitment and creativity. Mentoring and empowering followers helps workers to develop their full potential and thus contribute more effectively to the running of the organization (Eagly 2007). The traditional feminine communal behaviour of creating a sense of community, empowering subordinates, communicating and listening effectively, are seen to be more useful and appropriate in this new context.

However, effective leadership is not defined merely by collaboration. Among other important qualities of this coach/teacher model of leadership is the ability to inspire others to be creative and to go beyond the confines of their roles. In order to be able to inspire collective achievement and motivate workers, the new leader must fully develop the emotional intelligence competencies of social skills and social awareness. Emotional Intelligence is the ability to manage oneself and one's relationships effectively. In brief, emotional intelligence is built on five essential capabilities, each with its own set of corresponding competencies as Figure 3 shows (Goleman's 1995).

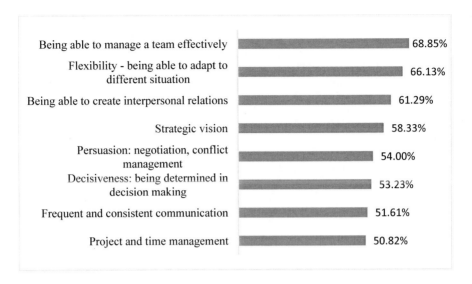

Figure 2. Percentage of female leaders who ranked each leadership skill with the highest score (5 points).

Figure 3. The principles of emotional intelligence.

In general, today's leaders need right-brain skills – empathy, inventiveness, and quest for meaning – to achieve professional success and personal satisfaction. In fact, the best MBA programs are moving in this direction and offering soft-skills training, such as how to build stronger teams and how to communicate more effectively. Traditionally, soft-skills such as effective communication or emotional intelligence are fields in which women have always performed well.

Consequently, in the current context we must create an environment that facilitates this new skill set for leaders. An organization must change its systems and the way it operates to allow people to collaborate and work more interdependently. Leaders are calling for rewards systems that focus on the balance of the individual, the team, and innovation (Martin et al. 2003).

STRENGTHS AND WEAKNESSES OF FEMALE LEADERS

Female leadership style is traditionally identified as a transformational style, characterized by letting go of a more traditional command and control approach in favour of more participative decision making, power sharing interactions and activities intentionally aimed at enhancing self-worth. This style of "interactive management" creates loyalty by signalling trust and respect for subordinates. Generally, a female style of leadership is described as one which shows concern for and understanding of people, seeks further personal development, and uses that knowledge and insight as a resource for managing, and adopting a participative approach. Post (2015) explores how female leadership can become an advantage, by analysing answers from 82 teams in 29 organizations. She finds that female leadership is more positively associated with cohesion on large and diverse teams, and with cooperative learning and participative communication on larger and geographically dispersed teams.

In general, men tend to view leadership as a series of transactions with subordinates, and use their position and control of resources to motivate their followers (transactional style). In contast, women wish to transform subordinates' self-interest into a concern for the whole organization. Furthermore, they report using personal traits like charisma, and interpersonal skills to help motivate others. This kind of woman leader practices more "interactive leadership" in an attempt to make every interaction with co-workers positive. She aims to involve all in the process by encouraging participation, sharing power and information and making people feel important. This leadership style is more successful at motivating employees, to turn their self-interest into the goals of the organization (Rosener 1990). As outlined, all these "transformational" characteristics are necessary for effective leadership in a modern economic context.

More recently, Montes and Roca (2016) interviewed six women who work as creative leaders in different advertising agencies in Spain. These women define their female leadership style as much more empathic, inclusive, sensitive, accessible and intuitive. They highlighted women's ability for observation, organization and action, as well as considering the needs and skills of their team to reach organization goals. Besides, women are known to be more adaptable. They define their leadership style as democratic, collaborative and based on an organic work system, both inspirational and transformational. Other characteristics worth mentioning include their abiltity to motivate and inspire their teams, and create freedom and an atmosphere of trust..

Although linking effective leadership styles to gender may be something of an over-simplification, studies indicate that differences in style do indeed exist. However, the issue is not whether women are more effective leaders than men. Instead the key question is whether those characteristics that were traditionally assigned to women are in fact more useful for successful leaders in a modern and sustainable organization. However, it is clear that both men and women can lead through either traditional or non-traditional styles, and that both genders can adopt and develop the necessary characteristics to become a more successful leader.

However, even if women seem to adopt these winning leadership skills more readily, they may face some extra obstacles. García-Retamero and López-Zafra (2008) studied the perception of female leadership. The authors analyzed whether the prejudice against women in leader positions was possibly due to an incongruence between the female role and the leader role. They compare perceptions with two surveys, one Spainsh, the other German. By and large, Spanish participants showed more prejudice against the female leader than their German counterparts.

It is known that even if women can develop and implement soft skills in their leadership style, in some contexts (normally in a traditionally masculine context) women may suffer from some prejudicial evaluations of their competences as leaders (Eagly et al. 2003). Interestingly enough, Lammers and Gast (2017) explain a counterintuitive theory: stressing that the advantages of female leadership can place women at a disadvantage. Despite the popular claim that female leadership skills such as empathy, communication or cooperativeness are better for the business world, some fear that women may use this advantage to steal men's overrepresentation in leadership. Four different experiments conclude that exaggerated and sensationalist claims may maintain gender inequality, since they undermine the support for affirmative action, reducing the probability that females are selected for leadership roles.

Another disadvantage for women is the problem of work-life balance.. Due to biological factors, when a woman decides to be a mother she must face a higher opportunity cost than a man. As a result, the competing demands of work and family are particularly difficult for those women who aspire to be at the top of any organization. Long hours, late evenings, weekend work, unplanned travel, after-hours socializing, lengthy out-of-town training, and high stress levels all presuppose that someone who wants to succeed in conventional terms will either have no serious life outside of work or will need to hire someone else to tend to the issues of house, home, and family (Hertz 2005, Montes and Roca 2016).

If a woman decides to take time off work while her children are young, her behaviour could be interpreted as a decision to disinvest in the organization. Balancing these two aspects is quite complicated.. If a woman decides to take time for motherhood, she could feel like a failure in professional terms. On the other hand, if she does not have children, she may feel like a failure in personal terms. As we said before, the opportunity cost of having a family used to be higher for women than for men. Even in a couple with parity task sharing, the biological component forced women to renounce, at least for a while, some parcels of their professional career. The problem becomes bigger when domestic tasks are not evenly distributed between partners. The fact is that still nowadays, the woman usually assumes a bigger portion of domestic responsibility, sometimes by choice but in other cases because she does not have the support of her partner. For men, however, it is easier to find somebody ready to devote time to the family, and so they do not have to renounce any parcel of their lives. Even today this decision making regarding work–life balance remains difficult. Bosses and coworkers still view part-timers as less committed employees, since they are less available and not fully part of the team.

Nevertheless, the idea of work-life balance (family, friends, hobbies, and so on) is crucial for all workers, whether men or women, whether part of a family or single. The worker who has time to invest in and develop his/her private life will be a more effective worker and will be more engaged with the firm. If we aim of have a good work-life balance, the enterprise needs to do all it can to change the work organization. These changes could include a range of measures such as encouraging flexible timetables, working from home using new technologies and so on. However, while this kind of flexibility is indeed possible, it only suits some kinds of jobs. Indeed becoming a successful leader still requires a singular passionate focus on work in many different work contexts.

Nowadays, business universities and MBA courses are full of female students but the top positions in organizations are still held by men,. This is a clear symptom of imbalance and evidence of the existence of the *glass ceiling*. Therefore, it is crucial to develop models for how organizations can best use women's talents, rather than forcing women to choose between work and family.

CONCLUSION

The current business environment has suffered substantial changes in recent years. Thus, the majority of modern enterprises require a manager to possess certain qualities that are no longer just the traditional ones. New social and business organizations are characterized by flexibility and continuous changes; they require flexible managers capable of motivating employees and creating new forms of loyalty towards the firm. The current socio-economic reality is immersed in constant change, where uncertainty and the fleeting nature of personal and work relationships make it more difficult to build trust and engagement. These new conditions have increased the complexity of an organization's mission, as well as adding to the diversity of the workforce. Therefore, contemporary approaches to good leadership not only recommend a reduction in hierarchy but also emphasize the need to place the leader more in the role of coach or teacher than in previous models of leadership.

According to the literature, women are more likely to follow a supportive or transformational style of leadership. Some of the main characteristics of these styles include motivating employees, encouraging participation and sharing power and information - characteristics which are now essential for a successful leader. The female style of leadership is very suitable for the new economic context, where job flexibility makes it very difficult to create a feeling of loyalty towards the firm. On the other hand, fast changes in organizations mean employees need to have more open and creative minds. So, the need to encourage participation and share power and information are all more effective in this context than in a traditional authoritative leadership style. Therefore, those characteristics that were typically attributed to a female leadership style are now becoming key strengths in modern leadership models.

However, when women face the problem of work-life balance, they usually find some limitation on career progression. Obviously, for them it becomes difficult to compete with other colleagues, women or men, whose main priority is their work. Therefore, the reconciliation of family and job is only possible in an organization which allows flexible timetables and proposes a reduction in the working timetable. However, it is not only organizations that need to become more balance-friendly. The key point is that there needs to be a cultural shift in society's view on gender parity. The support that women need to manage their work-life balance should come not only from the organizations in which they work, but specially from their partners at home. So where certain jobs require dedication, commitment and hard work, the only way to truly succeed in these fields is when someone shares all domestic responsibilities with you in a fair and just way. Traditionally, it has been easier for men to further their careers, enjoy their family or private lives, their hobbies and so on. So, why can't women do the same? At present, it should of course be possible for both men and women to achieve this work-life balance with real cultural change towards gender equality.

However, workers with family responsibilities are not the only ones who need time to reconcile their work with their private lives. People with different personal backgrounds also need time to pursue their private lives. It is well-known that the welfare of employees positively affects their work, productivity, creativity and ultimately their loyalty towards the firm.

The new economic context is modifying society and private life, so firms must respond to this transformation, both with a change in the style of leadership and in work organization. Therefore, we must create a suitable working environment for the professional development of both men and women, regardless of their personal choices or family cicumstances.

If society adopts a less traditional vision of women, where gender equality is promoted as a cultural value, the incongruence between the female role and the leader role will be reduced (García-Retamero and López-Zafra, 2008). As stereotypes become more dynamic and shapeable, traditional beliefs will be modified and leadership roles will be further redefined to incorporate those characteristics that used to be more typically associated with women.

REFERENCES

Bauman, Z. (2007). *Tiempos líquidos. Vivir en una época de incertidumbre.* [Liquid times. Living in an age of uncertainty.] Ensayo TusQuest editores S. A. Barcelona. Spain.

Cancedda, A. (2002). "Leadership femminile e azione sociale: implicazioni per la ricerca e per lo sviluppo delle carriere femminili." ["Female leadership and social action: implications for research and development of female careers."] Osservatorio europeo sulle buone prassi per l'eliminazione del "tetto di vetro." Commissione Europea. DG Occupazione e Affari Sociali.

Duffy, S. (2004). "Primary Field Comprehensive Examination Organization Behavior and Development. Leadership." *Women's Entrepreneurial Leadership Initiative.*

Eagly, A. and Johannesen-Schmidt M. (2001). The Leadership Style of Women and Men. *Journal of Social Issues*, Vol 57, No. 4, 2001, pp. 781-797.

Eagly, A. and Carli, L. (2003). "The female leadership advantage: An evaluation of the evidence" *The Leadership Quarterly* 14. 807 -834.

Eagly, A. (2007). "Female leadership advantage and disadvantage: resolving the contradictions." *Psychology of Women Quartely.* 31. 1-2.

FEPIC project (2010). "FEPIC – Female Engineers Pushing Innovation in Companies" www.fepic.eu.

García-Retamero, R. and López-Zafra, E. (2008). Atribuciones causales sobre éxito y fracaso y percepción del liderazgo femenino [Causal attributions about success and failure and perception of female leadership], *Estudios de Psicología*, 29(3), 273-287.

Goleman, D. (1995). *Emotional Intelligence: Why It Can Matter More Than IQ*, Bantam Books.

Guillén-Parra, M. (2006. *Ética en las organizaciones. Construyendo confianza.* [Ethics in organizations. Building trust.] Madrid, Pearson Education.

Hertz, R. (2005). "Tests of manhood." *Regional review.* Quarter 12. 2005. FRBB Federal Reserve Bank of Boston.

Kouzes, J. and Posner, B. (2001). *"Leadership Practices Investory. Chapter 3: The five Practices of Exemplary Leadership."* pp. 3-4. Jossey-Bass/Pfeiffer. Part Number: 0999-000365.

Lammers, J. and Gast, A. (2017). Stressing the advantages of female leadership can place women at a disadvantage, *Social Psychology*, 48(1), 28-39.

Martin, A., Willburn, P., Morrow, P., Downing, K. And Criswell, C. (2003). "The Changing Nature of Leadership." *CCL Research White Paper. Center for Creative Leadership*. http://www.ccl.org/wp-content/uploads/2015/04/NatureLeadership.pdf.

Martin, A., Global voice of Leadership Team and Lawrence, L. (2006). "Everyday Leadership." *CCL Research White Paper. Center for Creative Leadership*. https://www.ccl.org/wp-content/uploads/2015/04/EverydayLeadership.pdf.

Montes, C. and Roca, D. (2016). El liderazgo femenino en la creatividad publicitaria [Female leadership in advertising creativity], *Cuadernos.info*, 39, 113-131.

Post, C. (2015). When is female leadership an advantage? Coordination requirements, team cohesion, and team interaction norms, *Journal of Organizational Behavior*, 36, 1153-1175.

Sennet, R. (2001). *L'uomo flessibile. Le conseguenze del nuovo capitalismo sulla vita personale*. Feltrinelli.

Soto, Pineda, E. and Cárdenas Marroquín, J. A. (2007). *Ética en las organizaciones*. [Ethics in organizations.] México D. F., McGraw Hill.

Rosener, JB. (1990). "Ways women lead." *Harvard Business Review*. Nov-Dec; 68(6):119-25.

In: Modeling Social Behavior and Its Applications
Editors: L. A. Jódar Sánchez et al.

ISBN: 978-1-53613-666-1
© 2018 Nova Science Publishers, Inc.

Chapter 5

RANKING UNIVERSITIES THROUGH AN EXTENDED GOAL PROGRAMMING MODEL

Francisco Guijarro[1], Delimiro Visbal-Cadavid[2]
and Mónica Martínez-Gómez[3],*

[1]Institut de Matemàtica Pura i Aplicada,
Universitat Politècnica de València, Valencia, Spain
[2]Facultad de Ingeniería, Universidad del Magdalena,
Santa Marta, Colombia
[3]Departamento de Estadística e Investigación Operativa Aplicadas
y Calidad,Universitat Politècnica de València, Valencia, Spain

ABSTRACT

University rankings help educational authorities to properly allocate human and economic resources. Although this ranking can be performed by a single performance measure, the analysis generally involves a collection of performance measures. This paper introduces several goal programming models to handle performance variables and compute a global university performance measure. Two extreme approaches are compared, one favoring the consensus performance measures and another favoring the most independent and discordant performance measures. We applied this methodology to the Colombian State Universities and the results confirmed that the position of the best and worst Universities remains stable, regardless of the the goal programming model approach.

Keywords: ranking, goal programming, universities, performance

---

* Corresponding Author address: momargo@eio.upv.es.

INTRODUCTION

The Colombian educational system has for some time been called into question by educational monitoring agencies and institutions for its poor performance as regards the skills acquired by students in state-conducted quality tests. The results of higher education institutions are a possible indicator of inefficiency and educational failure, revealing that the universities' strategic mission of education, research and extension is not altogether being fulfilled. The OECD has recently claimed that "public resources are not allocated in a way that promotes efficiency, equity, or the established goals" of the higher education sector (OECD, 2016). The Columbian government has created a national system of tertiary education (SNET) and a national quality system (SISNACET)—among other reforms—that presumably aim to secure improvements (Visbal-Cadavid et al., 2017).

The government is concerned about the distribution of human and economic resources in the universities and how this distribution can affect their quality.

The purpose of this paper is to introduce a methodological framework that ranks universities according to the variables related to their output. This would enable those responsible for education to verify whether funding and economic resources are properly converted into higher educational standards, and if a positive relation can be elicited between economic investment and university rankings. Different approaches are established through a goal programming (GP) model.

The rest of the chapter is structured as follows: Section 2 gives the methodological framework for the ranking of Colombian universities. In Section 3 we present the database used in our analysis. Section 4 shows the main results and Section 5 gives the conclusions of the paper.

METHODS

GP was defined by Ignizio and Romero (2003) as a multicriteria technique that builds mathematical progamming models by combining linear and/or nonlinear functions, considering continuous and discrete variables, in which objective functions have been transformed into goals. Unlike classical mathematical programming models, GP is an example of "satisficing" models which provide good enough solutions in a reasonable computation time. In this regard, GP is in line with some heuristic algorithms proposed in the Artificial Intelligence area: they cannot ensure the optimal solution but do provide a nearly optimal one in far less time. From a mathematical approach, GP can be expressed as an optimization model that minimizes the deviation between the achievement of goals and their (optimal) aspiration levels. The model (1) – (2) expresses the classical goal programming model:

$$min \sum_{i=1}^{n} |f_i(X) - g_i| \tag{1}$$

$$s.t. \ X \in F \ (F \ is \ the \ feasible \ set) \tag{2}$$

where $f_i(X)$ is the function of the ith goal and g_i is its aspiration level.

Linares and Romero (2002) propose a GP-based methodology that allows the aggregation of individual preferences provided by several social groups toward different criteria. Because conflicting criteria must be handled simultaneously, the authors propose alternative GP models for the combination of these criteria. García et al., (2017) recently proposed the use of these GP models for constructing firm rankings according to economic and social performance. The aggregation of these variables is obtained through a GP model, which establishes the optimal weight for each variable according to different preferences. These authors, instead of ranking the firms by a single criterion, claim that GP enables simultaneously incorporating all the criteria. As some single-criterion performance measures are usually in conflict, they propose two opposed alternatives for determining multiple-criterion performance: the first calculates a consensus performance that reflects the majority trend of the single-criterion measures and the other calculates a performance that is biased toward the measures that show the most discrepancy with the rest.

We used these GP models to propose a university ranking considering different dimensions related to their performance. In the following we introduce the weighted and MINMAX GP models, as well as the extended GP model, which enables us to combine these two models. In all cases, the aim is to combine different university performance dimensions (single-criterion performance) into a global performance measure (multicriteria performance).

The weighted goal programming model (WGP) calculates the multicriteria performance by maximizing the similarity between this unifying performance and the other original performance measures considered as inputs to the model (3) – (6):

$$min \ Z = \sum_{i=1}^{n} \sum_{j=1}^{d} (\alpha_j n_{ij} + \beta_j p_{ij}) \tag{3}$$
$$s.t.$$

$$\sum_{k=1}^{d} (w_k c_{ik}) + n_{ij} - p_{ij} = c_{ij} \qquad i = 1, \ldots, n \ j = 1, \ldots, d \tag{4}$$

$$\sum_{j=1}^{d} w_j = 1 \tag{5}$$

$$\sum_{j=1}^{d} w_j c_{ij} = c_i \qquad i = 1, \dots, n \tag{6}$$

All the variables are assumed to be positive. The negative and positive deviation variables are n_{ij} and p_{ij}, respectively. If $n_{ij}(p_{ij})$ is unwanted then $\alpha_j = 1$ ($\beta_j = 1$). The variable to be optimized by model (3) – (6) is the weight or importance of each single-criterion, w_j. For each university i, as many equations (4) are created as criteria have been considered to measure their performance. In each of these equations the university's estimated multicriteria performance is compared to its performance in the jth criterion. The estimated multicriteria performance for University i, c_i, is computed as the weighted unicriterion performance $\sum_{j=1}^{d} w_j c_{ij}$ in Eq. (6), taking into account that the sum of the weights must equal 1, as shown in Eq. (5).

The aim of model (3) – (6) is to provide a global university performance measure in line with the single-criterion performances used in the analysis. However, this will be somewhat more complicated when the single-criterion performances are in conflict with each other, so that a high value in one dimension can suppose a low value in another. With universities, this could happen if teaching and research activities are competing for the same resources, so that improving one dimension would likely imply worsening the other. However, similar criteria (i.e., they belong to the same performance dimension) are favoured by model (3) – (6). In short, the multicriteria performance favours similar single-criterion performances, whilst it underweights those criteria which are independent of the rest.

The opposite approach favours the most independent criteria in such a way that the multicriteria performance is similar to these extreme criteria and different from the rest. In other words, the multicriteria performance penalizes those criteria in line with the general behaviour and favours those which do not conform to "common" behaviour. This model is known as the MINMAX or Chebyshev GP model (Romero, 2001), which minimizes the maximum difference between the estimated multicriteria performance and the unicriterion performances (7) – (12).

$$min \; D \tag{7}$$
$$s.t.$$
$$\sum_{k=1}^{d} (w_k c_{ik}) + n_{ij} - p_{ij} = c_{ij} \qquad i = 1, \dots, n \; j = 1, \dots, d \tag{8}$$

$$\sum_{j=1}^{d} w_j = 1 \tag{9}$$

$$\sum_{j=1}^{d} w_j c_{ij} = c_i \qquad i = 1, \dots, n \tag{10}$$

$$\sum_{i=1}^{n} (\alpha_j n_{ij} + \beta_j p_{ij}) = D_j \quad j = 1, \dots, d \tag{11}$$

$$D_j \leq D \qquad j = 1, ..., d \tag{12}$$

For each performance unicriterion the variable D_j computes the sum of the differences between the estimated multicriteria performance and the unicriterion performances. Hence, a high value in D_j indicates that there is a strong disagreement between the jth performance criterion and the estimated multicriteria performance. Small values indicate that the university's behaviour in that criterion is close to the global multicriteria performance. D, representing the maximum disagreement level, is the supremum for all D_j, and is the variable to be minimized in model $(7) - (11)$. The solutions of the WGP and MINMAX GP models represent extreme cases, with two contrasting strategies set against one another. In short, the WGP model gives priority to the general consensus between unicriterion performance measures, whilst the MINMAX GP model favours the conflicting performance measures.

Romero (2001) proposed a compromise solution between both approaches, the so-called extended GP model. This model is represented in $(13) - (19)$ and introduces a new parameter, λ, which widens the range of alternatives, giving compromise solutions between the extreme cases represented by the WGP and the MINMAX GP models. We obtain the same solution as the WGP model if we use $\lambda = 1$, whilst $\lambda = 0$ gives the solution of the MINMAX GP model. Intermediate values give compromise solutions between these two extreme approaches.

$$min \; \lambda \sum_{i=1}^{n} \sum_{j=1}^{d} \left(\alpha_j n_{ij} + \beta_j p_{ij} \right) + (1 - \lambda)D \tag{13}$$
$$s.t.$$

$$\sum_{k=1}^{d} (w_k c_{ik}) + n_{ij} - p_{ij} = c_{ij} \qquad i = 1, ..., n \; j = 1, ..., d \tag{14}$$

$$\sum_{j=1}^{d} w_j = 1 \tag{15}$$

$$\sum_{j=1}^{d} w_j c_{ij} = c_i \qquad i = 1, ..., n \tag{16}$$

$$\sum_{i=1}^{n} \left(\alpha_j n_{ij} + \beta_j p_{ij} \right) = D_j \quad j = 1, ..., d \tag{17}$$

$$D_j \leq D \qquad j = 1, ..., d \tag{18}$$

$$\sum_{j=1}^{d} D_j = Z \tag{19}$$

It should be noted that the variables must be normalized in all the models mentioned above. A common procedure is to use the zero-one normalization (Tamiz et al., 1998):

$$c_{ij}^* = \left(c_j^{max} - c_{ij}\right)/\left(c_j^{max} - c_j^{min}\right) \; i = 1, \dots, n \; j = 1, \dots, d \tag{20}$$

where c_{ij}^* is the normalized value of the jth performance criterion in the ith university, and c_j^{max} and c_j^{min} are the maximum and minimum values, respectively, of the jth performance criterion.

The extended GP model can obtain the optimal Pareto frontier of solutions, where other multicriteria models obtain a single solution. However, GP does not guarantee a Pareto optimal solution. In fact, it was not designed for the purpose of obtaining non-dominated solutions but was developed as a method of finding satisficing solutions (Romero 2014). If the intention of the decision maker is to achieve at least the goals' target values, then an optimal solution can be a non-efficient solution.

The extended GP model has previously been applied in different contexts to ranking firms, incorporating economic, financial and corporate social responsibility variables (García et al., 2010, 2013; Cervelló-Royo et al., 2017; García-Martínez et al., 2017)

DATABASE

We collected information from 32 Colombian state universities for the year 2016 and selected 13 variables to analyse their performance. All these variables can be clustered into 3 dimensions: Quality (Q), Success (S) and Admission (A). Table 1 gives a list of the universities and the variables used in the study.

Table 1. Database description

Universities	
UNIV01	Universidad Nacional de Colombia
UNIV02	Universidad Pedagógica Nacional
UNIV03	Universidad Pedagógica y Tecnológica de Colombia
UNIV04	Universidad del Cauca
UNIV05	Universidad Tecnológica de Pereira
UNIV06	Universidad de Caldas
UNIV07	Universidad de Córdoba
UNIV08	Universidad Surcolombiana
UNIV09	Universidad de la Amazonía
UNIV10	Universidad Militar-Nueva Granada
UNIV11	Universidad Tecnológica del Chocó-Diego Luis Córdoba
UNIV12	Universidad de los Llanos

Universities	
UNIV13	Universidad Popular del César
UNIV14	Universidad-Colegio Mayor de Cundinamarca
UNIV15	Universidad del Pacífico
UNIV16	Universidad de Antioquia
UNIV17	Universidad del Atlántico
UNIV18	Universidad del Valle
UNIV19	Universidad Industrial de Santander
UNIV20	Universidad de Cartagena
UNIV21	Universidad de Nariño
UNIV22	Universidad del Tolima
UNIV23	Universidad del Quindío
UNIV24	Universidad Francisco de Paula Santander-UFPS Cúcuta
UNIV25	Universidad Francisco de Paula Santander-UFPS Ocaña
UNIV26	Universidad de Pamplona
UNIV27	Universidad del Magdalena
UNIV28	Universidad de Cundinamarca UDEC
UNIV29	Universidad de Sucre
UNIV30	Universidad de la Guajira
UNIV31	Universidad Distrital Francisco José de Caldas
UNIV32	Universidad Nacional Abierta y a Distancia UNAD

Performance measure	Definition
Q1 – SaberPro Exam	Weighted number of students who obtained scores in the top quantile in the Saber PRO exams
Q2 – MSc Teachers	Number of full-time equivalent teachers with Master degree, including professors and lecturers
Q3 – PhD Teachers	Number of full-time equivalent teachers with Doctorate, including professors and lecturers
Q4 – Accredited programs	Number of accredited degrees over the total number of degrees offered by the University
Q5 – Accredited University	Dummy variables which indicate whether the University is accredited or not
S1 – Graduate ratio	Relative variation in the Graduation rate of undergraduate students
S2 – Researchers	Weighted number of researchers
S3 – Research groups	Weighted number of research groups
S4 – Published papers	Weighted number of published papers, according to journal impact
A1 –Undergraduate admissions	Weighted absolute variation of students enrolled by educational level and teaching methodology at undergraduate level
A2 –Postgraduate admissions	Weighted absolute variation of students enrolled by educational level and teaching methodology at postgraduate level
A3 –Retention rate	Relative variation in the retention rate
A4 –Social admission	Information related to the percentage of students admitted from depressed areas

Some of these variables are weighted in accordance with Colombian Law 1279, 19 June 2002. For example, S4 – "Published Papers" is the weighted number of indexed journals, calculated by the Ministry of National Education of Colombia as $15 \times A1 + 12 \times 2 + 8 \times B + 3 \times C$, where A1, A2, B and C represent the number of papers published in indexed journals according to their impact (this classification is done by the Colombian Institute *Colciencias*).

RESULTS AND DISCUSSION

This section presents the results obtained by applying the extended GP model to the database described in the previous section. As the extended GP model can be considered a generalization of the WGP and MINMAX GP models, we used it here to propose different university rankings by changing the values of parameter λ, to determine whether the rankings differ when parameter λ varies and study the evolution of the weight for each variable.

The extended GP model was solved for λ between 0 and 1 with 0.1 intervals. The results are summarized in Table 2. The estimated weights for the 13 unicriterion performances considered are collected in the first rows of Table 2. It can be seen that the importance of the variables changes with the value of λ, mainly in the lower values of this parameter. For $\lambda = 0$, the most important variable is IC1 (0.410). However, the relevance of the variables radically changes for higher values of λ. Thus, for $\lambda \in \{0.1, 0.2, 0.3\}$ the most important variable is IC3 (0.319, 0.195, 0.198), whilst for $\lambda \geq 0.4$ the most important is IL2. It is worth noting that some variables are indifferent to the value of λ: IC2 obtains a 0, and IL3 obtains 0 in all cases except for $\lambda = 0.0$. This does not necessarily mean that these variables are not related to multicriteria performance, but as they are also closely related to other variables they become irrelevant in the multicriteria performance computation; i.e., they are redundant because this effect has already been incorporated into other variables.

In the second part of Table 1 the maximum disagreement (D) is attached to variable IC1. This reveals that variable IC1 is quite independent of the rest of the variables and hence gives additional information not reported by the other dimensions in the database. Despite this variable being included in the IC dimension, we can conclude that it provides new information unrelated to the rest of the variables in its own dimension. IC5 also gets high values in its disagreement value for the same reason.

After ranking the importance of the variables in the extended GP model, the next step is to analyze the university ranking. The research question is *whether the position of the Universities varies with the approach associated with* λ.

Table 2. Results of the extended GP model

Weights

Lambda	Q1	Q2	Q3	Q4	Q5	S1	S2	S3	S4	A1	A2	A3	A4
0.0	0.410	0.000	0.000	0.000	0.366	0.000	0.000	0.223	0.000	0.000	0.000	0.000	0.000
0.1	0.079	0.000	0.319	0.179	0.196	0.024	0.048	0.000	0.000	0.007	0.135	0.013	0.000
0.2	0.102	0.000	0.195	0.049	0.127	0.070	0.208	0.000	0.036	0.000	0.041	0.098	0.074
0.3	0.076	0.000	0.198	0.063	0.094	0.041	0.195	0.000	0.067	0.054	0.050	0.076	0.085
0.4	0.057	0.000	0.207	0.050	0.063	0.060	0.247	0.000	0.065	0.064	0.047	0.096	0.045
0.5	0.049	0.000	0.218	0.056	0.056	0.059	0.242	0.000	0.060	0.057	0.056	0.094	0.053
0.6	0.050	0.000	0.216	0.057	0.055	0.058	0.242	0.000	0.062	0.058	0.056	0.093	0.053
0.7	0.045	0.000	0.215	0.069	0.049	0.049	0.255	0.000	0.091	0.074	0.046	0.096	0.011
0.8	0.042	0.000	0.210	0.071	0.049	0.043	0.247	0.000	0.105	0.070	0.050	0.099	0.014
0.9	0.042	0.000	0.207	0.067	0.050	0.044	0.242	0.000	0.104	0.064	0.052	0.101	0.027
1.0	0.031	0.000	0.209	0.068	0.050	0.043	0.231	0.000	0.103	0.055	0.054	0.106	0.050

D_j

Lambda	Q1	Q2	Q3	Q4	Q5	S1	S2	S3	S4	A1	A2	A3	A4	Z	D
0.0	9.913	6.857	7.667	8.242	9.913	6.852	9.913	9.311	9.170	6.815	5.598	8.463	6.715	105.430	9.913
0.1	10.521	5.896	5.255	7.008	10.521	5.518	8.335	7.670	7.295	6.616	4.950	7.862	4.948	92.396	10.521
0.2	11.128	5.056	4.389	8.035	11.128	5.356	7.201	6.532	6.311	6.543	5.596	7.678	3.754	88.709	11.128
0.3	11.318	4.912	4.073	8.205	11.318	5.420	7.024	6.355	6.095	6.505	5.737	7.667	3.489	88.118	11.318
0.4	11.565	4.764	3.814	8.562	11.565	5.359	6.719	6.051	5.800	6.452	5.953	7.603	3.460	87.668	11.565
0.5	11.602	4.748	3.728	8.562	11.602	5.386	6.682	6.013	5.759	6.495	5.966	7.649	3.426	87.618	11.602
0.6	11.604	4.750	3.727	8.561	11.604	5.388	6.681	6.012	5.755	6.496	5.965	7.652	3.418	87.616	11.604
0.7	11.752	4.859	3.730	8.600	11.557	5.355	6.563	5.894	5.597	6.502	6.080	7.589	3.465	87.543	11.752
0.8	11.809	4.900	3.742	8.571	11.495	5.371	6.533	5.864	5.541	6.566	6.084	7.597	3.453	87.526	11.809
0.9	11.821	4.902	3.726	8.568	11.479	5.401	6.520	5.851	5.528	6.608	6.080	7.620	3.422	87.524	11.821
1.0	11.907	4.932	3.658	8.557	11.410	5.511	6.439	5.770	5.446	6.733	6.128	7.675	3.355	87.520	11.907

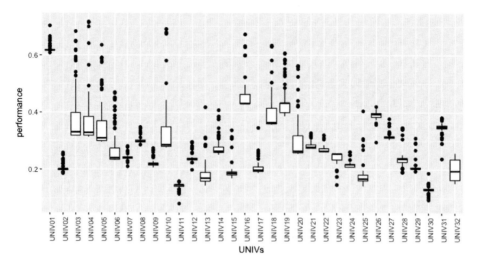

Figure 1. Ranking of Universities according to the extended GP model.

The multicriteria performance c_i for each University is shown in Figure 1. The boxplot gives the values obtained by the universities for a wider range of λ values. In this case, we ran the extended GP model for λ between 0 and 1 with 0.01 intervals, which gives 101 different multicriteria performance values for each university. Regardless of the value of λ, it can be seen that DMU01 (*Universidad Nacional de Colombia*) shows the best performance. In second place is the *Universidad de Antioquia*, and the third is the *Universidad Industrial de S*antander. The lowest classified are: *Universidad Tecnológica del Chocó – Diego Luis Córdoba* and *Universidad de la Guajira*.

It can therefore be concluded that the best and worst universities mainly remain unchanged, regardless of the value of parameter λ, and as the results are not conditioned by the parameter setting, the extended GP model can be considered robust. The conclusions on the leading universities in Colombian Higher Education are thus independent of the approach used in the GP model.

CONCLUSION

The Colombian educatuional authorities are concerned about the distribution of human and economic resources in their universities and how this distribution can affect their quality. Since a large percentage of the state budget is allocated to higher education, the government must monitor how public money is invested and the benefits to the population. This paper presents a mathematical model based on goal programming to rank the Colombian state universities. Even though the results can vary with the parameter used in the model, we verified that the best and worst universities maintain their positions, regardless of the value of this parameter. These results confirm that the

Universidad Nacional de Colombia, Universidad de Antioquia and *Universidad Industrial de Santander* show the best performance in the Colombian Higher Education System, whilst the worst classified are the *Universidad Tecnológica del Chocó – Diego Luis Córdoba* and *Universidad de la Guajira.*

ACKNOWLEDGMENTS

Mónica Martínez-Gómez has been funded by the research project GVA/20161004: Project of Conselleria d'Educació, Investigació, Cultura i Esport de la Generalitat Valenciana, through the project "Validación de la competencia transversal de innovación mediante un modelo de Medida formativo."

REFERENCES

Cervelló-Royo, R., Guijarro, F. & Martinez-Gomez, V. (2017) Social Performance considered within the global performance of Microfinance Institutions: a new approach. *Operational Research International Journal*, in press. DOI: 10.1007/s12351-017-0360-3.

García, F., Guijarro, F., & Moya, I. (2010). A goal programming approach to estimating performance weights for ranking firms. *Computers & Operations Research*, 37(9), 1597-1609.

García, F., Guijarro, F., & Moya, I. (2013). Monitoring credit risk in the social economy sector by means of a binary goal programming model. *Service Business*, 7(3), 483-495.

García-Martínez, G., Guijarro, F., & Poyatos, J. A. (2017). Measuring the social responsibility of European companies: a goal programming approach. *International Transactions in Operational Research*, in press. DOI: 10.1111/itor.12438.

Ignizio, J. P., & Romero, C. (2003). *Goal programming. Encyclopedia of information systems*, 2, 489-500.

Linares, P., & Romero, C. (2002). Aggregation of preferences in an environmental economics context: a goal-programming approach. *Omega*, 30(2), 89-95.

OECD (2016). *Education in Colombia*. OECD Publishing, Paris.

Romero, C. (2001). Extended lexicographic goal programming: a unifying approach. *Omega*, 29(1), 63-71.

Romero, C. (2014). *Handbook of critical issues in goal programming*. Elsevier, Amsterdam.

Tamiz, M., Jones, D., & Romero, C. (1998). Goal programming for decision making: An overview of the current state-of-the-art. *European Journal of Operational Research*, 111(3), 569-581.

Visbal-Cadavid, D., Martínez-Gómez, M., & Guijarro, F. (2017). Assessing the Efficiency of Public Universities through DEA. A Case Study. *Sustainability*, 9(8), 1416.

In: Modeling Social Behavior and Its Applications   ISBN: 978-1-53613-666-1
Editors: L. A. Jódar Sánchez et al.   © 2018 Nova Science Publishers, Inc.

Chapter 6

MODELING SOCIAL BEHAVIORS IN ORGANIZATIONS THROUGH SHAPING THE CULTURE FOCUSED ON ORGANIZATIONAL LEARNING

Mateusz Molasy[1],*, Katarzyna Walecka-Jankowska[2],†
and Anna Zgrzywa-Ziemak[2],‡
[1]Faculty of Mechanical Engineering
[2]Faculty of Computer Science and Management
Wrocław University of Science and Technology, Wrocław, Poland

ABSTRACT

This chapter describes a valid and current research area which is organizational learning processes as social behaviors in organizations. Many researchers emphasize that the organizational culture plays a key role in determining the processes of organizational learning. The purpose of this chapter is to demonstrate the method of modelling social behaviors in organizations to direct these organizations to learning through appropriate shaping of their organizational culture. Based on different theoretical views and empirical studies presented in the literature, the characteristics of an organizational culture that fosters and inhibits organizational learning are discussed. The sketch of the method forming organizational culture conducive to organizational learning is developed.

Keywords: organizational culture, organizational learning, method

---

* Corresponding Author Email: mateusz.molasy@pwr.edu.pl.
† Email: katarzyna.walecka-jankowska@pwr.edu.pl.
‡ Email: anna.zgrzywa-ziemak@pwr.edu.pl.

INTRODUCTION

Nowadays, the efforts of numerous theoreticians and practitioners are focused on the search for such social behavior models that will increase the effectiveness of modern organizations. It is recognized that functioning in complex and dynamic environment forces organizations to seek sources of their success not in specific products, technologies or sources of resources, but in the ability of the organization to develop more and more new and useful knowledge (Wu 2010). Therefore, organizational learning, learning faster and more efficient than the competition, is a prerequisite for survival and development of organizations (Santos-Vijande et al. 2012). There is one question left, namely how to increase the organization's ability to learn.

Since the breakthrough work by Fiol and Lyles (1985) on the nature of organizational learning, many researchers emphasized the fact that the organizational culture (OC) plays a key role in determining the processes of organizational learning and creating a learning organization (Marquardt 1996; Marquardt 1996; Pedler et al. 1997; Popper and Lipshitz 1998; Davenport and Prusak 1998; Garvin 2003; Schein 2004; Zgrzywa-Ziemak and Kamiński 2009; Sanz-Valle et al. 2011; Argote 2012; Liao et al. 2012). Triandis argues that not paying attention to the way culture influences social behavior is usually a mistake (Lonner and Malpass 1994). Organizational culture, combining the achievements of both psychology and sociology as well as anthropology, has become the subject of many discussions and considerations on the basis of science, as well as from the point of view of management practice. It is emphasized that organizational culture can both – facilitate learning or be a major barrier for it (Davenport and Prusak 1998; Sanz-Valle et al. 2011; Liao et al. 2012) and that different organizational culture can have different impact on organizational learning (Sanz-Valle et al. 2011).

The purpose of this chapter is to demonstrate the method of modelling social behaviors in organizations in such a way as to direct these organizations to learning through appropriate shaping of their organizational culture. The features of a culture that fosters and inhibits organizational learning will be discussed in the light of different theoretical views and in the view of the empirical study discussed in the literature. A practical dimension of presented sketch of the method based on seven steps gives it a transparent application dimension.

THE ORGANIZATIONAL CULTURE

Kroeber and Kluckhohn found 164 different definitions of culture (Sikorski 2002). Undoubtedly it is the result of processes that consist of dynamic interactions between individuals. The most commonly occurring in the literature definition of organizational culture defines this concept as *"a pattern of shared basic assumptions that the group learned as it solved its problems of external adaptation and internal integration, that has worked well enough to be considered valid and, therefore, to be taught to new members as the correct way to perceive, think, and feel in relation to those problems"* (Schein 1992, 12).

External manifestations of organizational culture are norms, artifacts, and symbols. Norms define what behavior is appropriate for organization and regulate conflict resolution and workplace uniforms. Norms are characterized by the extent of the norm and the weight expressed by the intensity of approval or disapproval for specific beliefs, attitudes and methods. Artifacts are material objects, layout and appearance of the workplace, technologies, language, patterns of behavior and organizational procedures and practices. Symbols reflect specific aspects of organizational culture, facilitate the interpretation of ambiguous events and motivate people to act, resulting in a specific emotional response (O'Reilly 2009; Jashapara 2011).

Values are the organization of the social dimension, which refers to the way of understanding reality and the experiences that characterize a given group, cognitive refers to the use of the experience of individuals forming these groups and the functional, which illustrates how these values translate into the actions of individuals and their relationships. Four types of organizational values have been distinguished (Lencioni 2002; Jashapara 2011):

- Core values - principles that determine the start-up of an organization from which the organization does not depart even in the name of economic benefits. Fundamental values require constant vigilance, so that they always express the essence of the organization. These rules were most often initiated by the founders of the company.
- Aspirational values - values necessary for the implementation of the new strategy. The company will need them in the future, but they do not currently have them.
- Permission-to-play values - minimum standards for attitudes and behaviors.
- Accidental values - values that arise automatically through the integration of workers. Possible to be both positive and negative.

Another element of an organization's culture is belief. Beliefs are different concepts that we accept as true. Persistent beliefs affect the value of an organization. Attitude is a combination of values and beliefs with feelings. He is taught the tendency to behave appropriately in certain circumstances. Attitude is more persistent than opinion and influences employee motivation (Rokeach 1973; Jashapara 2011).

The last element of culture are assumptions, which are the result of complicated interpretation of facts, conditioned by beliefs, values and emotions. Assumptions are kind of solutions to specific problems that are taken for granted. They are theories that facilitate routine behavior and adaptive learning. Assumptions are unconscious, which makes them difficult to verbalize (Arygyris and Schon 1978; Jashapara 2011).

THE ORGANIZATIONAL LEARNING

An analysis of a number of concepts of organizational learning, indicating the differences between them regarding the course of organizational learning processes, who is the subject, what is a stimulus to its occurrence, how researches see its results and to what extent it can be managed, will allow to determine basic features of organizational learning (Zgrzywa-Ziemak 2009):

- All organizations are learning systems, while learning is a continuous process as changes occurring in the organization and beyond it are constant. This opinion is not shared by all researchers[1].
- Learning organization is not only influenced by the organizations' interactions with the environment, but is also the outcome of the organization's internal aspirations.
- Learning process is a change in the knowledge of the organization as well as a parallel verification processes of existing knowledge and development of new knowledge (through simultaneous clash of exploitation and exploration processes).
- In addition to cognitive (technical) perspective, learning organization has social dimension. It takes place between levels: individual, group and organizational (and also inter-organizational), while sub-processes at individual levels have a different nature (Figure 1).
- Organizational learning is inseparably associated with action (cognition affects action and vice versa), however, the results of organizational learning should be viewed broadly – this can be a change not only in organizational behaviors, but also in potential behaviors. This prevents direct study of the results of organizational learning.

---

[1] For example, Crossan et al. (1999) believe that although all learning processes by individuals and groups can be considered as continuous, learning by the entire system has no such nature. It seems that this view is due to the way of seeing learning at the system level only through the prism of institutionalization understood as the implementation of knowledge created at lower levels into organizational routines, and thus – changing the organizational behaviour. Most organizational learning theories support the continuity of these processes.

- Learning organization cannot be a fully conscious process and therefore is the process that cannot be managed. The author believes that managers can influence learning organization, developing learning skills at all levels of learning. As a result, it is not possible to directly observe the organizational learning processes, but one can evaluate to what extent the conditions existing in the organization are conducive to these processes.

'Organizational learning' is often confused with the term 'learning organization'. It should be pointed out that „a learning organization is the ultimate goal that an organization strives to achieve, whereas organizational learning is the means through which a learning organization is attained; learning organization is the normative facet of organizational learning" (Firesonte and McElroy 2004 after: Karkoulian et al. 2013, 513).

The differences between organizational learning and the learning organization has been presented in Table 1.

LEVEL	PROCESS
individual	intuiting
group	interpreting
	integrating
organization	institutionalizing

Source: Own study based on: Crossan et al. (1999).

Figure 1. Sub-processes of organizational learning at individual, group and organizational levels.

Table 1. Distinctions between organizational learning and the learning organization

Organizational learning	Learning organization
Means	End
Process or activity	Idealized form
Attainable	Easily lost due to changes
Descriptive research	Prescriptive research
Inductive	Deductive (normative)
Academic and scholarly orientation	Practitioner and consultancy orientation
Predeminantly qualitative research	Predominantly quantitative research
Theoretical orientation	Action orientation

Source: Jashapara 2011, 160.

ORGANIZATIONAL CULTURE AND ORGANIZATIONAL LEARNING

Organizational culture is mostly seen as a facilitating factor or even an essential condition for organizational learning to occur and the cultural orientation towards learning is called learning oriented culture or learning culture. Learning culture can be defined as an organizational culture promoting and facilitating the individuals' learning, its share and dissemination, in order to contribute to organizational development and performance (Rebelo and Gomes 2011). There are the points of convergence among authors what are the characteristics that distinguish the learning culture.

The assumption of temporarily possessed knowledge fosters organizational learning. It leads to activities aimed at continuous improvement, building new knowledge and verifying the existing one (Zgrzywa-Ziemak 2009). Organizational learning researchers underline that learning should be one of the organization's core values (Schein 1992; Rebelo and Gomes 2011). This means not only orientation towards continuous development of all employees and their commitment to the improvement of the organization, its products and services (Marquardt 1996; Schein 2004; Pedler, Burgoyne and Boydell 1997; Popper and Lipshitz 1998; Senge 1990; Chang and Lee 2007), but also accountability which involves assuming responsibility for learning and active incorporation of the lessons learned into future action (Salk and Schneider 2009).

Organizational learning idea requires questioning of fundamental beliefs and work patterns (Schein 2004; Pedler et al. 1997; Senge 1990; Chang and Lee 2007) and opening to new ideas, knowledge coming from the inside of the organization as well as its surroundings (Leonard-Barton 1992). Organizational learning culture must include an assumption that solutions to problems arise from seeking the truth that can be found anywhere depending on the nature of the problem (as Schein's "commitment to truth through pragmatism and inquiry"). Many researches also emphasize the importance of issue orientation (Popper and Lipshitz 1998; Friedman et al. 2001).

According to Rijal (2010), the lifeblood of the learning organization is a free and open system for communicating information and knowledge as it encourages knowledge creation and enhances learning. Learning culture to promote open and intense communication, foster sharing ideas, information and knowledge, open dialogue (Senge 1990; Rijal 2010; Schein 2004; Chang and Lee 2007; Rebelo and Gomes 2011). Schein (1992) argues that it should be limited to "task-relevant" information (too much openness is, surprisingly, not helpful). Salk and Schneider (2009) find transparency, the ability to expose one's thoughts and actions to others to receive feedback as the most important. In transparent cultures pressure to distort or suppress unfavorable information is counteracted and openness to criticism and admission of error is facilitated (Salk and Schneider 2009).

Defining features of learning culture requires a reference to the nature of human actions which according to Schein (2004) should be proactive (not reactive), participants must be active in solving problems and learning, not passive. This view is recognized in the literature on learning organization (e.g., the concept of Friedman's organizational learning agent (2002) and Senge's personal mastery (1990)). Learning culture should stimulate to experimentation in every place of the organization by all its participants (Rijal 2010; Rebelo and Gomes 2011). Extensive experimentation is inevitably associated with risk, therefore willingness to take it is crucial for learning (Leonard-Barton 1992; Marquardt 1996; Pedler et al. 1997; Chang and Lee 2007). However, participants of the organization will show their readiness to take risk if they are encouraged to do so, the fear of failure is eradicated and they are given tolerance for errors (Schein 2004; Pedler et al. 1997; Rebelo and Gomes 2011). Taking into consideration learning perspective, a culture that does not require infallibility and perfection is needed. (Garvin, 2003). In addition, according to Schein (2004), learning requires positive assumptions about human nature, faith in people, belief that ultimately human nature is basically good and, in any case, malleable, and that they can change as they are able to improve themselves.

Characteristics of organizational culture as a learning-friendly organization require a reference to the essence of interpersonal relations. One of the fundamental values of the learning organization is egalitarianism that is equality of all participants of the organization (equality in expressing opinions, informing, requesting explanations, opportunities for promotion, development, etc.) (Leonard-Barton 1992; Senge 1990). Egalitarianism refers to the way of sharing power, participation and equal responsibility for achieving goals of the organization. According to Friedman (2001), egalitarianism opens communication channels, through which it promotes innovation and organizational learning, strengthens a sense of safety and justice, ensures that members of the organization are more willing to share their doubts and begin to inquire the truth.

A significant difficulty can be found in determining whether the essence of learning culture is collectivism or individualism. Learning organization idea assumes a large role of social interactions – team work, team solving of complex problems, joint exploration of reality and building goals (Rebelo and Gomes 2011). However, Sikorski believes (1999) that in a stream of constant changes, the lasting identity can only be individual. Contemporary team work should not lead to collectivist myths, cooperation and independent thinking are required. As a rule, the concept of the learning organization assumes that creating organizational goals must be strongly associated with personal goals of members of the organization and with an emphasis on self-development of its all participants (this is best seen in 'personal mastery' discipline of Senge (1990)). This view is in line with 'person-orientation' as an important feature of learning culture (Rebelo and Gomes 2011). For participants of the organization it is a tool for satisfying their personal needs of learning and development, and there is a close cooperation, mutual support and experience sharing; employees are not expected to act against their goals and values. Sikorski (1999, 2002) proposes the concept of collective and individual identity where the sense of collective identity is expressed in the belief that participation of an individual in the group should be exclusive, permanent and moral, and the purpose of participation is to find a safe place, and the sense of individual identity allows for parallel, temporary and calculative participation, and the goal here is to seek conditions favorable to achieving success. In this context, the sense of individual identity supports learning of the contemporary organization. Such relationships can only be built on the assumption of trust between members of the organization.

A number of authors highlight the importance of trust for the learning organization (Stata 1989; Leonard-Barton 1992; Senge 1990). Individuals and groups between which trust relationships occur, strive to avoid information distortions, eliminate emotional barriers that inhibit the free flow of information and knowledge, avoid secrets, share information for mutual assistance in solving tasks (Lyles 2001). Especially in the case of creating hidden knowledge it is required to move from an organizational culture oriented towards competing within the organization to a culture based on trust (Nonaka et al. 2001). Without trust, it would be impossible for participants of the organization to disclose their basic assumptions, and especially consent to their verification (which is important from the point of view of generative learning).

An important aspect of the organizational culture is how culture copes with organization-environment relation. Schein (2004)) argues that learning culture requires assumption that "the environment can be dominated," that organization can adapt to, and have some control over, rapidly-changing environment. However, the word 'dominance' can be misleading. Researches dealing with learning organizations indicate the fact that these organizations can shape their future in accordance with their dreams and aspirations (Senge 1990). The conviction about determination of the organization's activities by the environment imposes an attitude of reacting reactively to changes in the present and forecasted environment, which, especially in the dynamic and complex environment is not conducive to learning. Therefore, the conviction of many alternative futures should dominate as it requires activity in creating the future by the organization which stimulates generative learning. However, the freedom to decide about the future of the organization does not require striving to control and dominate the environment, but to cooperate with it to build the desired future (Zgrzywa-Ziemak 2009). For example, Rebelo and Gomes (2011) underline that one of the features of the learning culture is concern for all stakeholders.

Table 2. Organizational culture that inhibits and supports organizational learning

Culture that inhibits organizational learning	Culture that supports organizational learning
• negative attitude towards sharing knowledge and information • closure to one's own views, information and ideas • orientation to one, best way of perceiving reality • no possibility of expressing different views and opinions • criticism treated as threat • no violation of rules • no self-reliance • experimentation perceived as threat • risk avoidance • severe punishment for mistakes • no equal opportunities • full subordination of individual goals to group • stabilization resulting from external conditions of work • conformism • reluctance to take responsibility • exclusive, permanent and moral participation • lack of trust is dominant	• positive attitude towards sharing knowledge and information • orientation on exploration views of others • continuous search for new ideas • accepting plurality of ways of perceiving reality • freedom in expressing views and opinions • openness to criticism • orientation on the search for individualized solutions • self-reliance and freedom in making decisions • enthusiastic approach to experimenting • readiness to take risk • mistakes are opportunity to learn • equal opportunities • independence of individuals • person-orientation • stabilization based on knowledge and competence • independence of thinking, willingness to take responsibility • parallel, temporary and calculative participation • trust is dominant

Source: own study.

Although there is a wide discussion what the organizational culture that supports organizational learning is, the empirical research verifying developed concepts are very limited. They rarely go beyond case studies analysis. There are significant differences and inconsistencies in defining and measuring organizational culture and OL, which makes it difficult to compare achieved results. In case of the wider research, part of the research refers to selected characteristics of the organizational culture in the context of its influence on the OL, while the other part aims to determine the type of culture conducive to the organizational learning. Sanz-Valle et al. (2011) provide evidence for the positive link between organizational culture and organizational learning and that the impact of organizational culture on organizational learning varies with the type of organizational culture (the research was conducted on a sample of 451 Spanish organizations). It proved that the type of organizational culture which encourages organizational learning is adhocracy, while hierarchy culture is negatively associated to OL, and clan and market cultures were not significant for organizational learning. Cho, Kim, Park and Cho (2013) findings indicate that group, developmental, and rational cultures influence learning orientation, but hierarchical culture did not (study included 406 service providers in Korea). Rijal (2010) identified that dimensions of organizational culture significantly and positively related to learning organization are openness, confrontation, trust, authenticity, proaction, collaboration and experimenting, and that there was no significant correlation in case of autonomy dimension (8 organizations from the pharmaceutical industry from Nepal and India were investigated). According to Liao et al. (2012) study, an innovative culture and a supportive culture are important to influence the commitment to learning, open-mindedness and shared vision (in Taiwan's banking and insurance organizations). Salk and Schneider (2009) found out that two learning values were significant predictors to commitment to learning: accountability and valid information (they questioned 314 employees across 32 units of a public land management agency in the U.S.). Unfortunately, none of the empirical studies recognize *learning culture* in the theoretically presented complexity. What is more, with few exceptions, studies do not analyze the relationship between organizational culture and organizational learning in the context of other factors important for learning (other than organizational culture).

May the summary of the discussion on the features of a culture that supports and inhibits organizational learning be the characteristics shown in Table 2.

METHOD OF SHAPING THE ORGANIZATIONAL CULTURE THAT SUPPORTS ORGANIZATIONAL LEARNING

Knowing the elements of the culture that supports organizational learning it is worth considering how to shape desired culture of organization. The research that preceded presentation of the model (Molasy 2016) showed that organizations may build their organizational cultures on actions based mostly on human resources' management, as follows:

1. Development of model organizational culture.
2. Determining the "silhouette" of a desired employee.
3. Recruitment and selection.
4. Cultural adaptation of a new employee.
5. Pro-developmental assessment of the worker.
6. Motivation through special care for employees.
7. Actions from outside the area of human resources' management.

The set of actions for shaping the organizational culture has been presented on the Figure 2.

Source: Molasy 2016, 109.

Figure 2. Proposed set of actions for shaping the culture of organization.

To instill the desired organizational culture effectively in the company, first a culture pattern must be developed – the one that has been described previously described as culture that supports and inhibits organizational learning.

Based on the model organizational culture the "silhouette" of a desired employee should be developed. The concept of an individual as organizational learning agent seems to correspond to the presented pattern of culture that comes first of all from the concept of 'personal mastery' of Senge (1990), 'organizational learning agent' of Friedman (2001) and 'knowledge practitioners' of Nonaka and Takeuchi (1995). Friedman emphasizes that "individuals *at all levels in every organization encounter new ideas, mistakes, puzzles or other opportunities to learn every day*". He believes that *"people who decide to act based on their discoveries and make the organization interested in them are organizational learning agents"* (Friedman 2001, 412). 'Personal mastery' was recognized by Senge as one of five disciplines of the learning organization, according to him *"people who have achieved a high level of personal mastery constantly expand their ability to achieve in life what they really strive to"* (Senge 2000, 146), *while the organization will not teach as long as it does have at all levels of its structure people practicing individually such understood [as personal mastery] learning"* (Senge 2000, 148). In turn, mid-level managers who accumulate, create and update quiet and explicit knowledge are 'knowledge practitioners' in the opinion of Nonaka and Takeuchi (1995). The author of this research cannot agree with the view of Nonaka and Takeuchi who recognize that 'knowledge practitioners' can only become mid-level managers. The author believes that definition of Friedman best reflects the concept of organizational learning agent where every employee at any level of the organization can be involved in its improvement. Detailed analysis of the features of individuals which are important in the learning organization indicates that concepts presented by Friedman (2001) and Senge (2000) complement each other.

Organizational learning agent must be proactive, he should undertake to solve approached problems instead of expecting it from the organization (Friedman 2001). Moreover, Senge tells about the adoption of *"creative rather than reactive way of seeing the world"* (Senge 2000, 147) which requires mastering two types of skills. On the one hand, the ability for continuous determination which is important for the individual, i.e., creating personal vision of the future, with Senge points out that people who have achieved a high level of personal mastery have a special sense of purpose superior to their vision and intentions. Friedman states only that organizational learning agents are people of high aspirations. On the other hand, participants of the organization must master the ability to clearly perceive the surrounding reality. This is the reason why Friedman emphasizes that organizational learning agents demonstrate reflexivity, invest time and energy in investigating and analyzing the situation. Both authors indicate that individuals must be aware of the limitations present in complex organizational reality so that failures or resistance of the organization do not lead them to cynicism and discouragement. Friedman defines this feature as realism in the perception of limitations. Fritz states that *"A truly creative person knows that creativity consists in working among limitations. When there are no limitations, there is also no creativity"* (Senge 2000, 160). Senge believes that people who have achieved a high level of personal mastery can see a particular reality surrounding them as an ally and not as an enemy, therefore they can perceive and cooperate with forces leading to changes instead of fighting against these forces. They are characterized by perseverance which often results from faith and trust in their own strength.

Organizational learning agent should have critical approach towards the surrounding reality in order to perceive the gap between the goals set and the reality, to see more and more new problems to be solved (Friedman 2001). *"The essence of personal mastery is learning to create and maintain creative tension in our lives"* – this tension results from the difference between reality and vision (Senge 2000, 147). Friedman sees the need to link criticism in relation to the surrounding reality with commitment to its improvement.

An individual must be able to maintain his independence (independence of judgment and assessment), while cooperating with others in order to accomplish the goals set (Friedman 2001). Similarly, Senge states that people who have achieved a high level of personal mastery feel attached to others and to the whole of life around them, without denying any of their unique features.

Senge indicates that *"people who have achieved a high level of personal mastery never stop learning"* (Senge 2000, 148). Popper and Lipshitz (1998) mention the *"professionalism of organization members"* as significantly affecting organizational learning. Nonaka and Takeuchi (1995) indicate that high qualifications and skills expand the individual's ability to analyze and improve reality. Literature also includes a term 'orientation focused on development and learning,' which are defined by London (1983) as *"striving to develop possessed knowledge and skills"* (Bartkowiak 1998, 8), Kozłowski and Farr (1988) as *"participation [...] in specified forms of permanent learning, i.e., aimed at seeking knowledge and skills related to interests"* (Bartkowiak 1998, 8), while Bartkowiak as an attitude of employees towards their own development and learning together with three components: cognitive, emotional and behavioural. Senge (1990) associates developmental orientation with the *"subjective importance of having proficiency or even excellence in specific knowledge or skills"* (Bartkowiak 1998, 8).

By specifying "silhouette" of a desired employee it is assumed that the organization's development requires its employees to demonstrate not only high skills, but also to constantly deepen their knowledge and skills – not only related to the currently performed job, but also in the perspective of their future career. It is also assumed that they enhance their qualifications in order to learn and practice innovative behaviors. Naturally, *"acquiring knowledge by individuals does not guarantee [...] that the organization is learning"* (Senge 2000, 145), however, this is the foundation for their commitment to the improvement.

Subsequent actions are taken in the context of recruitment and selection. Whether the candidate possesses the characteristics specified in the "silhouette," can be verified in few ways: by analyzing the submitted job application, in manual tests and in technical exams. Skills of the candidate can be best verified in an interview. Questions asked in the middle of it better help to understand the true nature of the achievement, experience and capability for learning and will to deepening knowledge. So, the companies should carefully prepare a framework for interviews - for example, a set of questions to be asked by the recruiter.

Another contact with the elements of the organizational culture and increasing awareness of them, the new employees have during special implementation period to the company, which takes into account full adaptation, also its cultural aspect. Implementation trainings are meant largely to integrate the new employee with the organizational culture and they should be designed regarding this purpose. The training program provided for this time may include not only the training in the field of the future position on which a new employee will start work, but also from a wide range covering the value of learning and ways to cultivate deepening knowledge within the organization.

The next step in creating culture is cyclical assessment of an employee which should regularly verify matching of human resources to the predetermined silhouette of a desired employee. It should not take into account only measurable results achieved by an employee on his position and the quality of his work, but also an assessment of what the employee thinks, feels, and what actions he takes with regard to his own results, to the organization, to the environment, to the extent of his identification with the organization's culture, to his place in the structure of the company. This assessment should be pro-developmental in nature for employees and in a special way rewarding behaviors compliant with the learning capabilities. It can be carried out in the form of a assessment conversation based on the self-evaluation prepared in advance by the employee.

Based on the evaluation results and difficulties identified, activities should be designed aimed at improving performance and building development path. A good and effective practice seems to be development of schedules of active and comprehensive trainings, covering also the trainings helping in shaping appropriate attitudes and behaviors. Important in continuous learning are courses and trainings not only in the subject of work, but also trainings for the trainings themselves. To deepen and cultivate the skills of acquiring knowledge itself.

During creating organizational culture a special concern for the fate of the employees should be considered as the primary source of motivation. It embodies, inter alia, in activities in the field of building an adequate offer of social facilities, the sense of security thanks to the working conditions and planning beyond-organizational life of workers. Thanks to that action, the employees are stronger tied to the organization and the risk of leaving work by them is reduced. These activities are accompanied by the assumption that after the use of the earlier steps of the method of creating organizational culture. We employ workers who share organizational values and who are soaked with them.

Created organizational culture to some extent is also affected by other activities from outside the area of human resources management. Work should be organized in such a way and take place in such conditions of the physical space of the organization that it fosters learning. Not only separate spaces appropriately organized for individual and group work play an important role, but also places where employees will meet to informally exchange their knowledge.

Not without significance are the rationalization systems used that enhance the creativity of employees and their willingness to make special efforts and take voluntary additional measures for the organization. An example of such actions, outside the area of human resources management, are all sorts of suggestion systems in organizations. During the sessions, employees generate ideas for improvements in many areas of the organization which results in benefits not only for the organization, but also for employees. Knowledge and willingness to create is deepened in organizations, while implemented suggestions bring measurable economic benefits. Employees not only receive material benefits from the implemented ideas, but also cultivate and deepen their learning skills.

CONCLUSION

This paper demonstrates application dimension of shaping social behaviors in organizations. After applying presented seven steps in organizations, an organizational culture can be created that will be conducive to organizational learning. Presented sketch of the method requires further research. It may include both the specification of particular steps included in the method as well as the definition of a specific type of organizational culture in relation to a number of typologies found in the literature. A type of organizational culture conducive to learning would be accompanied by a specific approach to human resources management.

REFERENCES

Argote, Linda. *Organizational Learning: Creating, Retaining and Transferring Knowledge*. Springer Science & Business Media, 2012.

Argyris, Chris, and Donald Schön. *Organizational Learning: A Theory-in-Action Perspective*, Adison-Wesley, 1978.

Bartkowiak, Grażyna. Orientacja Nastawiona Na Rozwój I Uczenie Się Osób Zatrudnionych W Organizacji [Orientation Oriented On Development and Learning of People Employed in the Organization], Poznań: Wyd. AE w Poznaniu, 1998.

Chang, Su-Chao, and Ming-Shing Lee. "A Study on Relationship among Leadership, Organizational Culture, the Operation of Learning Organization and Employees' Job Satisfaction." *The learning organization* 14, no. 2 (2007): 155-185.

Cho, Insu, Joseph Kichul Kim, Heejun Park, and Nam-Heung Cho. "The Relationship between Organisational Culture and Service Quality through Organisational Learning Framework." *Total Quality Management and Business Excellence* 24, no. 7-8 (2013): 753- 68.

Crossan, Mary M., Henry W. Lane, and Roderick E. White. "An Organizational Learning Framework: From Intuition to Institution." *Academy of management review* 24, no. 3 (1999): 522–537.

Davenport, Thomas H., and Laurence Prusak. *Working Knowledge: How Organizations Manage What They Know*. Harvard Business Press, 1998.

Fiol, Marlene, and Marjorie A. Lyles. "Organizational Learning." *Academy of Management Review* 10, no. 4 (1985): 803–813.

Friedman, Victor, Raanan Lipshitz, and Wim Overmeer. "Creating Conditions for Organizational Learning." In *Handbook of Organizational Learning and Knowledge*, edited by Meinlf Dierkes, Adrane Berthoin Antal, John Child and Ikujiro Nonaka, 757–793. New York: Oxford University Press, 2001.

Friedman, Victor. "The Individual as Agent of Organizational Learning." In *Handbook of Organizational Learning and Knowledge*, edited by Meinlf Dierkes, Adrane Berthoin Antal, John Child and Ikujiro Nonaka, 398–414. New York: Oxford University Press, 2001.

Friedman, Victor. "The Individual as Agent of Organizational Learning." *California management review* 44, no. 2 (2002): 70-89.

Garvin, David, A. *Learning in Action: A Guide to Putting the Learning Organization to Work*. Harvard Business Review Press, 2003.

Jashapara, Ashok. *Knowledge Management: An Integrated Approach*. Pearson Education, 2004.

Kamiński, Robert. *"Spójność Kultury Organizacyjnej a Innowacyjność Przedsiębiorstwa."* ["Cohesion of Organizational Culture and Enterprise Innovation."] PhD diss, Wrocław University of Science and Technology, 2002.

Karkoulian, Silva, Leila Canaan Messarra, and Richard McCarthy. "The Intriguing Art of Knowledge Management and Its Relation to Learning Organizations." *Journal of Knowledge Management* 17, no. 4 (2013): 511-526.

Lau, Patricia Yin Yin Lau, G ary N. McLean, Yen-Chen Hsu, and Bella Ya-Hui Lien. "Learning Organization, Organizational Culture, and Affective Commitment in Malaysia: A Person-Organization Fit Theory." *Human Resource Development International* 20, no. 2 (2017): 159-179.

Lencioni, Patrick M. "Make Your Values Mean Something." *Harvard business review* 80, no. 7 (2002): 113-117.

Leonard-Barton, Dorothy. "The Factory as a Learning Laboratory." *Sloan Management Review*, Fall (1992): 23–38.

Liao, Shu-Hsien, Wen-Jung Chang, Da-Chian Hu, and Yi-Lan Yueh. "Relationships among Organizational Culture, Knowledge Acquisition, Organizational Learning, and Organizational Innovation in Taiwan's Banking and Insurance Industries." *The International Journal of Human Resource Management* 23, no. 1 (2012): 52-70.

Lyles, Marjorie A. "Organizational Learning in International Joint Ventures: The Case of Hungary." In *Handbook of Organizational Learning and Knowledge*, edited by Meinlf Dierkes, Adrane Berthoin Antal, John Child and Ikujiro Nonaka, 681–698. New York: Oxford University Press, 2001.

Marquardt, Michael J. *Building the Learning Organization: A Systems Approach to Quantum Improvement and Global Success*. McGraw-Hill Companies, 1996.

Molasy, Mateusz. "Modelling Human Behaviours by Shaping Organizational Culture." In *Modeling Human Behavior: Individuals and Organizations*, edited by Lucas Jódar Sánchez, Elena de la Poza Plaza and Luis Acedo Rodriguez. Nova Science Publishers, 2016.

Nonaka, Ikujiro, and Hirotaka Takeuchi. *The Knowledge – Creating Company.* New York: Oxford University Press, 1995.

Nonaka, Ikujiro, Ryoko Toyama, and Philippe Byosière. "The Theory of Organizational Knowlegde Creation: Understanding the Dynamic Process of Creating Knowledge." In *Handbook of Organizational Learning and Knowledge*, edited by Meinlf Berthoin Antal Dierkes, Adrane, John Child and Ikujiro Nonaka. 491–517. New York: Oxford University Press, 2001.

O'Reilly, Charles. "Corporations, Culture, and Commitment: Motivation and Social Control in Organizations." *California Management Review* 31, no. 4 (1989): 9-25.

Pedler, Mike, John Burgoyne, and Tom Boydell. *The Learning Company: A Strategy for Sustainable Growth.* Maidenhead: McGraw-Hill, 1997.

Popper, Micha, and Raanan Lipshitz. "Organizational Learning Mechanisms: A Structural and Cultural Approach to Organizational Learning." *The Journal of applied behavioral science* 34, no. 2 (1998): 161–179.

Rebelo, Teresa M., and Adelino Duarte Gomes. "Conditioning Factors of an Organizational Learning Culture." *Journal of Workplace Learning* 23, no. 3 (2011): 173-194.

Rijal, Sapna. "Leadership Style and Organizational Culture in Learning Organization: A Comparative Study." *International Journal of Management & Information Systems* (Online) 14, no. 5 (2010).

Rokeach, Milton. *The Nature of Human Values.* Free Press, 1973.

Salk, Raintry J., and Ingrid E. Schneider. "Commitment to Learning within a Public Land Management Agency: The Influence of Transformational Leadership and Organizational Culture." *Journal of Park & Recreation Administration* 27, no. 1 (2009): 70-84.

Santos-Vijande, María Leticia, José Ángel López-Sánchez, and Juan Antonio Trespalacios. "How Organizational Learning Affects a Firm's Flexibility, Competitive Strategy, and Performance." *Journal of Business Research* 65, no. 8 (2012): 1079-1089.

Sanz-Valle, Raquel, Julia C. Naranjo-Valencia, Daniel Jiménez-Jiménez, and Laureano Perez-Caballero. "Linking Organizational Learning with Technical Innovation and Organizational Culture." *Journal of Knowledge Management* 15, no. 6 (2011): 997-1015.

Schein, Edgar H. *Organizational Culture and Leadership.* San Francisco: Jossey–Bass Publishers, 1992.

Senge, Peter M. *The Fifth Discipline: The Art and Practice of the Learning Organization.* New York: Currency Doubleday, 1990.

Sikorski, Czesław. *Kultura Organizacyjna.* [Organizational Culture.] Warszawa: CH Beck, 2002.

Stata, Ray. "Organizational Learning-the Key to Management Innovation." *Sloan Management Review* 30, no. 3 (1989): 63–74.

Wu, Lei-Yu. "Applicability of the Resource-Based and Dynamic-Capability Views under Environmental Volatility." *Journal of Business Research* 63, no. 1 (2010): 27-31.

Zgrzywa-Ziemak, Anna, and Robert Kamiński. *Rozwój Zdolności Uczenia Się Przedsiębiorstwa.* [Development of Enterprise Learning Ability.] Warszwa: Difin, 2009.

———. "Model zdolności uczenia się przedsiębiorstw w świetle badań empirycznych." ["The model of learning of enterprises in the light of empirical research."] In: *Rozwijanie zdolności uczenia się przedsiębiorstwa*, edited by Anna Zgrzywa-Ziemak, and Robert Kamiński. 138-178. Warszawa: DIFIN, 2009.

———. *Organizational Culture and Leadership.* John Wiley & Sons, 2004.

———. *Zachowania Ludzi W Organizacji.* [Behavior of People in the Organization.] Warszawa: PWN, 1999.

In: Modeling Social Behavior and Its Applications
Editors: L. A. Jódar Sánchez et al.

ISBN: 978-1-53613-666-1
© 2018 Nova Science Publishers, Inc.

Chapter 7

ANALYZING COUNTRY RISK THROUGH THE FIXED-INCOME SECURITIES MARKET: THE CASE OF SPAIN AND GREECE

Héctor Ariza Gutiérrez and *Elena de la Poza Plaza*

Universitat Politècnica de València,
Faculty of Business Management and Administration,
Valencia, Spain

ABSTRACT

This chapter analyzes the country risk; that is, the risk of not facing debt payment liabilities incurred by two European powers, Spain and Greece, during the 2008-2015 period.

The crisis era the world has known since 2008 has been one of the clearest aggravating factors that has led the payment capacity of countries, companies and families to fluctuate. This study analyzes these fluctuations and why they came about. This chapter measures the country risk through the evolution of a country's risk premium. It analyzes the evolution of risk premium and its relation with the financing requirements of the Spanish and Greek States. For this purpose, it studies the awarded volume and the returns on national debt issued on the primary markets of both States, as well as the negotiated volume and its returns on public debt on the secondary market. This chapter also studies the private debt market and the dependence between it and the risk premium. Finally, it provides details of the repercussions that fluctuations in the risk premium have had on the Spanish and Greek societies.

Keywords: country risk, risk premium, Spain, Greece, national debt, primary market, secondary market

---

* Corresponding Author address. Email: toxichector@gmail.com.

INTRODUCTION

The international financing system is based on three fundamental pillars: financial agents, financial markets and assets. The world crisis that began in 2008 favoured a reduction in the payment capacity of families, companies and countries. Thus financial agents with a deficit of funds, regardless of them being families, companies or the State itself, turn to financial markets to seek sources of financing, and are willing to pay the cost that these sources would involve depending on the solvency they present to face the incurred payment liabilities. In turn, families, companies or organizations with acquired surplus find the chance on financial markets to make their funds profitable.

One of the financing sources most widely used by both public and private sectors (mainly large- and medium-sized companies) is debt (fixed-income financial assets) financing.

So when the State is the agent that seeks financing sources, it normally issues both short-term debt (Treasury Bills) and long-term debt (bonds and liabilities). In turn, once all these issued debts have been awarded, they generate a cost for the financing issuer, and lead to a certain profitability for those agents that buy the issued assets. Likewise, the private sector also issues and buys fixed-income assets to finance its activity.

This chapter analyses the country risk; that is, the risk of not being able to comply with the payment liabilities that result from the debts incurred by the States of the two European powers Spain and Greece during 2008-2015.

The country risk, i.e., the likelihood that the State cannot pay its payment liabilities, can be explained by relevant facts and specific events that have occurred nationally; for Spain, the Spanish real-estate bubble; for Greece, the fact that it almost withdrew from the Eurozone; for both States, repeated national and bank bail-outs.

One of the most widely used methods to study fluctuations in the risk of a country not being able to pay its payment liabilities is to analyze the evolution of the country's risk premium, a method which this study centers on.

After analyzing the evolution of the risk premium, its relation with the return made from financing public debt on the primary and secondary markets of both countries is measured. In other words, the awarded volume and the returns of public debt issued on the primary markets of both the Spanish and Greek States, and the negotiated volume and its returns on the secondary market are studied.

METHODOLOGY

To analyse the risk premium in Spain and Greece, we must define what the country risk consists in and explain the methodology used to study it.

The country risk is the possible insolvency situation of all a State's payment liabilities. In other words, it is the State's possible *default* situation when faced with the obligation of complying with the demands of it paying its debts.

We must understand the State as a whole that encompasses:

- The public sector, which receives financing directly from taxes and rates, among others.
- The private sector, where we include companies, professionals and families.

To measure a State's insolvency situation, we can use several methods:

- On the one hand, we find the *risk premium* that defines the portal as "the difference in the interest paid for a country's debt and that paid for another country's debt" (Infobolsa, an entity completely owned by Spanish Stock Exchanges and Markets). To specifically calculate the risk premium used in this study, the return made on the German 10-year bond on secondary markets is taken as a reference.

  The reason for using the return made on the German bond is its stability over the years. Although it has not always been completely constant, it is the most stable bond in analysis records.
- On the other hand, and in a more visual and simpler way, Standard & Poor's credit ratings that score on a preset scale the possibility of refunds being paid upon maturity from the bonds issued by the State, are used to analyze the country risk.

  Although the econometric models used by Standard & Poor's to obtain ratings are confidential, it is well-known that some of the main pillars to issue them are:
  - The management of public/private institutions
  - The financial/economic power of companies and the State
  - Companies' sectorial information
  - Future forecasts of the economy of institutions and their surroundings.
- Finally, Pearson's correlation coefficient is estimated, which allows to linearly relate quantitative variables, even though they are measured in different units.

ANALYZING THE SPANISH RISK PREMIUM

Figure 1 shows the evolution of the Spanish risk premium between January 2008 and December 2015, along with the ratings that Standard & Poor's gave Spain during the same period (Table 1).

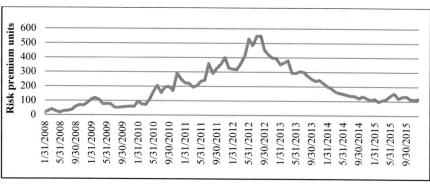

Source: The Authors according to "Infobolsa" and "Trading Economics".

Figure 1. Evolution of the risk premium in Spain.

Table 1. Credit Quality Rating of Spanish Public Debt according to S&P

Credit Quality Ratings of Spanish Public Debt according to S&P	
Date	Rating
January 2009	AA+
December 2009	AA+
April 2010	AA
October 2011	AA-
December 2011	AA-
January 2012	A
April 2012	BBB+
October 2012	BBB-
November 2013	BBB-
May 2014	BBB
October 2015	BBB+

Source: The Authors according to "Trading Economics".

Next we detail the most important historic facts that were recorded during our time horizon and which affected Spain in some way.

The bankruptcy of Lehman Brothers (September 2008), the fourth biggest investment bank in the USA and one of the most important in the world, favoured mistrust and instability on financial markets. This situation led to the fall of more financial/non financial institutions, and finally gave way to the world financial crisis in 2008, one of the worst ever recorded to date.

Meanwhile, the Spanish credit quality rating remained constant at AA+ from September 2008 to April 2010, after which time it began to drop. At that time, Spain went into recession as its gross domestic product (GDP) lowered in the two following trimesters.

On 2 May 2010, the first bail-out was passed for Greece, valued at 110, 000 million euros, in which Spain directly participated by means of bilateral loans that amounted to 6,650 million euros, and also indirectly through the International Monetary Fund (IMF), which loaned 20,100 million euros, where Spain participated at 1.7%. According to its percentage of participation in the financing institutions, the Spanish exposure to this bail-out came to 6,991.7 million euros.

From 2010 to 2012, the European Central Bank (ECB) bought Greek debt up to 20,000 million euros and, since Spain participated at 12.5%, the Spanish exposure amounted to 2500 million euros.

In May 2011, a bail-out for Portugal was passed, valued at 78,000 million euros, to which Spain contributed with 4 500 million euros.

On 9 June 2012 aid to Spain of 100,000 million euros was made public, which Spain had requested from the ECB to rescue its banking system. In the same year, Spain's credit quality rating went from A in January to BBB- in October.

In February 2012, more aid was granted to Greece by the Eurogroup, valued at 130 000 million euros. This time the bail-out came through the European Financial Stability Facility (EFSF), which lent 144,600 million euros, where Spain participated at 11.8%, which came to 12.7% because Ireland, Portugal and Greece were excluded from participating in this aid, and also through the IMF, which lent 19,100 million euros. So if we bear in mind Spain's participations in these institutions, Spain's exposure to this bail-out was 18,689 million euros.

Despite the banking system being not only rescued, but also an important news item to calm down the market and to confer stability, it was not until the end of August when the Spanish risk premium began to lower.

From 2012 to 2015, the risk premium continued to lower to almost 100 basic points, at which point Spain would enter a situation of political uncertainty. Strong rivalry among political parties existed immediately before the December 2015 elections in Spain. Immediately after these elections, no consensus was reached by these parties to form a government. This situation of political instability was transferred to the risk premium, which rose again, be it to a lesser extent, but did not go beyond 200 points.

Spanish Public Financing

On the primary public market we find awarded debt underwent many ups and downs. No large volume of awarded debt existed before the economic crisis that began in 2008, but it increased by 180% when the crisis began.

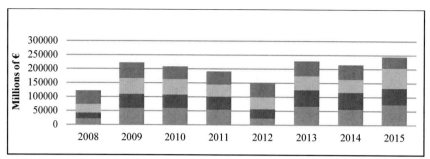

Source: The Authors according to "Bank of Spain". Blue: 1st quarter; red: 2nd quarter; green: 3rd quarter; purple: 4th quarter.

Figure 2. Awards in auctioning of the Spanish State - primary market.

Not only is the amount of awarded debt important, but also the type of awarded debt. From Figure 3 we can see that since the crisis began until it ended, Spain went from financing by short-term assets (Treasury Bills) to other longer-term assets (bonds and obligations). The quality of Spanish debt has, therefore, improved as the debt maturity has also increased, and Spain should face these payments during a longer time period.

Although it is true that quality has increased in general terms, we can see that in 2012, when Spain requested its banking system being bailed out, the most awarded assets were Treasury Bills, which obtained a rate of more than 60%.

Another variable that is important when issuing debt is the return it will make because, the higher its return, the higher the cost for the State's financing as the payment of interests is higher. In the graph below we can see the mean returns obtained from awarding debt. Specifically we use the quarter means of 3-and 5-year bonds and 10-year liabilities as they are the reference assets of investors.

If we bear in mind the performance curve theory of a financial asset, it can be concluded that the longer an asset's maturity, the higher the yield that investors expect. However due to inefficiencies on the market and lack of knowledge about auction bids, we observe that there are times when the performance of assets with a shorter maturity exceeds those with a longer maturity. It is noteworthy that the points where no information exists correspond to the time when this asset type is not awarded.

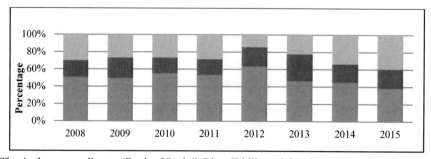

Source: The Authors according to "Bank of Spain". Blue: T-bills; red: bonds; green: obligations.

Figure 3. Spanish State Debt Awarded according to Financial Assets.

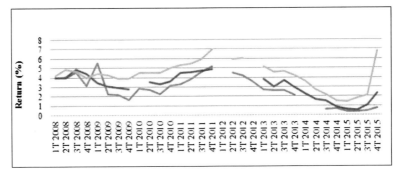

Source: The Authors according to "Bank of Spain". Blue: 3-Y Bonds; red: 5-Y Bonds; green: 10-Y Bonds.

Figure 4. Mean returns from auctioning the Spanish State's public debt.

If we apply Pearson's correlation coefficient to relate the risk premium with returns, we obtain the following results:

Table 2. Correlation coefficient between the return of public debt assets on the primary market and the risk premium – Spain

Correlation Coefficient between the Return on Public Debt Assets on the Primary Market and the Risk Premium – Spain	
3-Year bonds on the primary market (public sector)	0.36
5-Year bonds on the primary market (public sector)	0.32
10-Year liabilities on the primary market (public sector)	0.50

Source: The Authors according to "Bank of Spain".

For the assets with a shorter maturity (3- and 5-year bonds), it can be concluded that a moderate relation exists with the risk premium.

However for the assets with a longer maturity (10-year liabilities), a stronger linear relation exists. Thus an increase in the risk premium would affect the latter assets more, and vice versa.

If we look at the returns made with Spanish bonds, but this time on the secondary market, we also observe that they have their ups and downs:

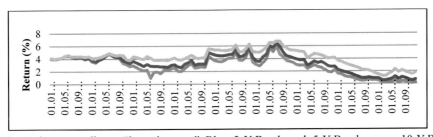

Source: The Authors according to "investing.com". Blue: 3-Y Bonds; red: 5-Y Bonds; green: 10-Y Bonds.

Figure 5. Return on Spanish public debt on the secondary market.

In this case, and on occasion, the yield of assets with a shorter maturity exceeds that of assets with a longer maturity. This is because information for investors on secondary markets is more accessible than in auctions.

If we consider the correlation coefficients for the return made with assets on the secondary market and also the Spanish risk premium, then:

Table 3. Correlation coefficient between the return on public debt assets on the secondary market with the risk premium – Spain

Correlation Coefficient between the Return on Public Debt Assets on the Secondary Market with the Risk Premium - Spain	
3-Year bonds on the secondary market (public sector)	0.49
5-Year bonds on the secondary market (public sector)	0.55
10-Year bonds on the secondary market (public sector)	0.64

Source: The Authors according to "Bank of Spain".

Once again assets with a longer maturity are those that most correlate with the risk premium. As the risk premium is calculated with the performance of the 10-year bonds on the secondary market, the correlation coefficient between the risk premium and the profitability on the secondary market is expected to be higher than the correlation coefficient that corresponds to the primary market. As the return on the 10-year German bonds has never been zero, and has varied over the years, the coefficient shows no perfect correlation.

ANALYZING THE GREEK RISK PREMIUM

As we have done with the Spanish risk premium, we analyze the Greek risk premium with its more relevant milestones, while we can see the ratings that S&P issued for Greek bonds.

As we can see, after the world crisis began, the risk premium began to rise about 1 year later, but it was not until 2010 that the plan of Goldman and Shachs (one of the world's biggest investment and securities financial groups) that it carried out to hide the millions of euros of Greek public debt from the European Commission came to light. At the time, issued Greek public debt was below the so-called junk bonds, and it would not go over this point during our time horizon.

After several months of negotiations, on 2 May in the same year, the European Union (EU) awarded Greece a plan with aid valued at 110,000 million euros, which would mainly come from the IMF. This plan would make Greece take macroeconomic adjustment measures, like increasing VAT or making government cuts that would affect civil servants. Nonetheless, its risk premium continued to increase even after announcing economic aid to financially help Greece.

In 2011 the situation became worse because Greece did not have enough liquidity to pay civil servants and pensioners beyond October. So public entities were privatized and certain taxes were amended, like property tax, which triggered citizen disturbances and, therefore, created economic, social and political instability, which led to anticipated General Elections being announced at the end of the year to take place in February 2012. Credit rating agencies continued to lower the ratings for Greek bonds, which were virtually at minimum levels on the scale, and the returns of bonds were at all-time maximums ever known to date.

In 2012 another lot of rescue aid for Greece was passed, valued this time at 130,000 million euros, which was to be made through the EFSF and the IMF. This time it led to a brusque drop in the Greek risk premium, which had an all-time maximum figure of almost 3500 points in February and then lowered to 1900 points. Although it is true that the risk premium rose again in May, it once again lowered gradually and approached the 1000 points limit at the end of the year, which led to credit rating agents improve the score of Greek bonds.

Over the next 2 years the risk premium had its ups and downs owing to constant market instability, and although it reached the same levels as those at the beginning of 2010, it rose in August 2013 and June 2014. From this point it went above 1000 basic points in 2015.

Rumors started circulating at the time about Greece possibly withdrawing from the Eurozone. The risk premium once again increased, while credit rating agencies once again started to make the scores of bonds worse due to the country's economic and political volatility given the possibility of it withdrawing from the EU.

On 5 July, the famous referendum was held to learn the public's opinion about whether to accept or not the conditions imposed by the EU. After "NO" won, negotiations for new rescue aid began, which ended in an agreement in August about 86 000 million euros being paid over 3 years. This resulted in the risk premium once again going below the threshold of 1000 basic points.

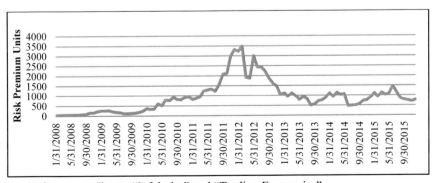

Source: The Authors according to "Infobolsa" and "Trading Economics".

Figure 6. Evolution of the risk premium in Greece.

Table 4. Credit Quality Rating of Greek Public debt according to S&P

Date	Rating
January 2009	A-
December 2009	BBB+
March 2010	BBB+
April 2010	BB+
December 2010	BB+
March 2011	BB-
May 2011	B
June 2011	CCC
July 2011	CC
May 2012	CCC
August 2012	CCC
December 2012	B-
December 2014	B
January 2015	B
April 2015	CCC+
June 2015	CCC-
July 2015	CCC+
January 2016	B-

Source: The Authors according to "Trading Economics".

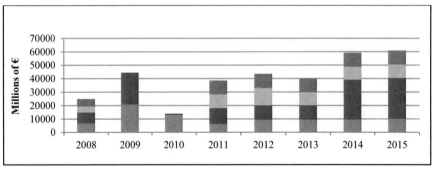

Source: The Authors according to the "Public Debt Management Agency".
Blue: 1stquarter; red: 2nd quarter; green: 3rd quarter; purple: 4th quarter.

Figure 7. Awards in Greek State auctions – primary market.

Greek Public Financing

As we can see, auction awards of Greek public debt on the primary market were irregular. We see sharp growth of 177% from 2008 to 2009, which drastically drops in 2010. From this point, it strongly increases and constantly follows a general growth tendency until 2015.

It is noteworthy that the State does not award debt in the last two quarters.

Regarding the quality of debt from the maturity viewpoint that Greece emitted, Figure 8 shows that it went from being financed in the long term to the short term.

Therefore, its quality has worsened and it will have to face making payments in less time. It is worth stressing that assets were divided in this way to resemble the Spanish case.

As we can also see in Figure 8, the change in tendency was drastic, which could be due to investors' lack of trust in Greece's future, plus the possibility of the country announcing its "default" situation. What it did was to not allow the purchase of any long-term bonds, and Greece's lack of liquidity meant that it had to issue short-term debt.

When we look at the returns we see there are no data at different points of Figure 9, which correspond to the times when the State auctioned no debt type.

As expected, the return on issued Greek public debt also had its ups and downs, and what occurred in the Spanish case also took place: the yield of assets with a shorter maturity exceeded those with a longer maturity.

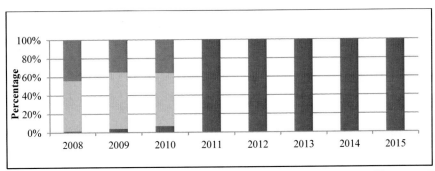

Source: The Authors according to the "Public Debt Management Agency. Blue: Bills; green: Bonds up to 5-Y; red: Bonds over 5-Y.

Figure 8. Greek State's Debt Auctioned according to Financial Assets.

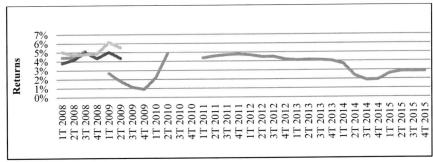

Source: The Authors according to the "Public Debt Management Agency. Blue: Bills; green: Bonds up to 5-Y; red: Bonds over 5-Y.

Figure 9. Greek State's Debt Auctioned according to Financial Assets.

If we calculate the correlation coefficients between the return and the Greek risk premium, we obtain the following results:

Table 5. Correlation coefficient between the return on public debt assets on the primary market with the risk premium – Greece

Correlation Coefficient between the Return on Public Debt Assets on the Primary Market with the Risk Premium – Greece	
Bills on the Primary Market (Public Sector)	0.46
Bonds Up to 5-Y on the Primary Market (Public Sector)	0.79
Bond over 5-Y on the Primary Market (Public Sector)	0.90

Source: The Authors according to the "Public Debt Management Agency".

In this case the degree of correlation is much higher than in the Spanish case. We observe a moderate correlation in the short-term assets which increases in the mid-term ones and rises again with the long-term ones, by approaching the unit, which would be the maximum degree of correlation.

If we focus on secondary markets, we obtain the following returns:

As we can see, the performance of the short-term assets has increased uncontrollably since 2011.

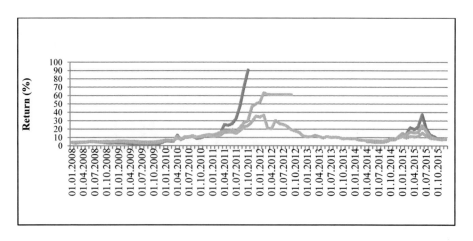

Source: The Authors according to "infobolsa" and "investing.com". Blue: 2-Y Bonds; green: 5-Y Bond; pale blue: 10-Y Bonds.

Figure 10. Return on Greek public debt on the secondary market.

If we exclude the sharp rise in the performance of the 2-year bonds, we observe the same tendency as in the Spanish case, where the performance of the bonds with a short maturity once again exceeds those with a longer maturity. This is particularly due to inefficiencies on the market, the country's instability and the fact that its future is so volatile.

The performance tendency of bonds has followed practically the same pattern as the changes in the risk premium, especially for those assets with a longer maturity as the following correlation coefficients show:

Table 6. Correlation coefficient between the return on public debt assets on the secondary market with the risk premium – Greece

Correlation Coefficient between the Return on the Public Debt Assets on the Secondary Market with the Risk Premium - Greece	
2-year bonds on the Secondary Market (Public Sector)	0.79
5-year bonds on the Secondary Market (Public Sector)	0.90
10-year bonds on the Secondary Market (Public Sector)	0.91

Source: The Authors according to the "Public Debt Management Agency".

We observe that the correlation coefficient on the secondary markets increases compared with that of the primary market. This is evidenced by the fact that the risk premium is calculated by means of the yields obtained on secondary markets.

COMPARISON OF THE SPANISH AND GREEK RISK PREMIUM

After separately analyzing both risk premiums, in the next graph we observe how both have evolved with time.

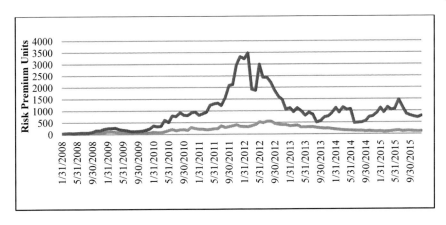

Source: The Authors according to "infobolsa" and "Trading Economics". Blue: Spain's Risk Premium; Red: Greece's Risk Premium.

Figure 11. Comparison of the risk premium between Spain and Greece.

At a glance we see that the tendency is similar. When using the correlation coefficient between both countries' risk premiums, we find a good correlation of 0.79, which allows us to confirm that the evolution of both premiums is similar. This may be due to the fact that Spain acted as a lender or guarantor in the bail-out aid constantly awarded to Greece.

Although we find a similar tendency between both, it is worth stressing that the Spanish risk premium is more stable over time. Despite the sudden rises appearing for Spain, they are not as sharp as they are for Greece.

CONCLUSION

After performing this study, we can state for the 2008-2015 period that both the Spanish and Greek States were entities with deficit of funds. So they needed sources of financing to deal with their expenditures. As a result of this situation, the country risk arises, which measures the likelihood of the State not paying its liabilities. The risk premium, among other methods, is used to measure this, which is merely the difference in the cost of financing among several countries, and we find that the credit rating agencies are a more visual aspect of this measurement.

As we have seen, both the Spanish and Greek premium risks have had their ups and downs during our study period owing to financial markets' predominant instability situation which results in uncertainties not only in the future, but also in the present, and in financial difficulties, and even in insolvency situations, for some countries. All this is especially marked by constantly bailing out banks.

If we focus on ratings, we see that they tend to worsen when the risk premium rises. Yet when the risk premium lowers, rating agencies, specifically Standard & Poor's, are most reluctant to improve ratings, which are maintained due to countries' poor future expectations.

Indeed Spain's risk premium has gone from very low figures immediately before the crisis to very high ones during the crisis, with maximum figures in 2012.

Moreover for Spain, despite its State's financed quantity having increased on markets, this has gradually transformed its' debt maturity from short term to long term. Thus its quality has improved in maturity terms.

As for this debt return on the primary market with the risk premium, although a good positive correlation between the return of this debt and the risk premium has been maintained, it is not excessively strong. The correlation coefficient of the profitability of public debt assets on the primary markets with the Spanish risk premium has moderate values that do not come close to the unit. This shows that the return on the German bond has fluctuated and does not equal zero.

If we look at yields on the secondary market where investors have more information about whether to buy assets or not, the degree of the correlation increases, especially for the 10-year bonds. This is logical given the way in which the risk premium is calculated.

The analysis performed on Greece shows that, although the premium risk fluctuations are more marked than Spanish ones, they have followed the same pattern, which has evolved from values close to zero with more marked peaks in the same year as Spain. However in the final part of the Greek risk premium analysis, the risk premium has remained considerably higher than the Spanish one owing to the more serious problems that Greece is currently facing.

The amount of the Greek State's public debt has increased from 2008 to 2015. However in 2010, it drastically dropped as the EU passed a package of aid to Greece, after which it continued to increase.

The problem with the Greek State's financing lies in the fact that the quality of debt has considerably worsened as it has gone from being financed in the mid and long terms in 2008 to being exclusively financed in the short term, which means that it has to face its financing maturities in very short time periods.

It has been observed how yields on the primary market have continued to positively and strongly relate with the premium risk. Thus the longer maturity debt has, the greater the linear relation with the premium risk. However, we must centre more on assets with a shorter maturity because long-term fixed-income assets have not been negotiated since 2010 given the investor's mistrust, the market's instability and the uncertain future as to whether Greece will receive more aid from the EU and will remain a Member State of the European Economic Community.

The negotiated Greek public debt on the secondary market is particularly noteworthy as its return, compared to its risk premium, obtains a correlation index over 0.79. This means that the risk premium's fluctuations have been very strongly transferred to the secondary market of Greek public debt.

From the financial markets' interconnection we see that both powers share economic, political and social links and, consequently, a close relation exists between both their risk premiums.

As previously mentioned, given the world relation among financial markets, the risk premium of countries with similar characteristics to Spain and Greece is also likely to fluctuate in the same way.

REFERENCES

Alonso, A. (2012, julio 20). Evolución histórica de la prima de riesgo. [Historical evolution of the risk premium] *El País*, p. 1.

Ayuso, J. (2013). *Un análisis de la situación de crédito de España.* [An analysis of the credit situation of Spain.] Dirección General del Servicio de Estudios, Banco de España.

Banco Central Europeo. (2015). *Informe anual de 2014.* [Annual report for 2014.] Madrid.

Banco de España. (2002). *Memoria sobre la actividad de la central de Anotaciones y de los Mercados de Deuda Pública.* [Report on the activity of the Central of Annotations and the Public Debt Markets.]

Banco de España. (2015). *Mercado de deuda pública 2014.* [Public debt market 2014.] Madrid.

Banco de España. (n.d.). *BIEST.* Retrieved September 18, 2016, from http://app.bde.es/ bie_www/faces/bie_wwwias/jsp/op/Home/pHome.jsp.

Bank of Greece. (n.d.). *Bank of Greece.* Retrieved November 20, 2016, from http://www.bankofgreece.gr/Pages/en/Publications/FinStability. Aspx.

Bolsas y Mercados Españoles. (n.d.). *Bolsas y Mercados Españoles, Estudios y Publicaciones.* [Spanish Markets and Markets, Studies and Publications.] Retrieved October 10, 2016, from https://www.bolsasymercados.es/esp/Estudios-Publicaciones.

Comisión Nacional del Mercado de Valores. (n.d.). *Informe anual sobre los mercados de valores y su actuación.* [Annual report on the securities markets and their performance.] Retrieved November 20, 2016, from http://www.cnmv.es/ portal/Publicaciones/Informes.aspx.

El País. (2014, Jan 3). Evolución de la prima de riesgo española. [Evolution of the Spanish risk premium.] *El País*, p. 1.

El País. (2015, Jan 2). Evolución de la prima de riesgo española. [Evolution of the Spanish risk premium.] *El País*, p. 1.

Encinas, C., Tugores, J., Paluzie, E., Tsounis, N., Polychronopoulos, G., Reyes, J. F., et al. (2015). *La crisis del euro y su impacto en la economía y la sociedad.* [The crisis of the euro and its impact on the economy and society.] Barcelona: Universidad de Barcelona.

Eurostat. (n.d.). *Eurostat.* Retrieved September 12, 2016, from http://ec.europa.eu/ eurostat/data/database.

Expansión. (2013, diciembre 31). La prima de riesgo termina 2013 en mínimos desde hace más de 2 años. [The risk premium ends 2013 at minimums for more than 2 years.] *Expansión*, p. 1.

Gil-Ruiz Esparza, C. L. (2007). El gasto público en un contexto descentralizado. [Public spending in a decentralized context.] *Presupuesto y gasto público, Instituto técnico de Estudios Fiscales*, 22.

Hellenic Statistical Authority. (2012). *Press release about General Government déficit/surplus and debt levels and provision of associated data, General Government balance, expenditure, revenue, for the years 2008-2011.*

Hellenic Statistical Authority. (2016). *Press release about General Government déficit/surplus and debt levels and provision of associated data, General Government balance, expenditure, revenue, for the years 2012-2015.*

Hellenic Statistical Authority. (n.d.). *Hellenic Statistical Authority.* Retrieved noviembre 10, 2016, from http://www.statistics.gr/en/home/

Infobolsa. (n.d.). Retrieved September 7, 2016, from http://www.infobolsa.es/prima-riesgo/historico-espana?

Investing. (n.d.). *Investing.com.* Retrieved September 20, 2016, from https://www.investing.com/rates-bonds/world-government-bonds.

Martínez Paricio, I. (2012). Definición y cuantificación de los riesgos financieros. [Definition and quantification of financial risks.] *Global Risk Management BBVA*, 4.

Ontiveros Baeza, E., & Valero López, F. J. (2012). Crisis financieras en la historia. [Financial crisis in history.] *Revista de la Historia de la Economía y de la Empresa*, 42.

Pérez, C. (n.d.). *La crisis en España: cronología desde 2008.* [The crisis in Spain: chronology since 2008.] Retrieved September 8, 2016, from http://www.rtve.es/noticias/20120605/crisis-espana-cronologia-desde-2008/533400.shtml.

Public Debt Management Agency. (n.d.). *Public Debt Management Agency.* Retrieved September 20, 2016, from http://www.pdma.gr/ index.php/en/debt-instruments-greek-government-bonds/issuance-calendar-a-syndication-and-auction-results.

Quirós Gómez, G., Esteban Velasco, J., Iglesias Araúzo, I., Martínez Resano, J. R., Miras Martínez, R., & Santos Sanza, R. (1998). *Mercado español de deuda pública. Dirección general del servicio de estudios* [Spanish public debt market. General direction of the study service], Banco de España.

Spanish Institute of Statistics. (n.d.). *Instituto Nacional de Estadística.* [Statistics National Institute.] Retrieved September 10, 2016, from http://www.ine.es/

Ramón Rallo, J. (2011, febrero 11). Grecia sí le debe a España más de 26.000 millones. [Greece owes Spain more than 26,000 million.] *Libre Mercado.*

RTVE.es. (n.d.). *Cronología de la crisis de Grecia.* [Chronology of the crisis in Greece.] Retrieved September 8, 2016, from http://www.rtve.es/noticias/20170804/cronologia-crisis-grecia/329528.shtml.

Trading Economics. (n.d.). *Calificación crediticia.* [Credit rating] Retrieved febrero 10, 2017, from https://es.tradingeconomics.com/country-list/rating.

Yahoo Finance. (n.d.). *Yahoo finance.* Retrieved September 18, 2016, from https://es.finance.yahoo.com/

In: Modeling Social Behavior and Its Applications   ISBN: 978-1-53613-666-1
Editors: L. A. Jódar Sánchez et al.   © 2018 Nova Science Publishers, Inc.

Chapter 8

Constructive Capitalization Model of Operating Leases: The Impact of IFRS 16 in European Companies

Francisca Pardo[*], *David Pla and Paloma Merello Giménez*
Department of Accounting, University of Valencia, Valencia, Spain

Abstract

The accounting treatment of leases has been subject of a great controversy. IFRS 16 entries into force in January 2019 and those companies applying the international accounting standards of the International Accounting Standards Board will recognize in the balance sheet their operating lease contracts and many financial and economic effects are expected. The capitalization of all non-cancellable lease contracts is expected to have an impact on financial indicators. The empirical part of this chapter focuses on the estimation of the assets and liabilities that the largest European listed companies, included in the Stoxx All Europe 100 Index, should include in the balance sheet as a consequence of the recognition of leases currently classified as operating. The constructive capitalization model has been used for the estimation. The results show an average increase of the assets and liabilities of 4.48% and 11.98%, respectively. Furthermore, after the adjustment, the largest European companies show a larger leverage, lower liquidity, and a decrease in their economic profitability ratio (return on assets), although there are industry differences. In addition, the study confirms an increasing trend in the use of operating leases in the period analyzed despite the forthcoming regulatory change.

Keywords: capitalization model, operating leases, accounting standards, European Union

---

[*] Corresponding Author Email: francisca.pardo@uv.es.

INTRODUCTION

Leases are an alternative to buying that is interesting for companies, because they allow assets to be available without the need to have the total amount of money at the initial moment and offer greater flexibility during the contract to extend, rescind or adapt payments. In addition, they allow reducing risks associated with asset ownership, such as obsolescence, and offer interesting tax incentives.

In Europe, according to the Leaseurope 2016 Annual Survey, leasing of new production amounted to more than €333 billion in 2016 (Leaseurope, 2016), while equipment rental companies and other companies providing rental services generated a total rental turnover of more than €24.29 billion in 2015 (European Rental Association, 2016).

The accounting treatment of leases has historically been subject of debate. There are two different positions, register assets and liabilities in the balance sheet or show information in the notes to the financial statements. In Europe, International Accounting Standard (IAS) 17 (IASB, 2003) includes a model that classifies leases as finance leases (which involve recognition of assets and liabilities in the balance sheet) or operating leases (which only imply the recognition of an expense in the income statement). However, operating leases are widely used in some industries such as airline, retail or travel and leisure, implying difficulty when companies are compared.

IAS 17 and Statement of Financial Accounting Standard (SFAS) 13 (FASB, 1976) have received numerous complaints for two main reasons, the inconsistency of the standard with the definitions of assets and liabilities found in the conceptual framework of accounting, and the increasing use of operating leases since its implementation with the objective of treating them as off-balance debt.

During the last decades, different models have arisen with the purpose of assessing the impact on accounting numbers if operating leases were capitalized. The great precursor was the constructive capitalization model by Imhoff et al. (1991).

Several versions of the constructive capitalization model have been developed from this model. Gritta et al. (1994) estimated operating lease liabilities and their effect on debt in the US airline sector in 1991. Goodacre (2003b) conducted a study on 102 companies in the retail sector in the United Kingdom (UK).

Other studies, however, have focused on analyzing the effect on different industries of the same country. Bennett and Bradbury (2003) analyzed operating leases in 38 companies listed in the New Zealand Stock Exchange in 1995 applying heuristic models (Imhoff et al. 1993; Ely, 1995) as well as the constructive capitalization method (Imhoff et al. 1991, 1993, 1997). Durocher (2008) analyzed the 100 largest Canadian listed companies. Duke et al. (2009) conducted a study in the US companies included in the S&P 500 index with the purpose of estimating the amount of debt not recognized in their balance sheets. Fitó et al. (2013) studied the effect of capitalization in Spanish listed companies. Wong and Joshi (2015) examined the impact of capitalization of leases in a sample of 107 listed Australian companies from different sectors. Fülbier et al. (2008) considered in their study the effect on financial ratios of German listed companies. Barral et al. (2014) compared two countries with different accounting tradition to test whether the capitalization of leases have a different impact. Giner and Pardo (2017) studied why companies choose operating lease as a way of financing.

All studies agree that the off-balance treatment of leases has a significant impact on company's risk and on leverage, profitability and liquidity ratios. Therefore, companies could use this type of leasing as an advantage that allows them to show a better economic and financial position at the same time that it facilitates compliance with covenants.

In 2006, the IASB (International Accounting Standards Board) and the FASB (Financial Accounting Standard Board) initiated a process of change towards the recognition of all leases in the balance sheet, that culminated in the approval of the standards in 2016: IFRS 16 (IASB, 2016a) and Accounting Standards Update (ASU) No. 2016-02 (Topic 842) (FASB, 2016). In January 2019, both standards will come into force. The recognition of assets and liabilities of operating leases in the financial statements will have an effect on the balance sheet, the income statement and the statement of cash flows (for classification and presentation purposes), as well as in the notes to the financial statements. It is necessary to evaluate if some economic decisions will be modified, since leases may become a less attractive option of financing (Goodacre, 2003a; Beattie et al. 2006; IASB, 2016b).

Although it is expected that the total demand for leases will not be modified, the lease contracts could contain more variable payments or be considered as short-term contracts to minimize the debt recognized in the balance sheet (Europe Economics, 2017). Regarding the possible impact on the cost of debt, the IASB argues that the new standard will not change the economic position of the companies, but will mean an improvement of the quality of financial reporting (IASB, 2016b). Most of the covenants agreed with financial institutions are based on the financial information reported by the companies, so it is estimated that IFRS 16 will cause many companies may break their covenants.

The aim of the chapter is to analyze this standard change from the empirical point of view in a sample of European companies by estimating the effect that the new accounting standard will have on the balance sheet, the financial indicators and the possible decisions that companies should make when IFRS 16 comes into force.

The study may be useful for company managers to try to reduce the expected impact, for accounting standard setters and any user of financial information, such as investors, to understand the changes in the financial statements of companies and in their economic decisions.

The chapter is organized as follows. In this section, the main topic is introduced. Next section contains a brief review of the standard in force (IAS 17) and the most relevant changes of the new one (IFRS 16). The third section describes the sample and capitalization models used in the empirical work. The fourth section deals with the numerical results. To conclude, the last section presents the main remarks.

THEORETICAL BACKGROUND: ACCOUNTING REGULATION

The current IAS 17, applied in the European Union, entered into force on January 1, 2005 for the consolidated financial statements of all listed groups. According to IAS 17, a lease is an agreement whereby the lessor conveys to the lessee in return for a payment or series of payments the right to use an asset for an agreed period of time.

The classification of a lease according to IAS 17 is determined by the transference of substantially all the risks and rewards incidental to ownership of an asset to the lessee. In this way, any contract in which the risks and rewards inherent to ownership are transferred to the lessee will be classified as a finance lease; otherwise, the lease will be considered as an operating lease.

Therefore, for classifying a lease, it must be taken into account, more than the form of the contract, the economic nature of the transaction. The recognition of a finance lease implies the recognition of the leased asset as non-current asset and the future lease payments as liability in the balance sheet. However, the accounting treatment of operating leases implies the recognition of lease payments as an expense in the income statement.

To lessors, the accounting of a lease will also depend on its classification. If the lease is classified as finance, the lessor must recognize a receivable at an amount equal to the net investment in the lease. In the case of an operating lease, the lessor will keep the asset in the balance sheet according to its nature and will recognize the lease income as income in the income statement.

In 2006, the IASB and FASB (2006) signed up the "Memorandum of Understanding" (MoU) which enhanced their commitment from a "compatible" to a "common" set of high quality standards. The MoU, which constituted a definite step forward in the convergence process, included, among the topics that were considered critical to the convergence, the accounting of leases. This MoU was the start of a joint project of both organizations whose main objective was to improve current lease accounting and eliminate the controversial duality between finance and operating leases.

As a result of this process, the IASB issued IFRS 16 in January 2016. Its main objective is to improve transparency and comparability for the users of financial information regarding the leasing activities.

With the aim of significantly reducing the cost of applying the new standard, the IASB decided that it will not apply to short-term leases nor to leases for which the underlying asset is of low value.

Regarding the definition of a lease, the new standard considers a contract as a lease if the contract conveys the right to control the use of an identified asset for a period of time in exchange for consideration. It is considered that there is control if the lessee has both the right to obtain substantially all of the economic benefits from use of the identified asset and the right to direct it use. IFRS 16 emphasizes the need to separate within the same contract the lease and non-lease components.

The new standard will not modify equally the accounting of the lessee and the accounting of lessor, as the latter will not change significantly with respect to IAS 17. Specifically, IFRS 16 substantially carries forward the lessor accounting, that is, the dual model (finance leases and operating leases), while introduces a single lessee accounting model.

At inception of a contract, the lessee is required to recognize a right-of-use asset representing its right to use the underlying leased asset and a lease liability representing its obligation to make lease payments.

Assets and liabilities arising from a lease are initially measured on a present value basis. The initial valuation of these two elements, although related, will not follow the same pattern. The subsequent measurement of the right-of-use assets will be similar to other non-financial assets and lease liabilities similar to other financial liabilities. As a consequence, a lessee recognizes depreciation (and its possible impairment) of the right-of-use asset and interest on the lease liability (using the effective interest method).

MATERIALS AND METHOD

The Sample

The sample comprises the companies included in the Stoxx All Europe 100 Index (n.d.) on January 4, 2016. This index includes the 100 largest companies in Europe. Financial and insurance entities have been eliminated from the sample (26 companies) due to the special nature of their activities (Giner & Pardo, 2017). Consequently, the initial sample consists of 370 firm-year observations, which corresponds to 74 companies in a five-year period (2011–2015). However, 12 companies were excluded, as they do not disclose information on operating lease expense. In addition, two of the companies do report the operating lease expense, but not the future minimum lease payments. Furthermore, it has not been possible to obtain information about another company, since it has been acquired and there is only available information in the last two years (2014-2015). Therefore, complete information is available for 60 companies, and the final sample is a data set of 297 observations.

The data have been hand-collected from the notes to the consolidated financial statements for a five-year period (2011-2015), and and from the financial information database Orbis (n.d.).

Table 1. Distribution of the companies in the sample by country and industry

Country	N. Companies	Industry	N. Companies
United Kingdom	21	Chemicals & Health Care	12
Germany	11		
France	8	Utilities, Basic Resources, Oil & Gas	11
Switzerland	6		
Sweden	4	Food & Beverage & Personal & Household	10
Spain	3	Goods	
Italy	2	Industrial Goods & Services	6
Netherlands	1		
Ireland	1	Telecommunications & Media	6
Denmark	1	Technology	5
Belgium	1	Automobiles & Parts	4
Finland	1	Construction & Materials	4
		Retail	2
TOTAL	60	TOTAL	60

The companies of the sample belong to 12 European countries (Table 1) and are classified into nine industries (Stoxx All Europe 100 Index, n.d.). Companies report the information in different currencies (US dollar, British pound, Swedish krona, Swiss franc, Danish krone); thus, data have been converted into euros according to the historical exchange rate at each closing date of the corresponding year (European Central Bank).

According to IAS 17, firms should disclose in the notes to the financial statements the following details about operating leases: future minimum lease payments for the following year, for years 2 to 5, and the total future minimum lease payments for the years after the fifth. However, some companies offer more detail. The future minimum payments have been hand-collected from the notes to the financial statements and have been converted into annual periods.

Financial Ratios

The financial ratios considered are the following:

$$Leverage\ 1 = \frac{Total\ Liabilities}{Equity + Total\ Liabilities}, \tag{1}$$

$$Leverage\ 2 = \frac{Total\ Liabilities}{Equity}, \tag{2}$$

$$Debt\_quality = \frac{Current\ Liabilities}{Total\ Liabilities}, \tag{3}$$

$$Solvency = \frac{Total\ Assets}{Total\ Liabilities}, \tag{4}$$

$$Liquidity = \frac{Current\ Assets}{Current\ Liabilities}, \tag{5}$$

$$Non - Current\ Asset\ Turnover = \frac{Net\ Sales}{Average\ Non-Current\ Assets}, \tag{6}$$

$$ROA = \frac{EBIT}{Average\ Total\ Assets}, \tag{7}$$

$$ROE = \frac{Net\ Income}{Average\ Equity}. \tag{8}$$

where EBIT is earnings before interest and taxes; ROA is return on assets; and ROE is return on equity.

Ratios (1), (2), (3) and (4) are related to the firm financial structure; while ratio (5) analyses the capacity of companies to deal with their short-term debts; ratio (6) measures the efficiency with which a company is deploying its assets in generating revenues; and ratios (7) and (8) measure firm performance either from the total firm perspective as a whole, ROA, or from the shareholders' perspective, ROE.

Capitalization Methods

The reference model for most studies is the constructive capitalization model developed by Imhoff et al. (1991), which estimates the effect of the operating lease capitalization (which will happen, when IFRS 16 comes into force). Due to its complexity, some investors and analysts have used other models such as factor or heuristic methods (Imhoff et al. 1993; Bennett and Bradbury, 2003). The latter methods are less reliable, but they have been used by some users of information, such as rating agencies, since the estimates are simpler, but they substantially overstate the potential lease liabilities. However, the results obtained by the constructive capitalization model enjoy greater reliability.

The Constructive Capitalization Model

The constructive capitalization model began to be used in order to evaluate the consequences of capitalization in US companies from different industries. The model assumes that there are assets and liabilities that are omitted and modify the accounting figures and ratios.

The following accounting figures must be defined: CA_o: original current assets; NCA_o: original non-current assets; CL_o: original current liabilities; NCL_o: original non-current liabilities; and E_o: original equity. After the lease capitalization, we have: CA_a: adjusted current assets; NCA_a: adjusted non-current assets; CL_a: adjusted current liabilities; NCL_a: adjusted non-current liabilities; and E_a: adjusted equity. The variables after capitalizing the operating lease payments follow the following expressions,

$$CA_a = CA_o, \tag{9}$$

$$NCA_a = NCA_o + adjustment_A, \tag{10}$$

$$CL_a = CL_o + net\_adjustment_{CL}, \tag{11}$$

$$NCL_a = NCL_o + net\_adjustment_{NCL}, \tag{12}$$

$$E_a = E_o - net\_adjustment_E, \tag{13}$$

where the adjustment of the liability is defined as,

$$adjustment_L = (mlp(1) \times (1 + i)^{-1}) + (mlp(2) \times (1 + i)^{-2}) + (mlp(3) \times (1 + i)^{-3}) + \cdots + (mlp(y) \times (1 + i)^{-y}), \tag{14}$$

where $mlp(y)$ is the future minimum lease payments in year y, and i is the interest rate.

The value of the right-of-use asset (non-current asset) will be a percentage of the value of the debt. This percentage will be higher or lower depending on the total life (TL) and remaining life (RL) of the lease contract, and the discount interest rate. Thus, the adjustment of the asset takes the following form,

$$adjustment_A = R \times adjustment_L, \tag{15}$$

$$R = \frac{RL}{TL} \times \frac{1-(1+i)^{-TL}}{1-(1+i)^{-RL}} \qquad (16)$$

where R is the ratio of any lease asset to the corresponding lease liability at any time during the contract period.

The adjustment of the liability must be calculated net of tax effect,

$$net\_adjustment_L = adjustment_L - (adjustment_L - adjustment_A) \times t, \quad (17)$$

where t is the effective tax rate. The tax rate is obtained dividing the tax expense by earnings before taxes (EBT) for each year. When EBT is negative, we use the median of the estimated tax rates, 23.86%.

The amount of the adjustment of the short-term lease liability is calculated as the present value of the minimum lease payment for $y = 1$ net of tax effect, equation (18), and the adjustment of the long-term lease liability is shown in equation (19).

$$net\_adjustment_{CL} = (mlp(1) \times (1 + i)^{-1}) - [(mlp(1) \times (1 + i)^{-1}) - R \times (mlp(1) \times (1 + i)^{-1})] \times t, \qquad (18)$$

$$net\_adjustment_{NCL} = net\_adjustment_L - net\_adjustment_{CL}, \quad (19)$$

Finally, because of the difference between the adjustment of liabilities and assets, a negative adjustment of equity is obtained.

$$net\_adjustment_E = (adjustment_L - adjustment_A) \times (1 - t), \quad (20)$$

The equity is reduced by the difference between the adjustment of the liabilities and the adjustment of the assets minus the deferred tax decrease. This adjustment is due to the accumulated difference in previous years between the expenses recognized when operating leases are capitalized (amortization and interest) and when they are not (rental expenses).

The general hypotheses of the model are: (i) at the beginning of the contract, the liability and the asset are equal to the present value of the future lease payments; (ii) the debt is valued at amortized cost at the effective interest rate (which will be the predetermined discount interest rate), (iii) the asset will be amortized in a straight-line method; (iv) if the company is in operation, the operating lease portfolio will be constantly renewed, so we will assume that the assets are in the middle of their useful life (50%), then $RL/TL = 0.5$; (v) at the end of the contract the value of the asset and the debt will be zero.

In this study, the following simplifications to the model are assumed. A discount rate of 5% is considered, more in line with the period analysed (Giner & Pardo, 2017). The remaining life of the lease is obtained by rounding up the result of dividing the future lease payment reported in the notes to more than 5 years, by the amount of the fifth year payment.

Heuristic or Factor Models

We also use standard "rule of thumb" procedures for capitalizing operating leases as a simpler alternative to estimate the obligations and assets to be recognized in the balance sheet (Imhoff et al. 1993; Bennett and Bradbury, 2003). It is interesting to compare the results obtained with a heuristic or factor model with a capitalization method in the case of European companies, since it has been previously done in the US.

In this model, the definition of the original variables remains identical. The fundamental variation occurs in the formula to obtain the adjustment of the liability ($adjustment_L$), which will be defined as,

$$adjustment_L = F \times operating\_leases \qquad (21)$$

where $operating\_leases$ is defined as the total operating lease expenses stated in the notes to the financial statements, and F is a multiplicative factor. In this study, $F = 8$ and $F = 6$ are considered. As a consequent simplification of the model, the asset adjustment is stated equal to the liability adjustment: $adjustment_A = adjustment_L$. Thus, the new adjusted variables are:

$$NCA_a = NCA_o + adjustment_A;$$

$$L_a = L_o + net\_adjustment_L.$$

where L_o is original liabilities; and L_a is adjusted liabilities.

There is another heuristic method that involves a multiplicative factor and maintains all the aforementioned simplifications, but the lease variable considered is $mlp(1)$. Thus, the liability adjustment is as follows,

$$adjustment_L = F \times mlp(1) \qquad (22)$$

where $mlp(1)$ is the minimum lease payment of the next period. In that case, $F = 6$ has been considered as in Bennett and Bradbury (2003).

RESULTS

Evaluation of Differences between Models

As we have seen in previous section, the differences between the constructive capitalization model by Imhoff et al. (1991) and the heuristic ones are remarkable in terms of mathematical notation. Bennett and Bradbury (2003) concluded that the results obtained by the heuristic methods were imprecise and overstated, since these methods were raised in the US context, where the term of leases is usually lower than in the rest of the world.

The objective of this section is to empirically evaluate the differences between both models in the European context and propose a multiplicative factor (F) for the largest European listed companies.

Through an example, we can see the differences in the case of a particular company (Siemens) in Table 2.

Table 2 shows a clear overstatement of the liability heuristic methods in comparison with the constructive model. Indeed, the adjustment of liabilities is even larger in the heuristic methods than the original total (non-discounted) lease liability of €3,428 million (as disclosed in the notes to the financial statements).

In order to compare the results of both methods, the difference (in millions of €) of the estimated adjustment of the liability between the constructive capitalization method and the heuristic methods has been calculated. Table 3a shows the descriptive statistics of this difference.

Table 2. Comparison of the adjustment (in millions of €) according to different capitalization methods of Siemens company, 2015. The third and fourth columns are calculated with the operating lease expenses

	Constructive	Heuristic F = 8	Heuristic F = 6	Heuristic $F_{mlp(1)} = 6$
Adjustment of liabilities	2,899.34	9,504.00	7,128.00	4,638.00

The results shown in Table 3a are repeated throughout the sample (Table 3b), so it seems reasonable to state that the heuristic methods are overvaluing and it is disregarded to analyze the results according to these methods. The average effect on the balance sheet is much larger than applying the constructive capitalization model for the three heuristic methods considered.

Table 3b shows a relative measure of the difference between both methods in order to analyze the difference in relative terms.

Table 3a. Descriptive statistics of the difference (in millions of €) of the estimated adjustment of the liabilities between the constructive capitalization method (CCM) and the heuristic methods ($F = 8, F = 6$, and $F_{mlp(1)} = 6$). The difference has been calculated as:

$$adjustment_L(heuristic) - adjustment_L(CCM)$$

Difference with CCM	Average	Standard deviation	Minimum	Maximum
$F = 8$	3,216.06	5,277.60	-4,358.16	32,513.62
$F = 6$	1,780.40	3,441.27	-6,252.16	21,476.60
$F_{mlp(1)} = 6$	1,326.48	3,173.11	-2,916.16	27,250.89

Table 3b. Descriptive statistics of the percentage difference of the estimated adjustment of liabilities between the constructive capitalization method (CCM) and the heuristic methods ($F = 8, F = 6$, and $F_{mlp(1)} = 6$. The percentage difference has been calculated as:

$$(adjustment_L(heuristic) - adjustment_L(CCM))/adjustment_L(CCM)$$

% Difference with CCM	Average	Standard deviation	Minimum	Maximum
$F = 8$	173.9%	130.2%	-36.5%	825.5%
$F = 6$	105.4%	97.7%	-52.4%	594.1%
$F_{mlp(1)} = 6$	57.1%	46.7%	-48.8%	237.8%

After analysing Table 3b, we estimate a factor of $F = 3.52$ for expression (21) and $F = 3.93$ for expression (22) in the case of the largest European listed companies. The first factor is the result of dividing the mean operating lease liability estimated by the constructive method (€2,526.57 million, Table 4) by the mean operating lease expense (€717.83 million). The second factor is the result of dividing the mean operating lease liability estimated by the constructive method (€2,526.57 million, Table 4) by the mean next period's minimum lease payment (€642.18 million). These factors are obtained as the factors that replicate the results obtained by the constructive method. The values proposed for the factors can be rounded up to $F = 4$, in order to generalize these methods. Thus, standard "rule of thumb" procedures for capitalizing operating leases are likely to be very inaccurate in a different context like Europe.

Impact of Operating Lease Capitalization in European Companies

This section analyzes whether the regulatory change will have a significant effect on the balance sheet of European companies with operating lease contracts.

Therefore, the assets and liabilities that will be recognized in the balance sheet have been estimated using the constructive capitalization model (Imhoff et al. 1991) for the sample of the largest listed European companies, as well as the changes in the main financial ratios according to the information of the future obligations derived from operating leases reported in the notes to the financial statements.

Table 4. Impact of operating lease capitalization on assets, liabilities, and equity (in millions of €)

	Average	Median	Minimum	Maximum
Current liabilities	586.28	240.61	17.62	6,220.70
Non-current liabilities	1,940.29	842.35	39.05	16,175.84
Total liabilities	2,526.57	1,071.62	61.02	20,661.10
Assets	2,193.62	910.81	46.01	18,014.41
Equity	-332.95	-147.05	-2,646.69	-6.69

Table 4 shows the variation in millions of euros in the balance sheet figures due to the capitalization of operating leases. As we can see in Table 4, the differences between the maximum and minimum values are very large. While the maximum adjustment of the liability is around €20 billion, the minimum is around €61 million. For the assets, a similar result is obtained, and for equity, the reduction of its value goes from approximately €2.6 billion to less than €7 million. Due to this dispersion, we also report the median to avoid extreme values distorting the average results.

If we analyze the values obtained from the capitalization with respect to the original values of assets, liabilities and equity before the adjustment, we obtain the increase or decrease in relative terms (Table 5).

As we can see, in relative terms, the median of the adjustment involves an increase of assets by 1.85%, increase of liabilities by 3.79%, and a decrease of equity by 0.72%.

Table 6 shows the median of the main financial ratios before and after operating lease capitalization, and its variation in relative terms. To test if its variation is statistically significant, we apply the non-parametric Wilcoxon test (as data are non-normally distributed).

Table 5. Impact of operating lease capitalization in relative terms

	Average	Median	Minimum	Maximum
% Variation of assets	4.48%	1.85%	0.21%	74.58%
% Variation of liabilities	11.98%	3.79%	0.35%	288.17%
% Variation of equity*	-2.39%	-0.72%	-128.21%	-0.02%

* In the case of the variation of equity, two observations have been excluded, since their original equity was negative.

**Table 6. Impact of operating lease capitalization on median ratios
and Wilcoxon test (* denotes significance at 1%)**

Ratio	Before	After	Variation	Wilcoxon test
Leverage 1	0.5976	0.6208	3.88%	-14.937*
Leverage 2	1.4704	1.6000	8.81%	-14.738*
Debt maturity	0.4643	0.4534	-2.35%	14.887*
Solvency	1.6734	1.6109	-3.73%	14.937*
Liquidity	1.1519	1.1164	-3.08%	14.937*
Non-current asset turnover	0.9878	0.9723	-1.57%	14.937*
ROA	0.0876	0.0848	-3.20%	14.430*
ROE	0.1564	0.1570	0.38%	-13.498*

As we can see, leverage (1 and 2) ratios increase after capitalization; thus, companies will show a greater leverage in their financial structure. In addition, the debt maturity decreases so liabilities will increase more in the long term. The solvency and liquidity ratios after capitalization decrease (3.73% and 3.08%, respectively), which indicates a lower capacity to deal with both long and short-term debts. On the other hand, turnover of non-current assets decreases by 1.57%, which indicates a lower efficiency of assets. Profitability indicators reveal opposite effects. On the one hand, the return on assets (ROA) decreases by 3.20%, while the financial profitability (ROE) increases slightly (0.38%) due to the decrease in equity as a consequence of the capitalization.

In the last column of Table 6, the Wilcoxon test shows that all changes produced by capitalization are statistically significant. Therefore, we can state that the regulatory change will have a significant effect on financial and economic ratios of companies with operating leases.

Impact of Operating Lease Capitalization by Industry

Some authors, such as Goodacre (2003a), Durocher (2008), Barral et al. (2014), or Giner and Pardo (2017), stated that industry is a determinant factor in the use of operating leases. Therefore, if the effect of the new standard is significant on accounting figures, companies that operate in industries with greater use of operating leases will have a larger impact on their financial statements and ratios. Therefore, this section analyzes whether the expected effect of capitalization of operating leases is different depending on the industry.

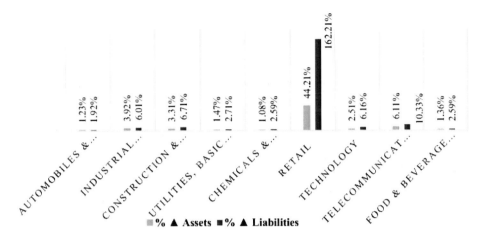

Figure 1. Median increase in assets and liabilities by industry.

Figure 1 shows the median increase in assets and liabilities due to capitalization in relative terms. Note that the increase differs considerably depending on the sector, with the retail sector being the most affected, given that, due to their characteristics, these companies frequently use operating lease contracts. In this industry, the mean increase in assets and liabilities is 44% and 162%, respectively. Other industries have a rather smaller impact, as shown in Figure 1.

Thus, a similar result is obtained in the main financial ratios. There is a difference by industries in all ratios analyzed, however, in Figure 2 only the Leverage 1 ratio, solvency ratio, and ROA are represented to illustrate this difference. These three indicators offer an overview of the change in leverage, solvency and profitability by industries.

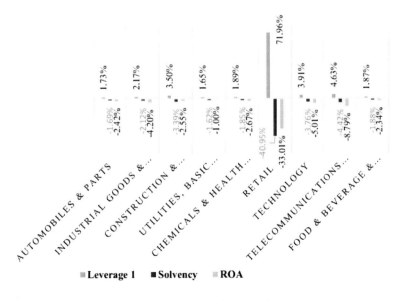

Figure 2. Impact of operating lease capitalization on ratios by industry.

According to the analysis, the most affected industry will be the retail, which will see its economic and financial structure significantly modified. Other industries that also show relevant changes, although lower, are Telecommunications & Media, Technology, and Construction & Materials.

Therefore, according to the obtained results, industry is an important factor in the use of operating leases and in the expected impact of operating lease capitalization.

Evolution of the Use of Operating Leases

Finally, we analyze whether there is a significant reduction in the use of operating leases during the period under study as a consequence of the regulatory change. We assume that a possible preparatory effect can occur in anticipation to a regulatory change, since companies can adapt their lease policies in advance. For this, the evolution in the use of operating leases between 2011 and 2015 is analyzed in order to verify the trend during this period (Figure 3).

Companies in the sample have not reduced the use of operating leases as a preventive measure to the changes expected from the entry into force of IFRS 16 (Figure 3). This result suggests that, although the operating leases will no longer be so attractive with the new standard, they may continue to be used for the rest of the advantages they offer besides the current off-balance sheet treatment. However, because the regulation will be in force in 2019, companies may still change their lease policy in the following years.

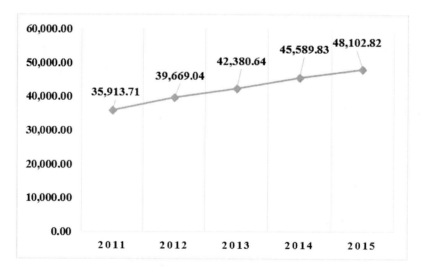

Figure 3. Evolution of total operating lease expenses in millions of euros.

CONCLUSION

The new IFRS 16, unlike the current standard, requires operating leases to be capitalized in the balance sheet in the same way as finance leases. Therefore, companies must understand the new standard and evaluate the importance of changes, to subsequently make the necessary decisions and properly implement IFRS 16.

Our study applies the constructive capitalization model by Imhoff et al. (1991) on a final sample of 60 listed European companies included in the Stoxx All Europe 100 Index in a five-year period (2011-2015). The results obtained are in line with previous studies such as Goodacre (2003b), Bennett and Bradbury (2003), Durocher (2008) or Duke et al. (2009). The average increase in assets and liabilities is 4.48% and 11.98%, respectively, while equity decreases by 2.39%. The debt-to-equity ratio (leverage 2) increases by 8.81%, while the ROA decreases by 3.20%. These results confirm that IFRS 16 will have a significant impact on financial indicators of companies. Although, some industries such as retail will experience a higher impact due to its greater use of this type of contracts. The evolution of the operating lease expense in the period analyzed shows an increasing trend, which indicates that, despite knowledge of the regulatory change, companies have continued to use operating leases.

Furthermore, the constructive capitalization method has been compared with other heuristic methods in the European context. An overstatement of lease liabilities has been evidenced and some news factors have been proposed for this context.

The study contributes to document the impact that the capitalization of operating leases can have as a consequence of the new regulation, and serves as a guide to anticipate the expected impact of this change, in such a way that the repercussion caused to companies is minimized.

REFERENCES

Banco Central Europeo (n.d.). *Euro Foreign Exchange Reference Rates*. Retrieved from: http://www.ecb.europa.eu/stats/eurofxref/.

Barral, A., Cordobés, M., & Ramírez J. N. (2014). Los arrendamientos operativos: impacto de su reconocimiento en los estados financieros y en la política de financiación de las compañías españolas y del Reino Unido. *Revista de Contabilidad*, 17 (2), 212-223. [Operating leases: Impact of operating leases recognized on financial statement and on financial policy in Spanish and British companies. *Spanish Accounting Review*, 17 (2), 212-223].

Beattie, V., Goodacre, A., & Thomson, S. J. (2006). International lease accounting reform and economic consequences: The views of UK users and preparers. *International Journal of Accounting*, 41 (1), 75-103.

Bennett, B. K., & Bradbury, M. E. (2003). Capitalizing non-cancelable operating leases. *Journal of International Financial Management and Accounting*, 14, 101-114.

Duke, J. C., Hsieh, S.-J., & Su. Y. (2009). Operating and synthetic leases: Exploiting financial benefits in the post-Enron era. *Advances in Accounting*, 25 (1), 28–39.

Durocher, S. (2008). Canadian evidence on the constructive capitalization of operating leases. *Accounting Perspectives*, 7 (3), 227–256.

Ely, K. M. (1995). Operating lease accounting and the market's assessment of equity risk. *Journal of Accounting and Research*, 33 (2), 397-415.

Europe Economics (2017). *Ex ante impact assessment of IFRS 16,* February. Retrieved from: http://www.europe-economics.com/publications/15/1/2017/publications.htm.

European Rental Association (2016). *ERA Market Report 2016.* Retrieved from http://erarental.org/en/publications/era-annual-reports/annual-report-2016.

Financial Accounting Standards Board (FASB) (1976). Statement of Financial Accounting Standards No. 13: *Accounting for Leases*. FASB, Norwalk, CT.

Financial Accounting Standards Board (FASB) (2006). *Memorandum of understanding.* Retrieved from: www.fasb.org/intl/mou02-06.

Fitó, M. A., Moya, S., & Orgaz, N. (2013). Considering the effects of operating lease capitalization on key financial ratios. *Spanish Journal of Finance and Accounting/Revista Española de Financiación y Contabilidad*, 42 (159), 341-369.

Fülbier, R. U., Silva, J. L., & Pferdehirt, M. H. (2008). Impact of lease capitalization on financial ratios of listed German companies. *Schmalenbach Business Review*, 60, 122-144.

Giner, B., & F. Pardo. (2017). Operating lease decision and the impact of capitalization in a bank-oriented country. *Applied Economics*, 49 (19), 1886-1900.

Goodacre, A. (2003a). Assessing the potential impact of lease accounting reform: A review of the empirical evidence. *Journal of Property Research*, 20 (1), 49-66.

Goodacre, A. (2003b). Operating lease finance in UK retail sector. *The International Review of Retail, Distribution and Consumer Research*, 13 (1), 99-125.

Gritta, R. D., Lippman, E., & Chow, G. (1994). The impact of the capitalization of leases on airline financial analysis: An issue revisited. *Logistics and Transportation Review*, 30 (2), 189–202.

International Accounting Standards Board (IASB) (2003). Revised *International Accounting Standard No. 17.* Leases, London: IASCF.

International Accounting Standards Board (IASB) (2016a). *International Financial Reporting Standard 16.* Leases. London: IASCF.

International Accounting Standards Board (IASB) (2016b). *Effects Analysis.* IFRS 16 Leases. London: IASCF.

Imhoff, E. A., Lipe, R. C., & Wright, D. W. (1991). Operating leases: Impact of constructive capitalization. *Accounting Horizons*, 5, 51-63.

Imhoff, E. A., Lipe, R. C., & Wright, D. W. (1993). The effects of recognition versus disclosure on shareholder risk and executive compensation. *Journal of Accounting, Auditing and Finance*, 8 (4), 335-368.

Imhoff, E. A., Lipe, R. C., & Wright, D. W. (1997). Operating leases: Income effects of constructive capitalization. *Accounting Horizons*, 11 (2), 12-32.

Leaseurope (2016). *Leaseurope Annual Survey 2016*. Retrieved from: http://www.leaseurope.org/uploads/documents/stats/European%20Leasing%20Market%202016.pdf.

Orbis (n.d.). *Database of company information around the globe*. Retrieved from: http://www.bvdinfo.com/es-es/our-products/company-information/international-products/orbis.

Stoxx All Europe 100 Index (n.d.). Retrieved from: https://www.stoxx.com/index-details?symbol=SXEBCP.

Wong, K., & Joshi, M. (2015). The impact of lease capitalization on financial statements and key ratios: Evidence from Australia. *Australasian Accounting, Business and Finance Journal*, 9 (3), 27-44.

In: Modeling Social Behavior and Its Applications
Editors: L. A. Jódar Sánchez et al.

ISBN: 978-1-53613-666-1
© 2018 Nova Science Publishers, Inc.

Chapter 9

MANAGEMENT BEHAVIOUR AND CAPITAL STRUCTURE APPLYING THE ACCOUNTING METHODOLOGY OF RADAR CHARTS: EVIDENCE FROM ITALY

Miguel Ángel Pérez-Benedito*, Luis Porcuna-Enguix and Rubén Porcuna-Enguix

Accounting Department, University of Valencia, Valencia, Spain

ABSTRACT

This manuscript aims to define the management behaviour of companies modelling the activity of firms throughout the application of the new Accounting Methodology of Radar Charts (AMRC). The study is based on the behavioural economics and the corporate governance field. This analysis approaches the management behaviour through the definition of the kind of management adopted by firms according to their ordinary activity. Thus, kinds of management do not show whether companies are properly performing their ordinary activity, but the achievement of optimal management (financial sufficiency and liquidity on transactions) in the considered areas does. Our results validate the application of AMRC on companies to understand the effect of making decisions. When a company adopts positive kinds of management needs external financing, and when it adopts negative kinds of management financing from shareholder funds (financial autonomy) is relevant to maintain activity when optimum of management is not satisfied. When the activity of a company achieves optimal management, it allows to continue its own activities without requiring external financing.

---

* Corresponding Author: miguel.a.perez@uv.es.

Keywords: AMRC, accounting, radar charts, management behaviour, kind of management

INTRODUCTION

Management is widely defined as the administration of an organization, either it is a profit-business or not-for-profit organization. In the extensive financial and organizational literature, firms' strategic activities and their orientation are supposed to affect firms' performance (Mariadoss et al., 2014). As well, the analysis of the microeconomic scenario is based on the different perception of rationality which, from an economist perspective, is the appreciation of human behaviour that underpins all economic matter (Simon, 1978).

It is well-known the necessity of simplifying the economic and business reality, because its complexity could lead to misleading conclusions. As a consequence, stakeholders are more likely to trust simple heuristic indicators rather than those that are trickier to disentangle (Burgstahler and Dichev, 1997). Stakeholders usually make their own decisions based on mental shortcuts ("rule of thumb") and framing, that is, the way that a problem is presented (Shrefin, 2002). Traditionally, empirical studies have attempted to classify firms' management behaviour addressing this splitting firms' behaviour into two groups: more or less aggressive (e.g., tax avoidance), more or less conservative (e.g., earnings management), more or less risk aversion (e.g., credit supply), more or less profitable, etc. As well, some literature has also used clustering models and other statistical methods so as to group firms according to a set of attributed variables (e.g., Birley and Westhead, 1990).

The Accounting Methodology of Radar Charts (AMRC) aims to assess companies' behaviour by employing accounting information and applying mathematical assumptions related to trigonometry and geometry (the cosine and sine theorems). AMRC develops a radar chart according to the three basic areas related to the operative activity of firms, that is, sales area, treasury area and purchases area. To develop it, the average periods of maturation are represented on axes of a radar chart, because they are dynamic accounting variables which can explain activities of companies. The effect of this representation is basically the kind of management (KM) adopted by a firm, because the accounting KMs are the own answers of companies to changes in the economic and financial environment (Pérez et al., 2017a; 2017b). KM allows analysing changes on financial structures and other variables associated with management of companies.

The application of cosine and sine theorems allows to build necessary and sufficiency conditions to explain the decisions adopted by companies. The fulfilling of these conditions defines companies' performance and financial structure. So that, there is a cause-effect relationship between KMs adopted by companies and the information from their financial statements, due to the proportional relation among average periods of maturation and accounting variables. Consequently, the AMRC implicitly measures the rationality of decisions adopted by companies on an economic environment. The analysis of radar chart image by stakeholders is similar to medical diagnosis. The first opinion about the radar chart image is contrasted by indicators associated to knowledge.

The available indicators until today take into consideration several assumptions for their generalization, leaving aside some characteristics (irrationalities) that could be crucial in order to describe more accurately firms' management behaviour. Therefore, AMRC acts as a nudge that may help stakeholders' decision-making. This is possible because AMRC works with indicators whose main characteristics are: (i) normalized, that is, applicable to whatever situation; (ii) independent, that is, data used in the analysis is not previously treated and there is no subjectivity implied in the methodology applied due to is a mathematical deduction; (iii) objective, the indicators are not influenced by the decisions of the researcher; and (iv) positive, that implies the indicators cannot take negative values in any case, so it avoids a possible compensation of values.

In short, AMRC considers multidirectional effects of decisions, because a decision adopted in a management area has an effect on the rest of areas represented on a radar chart.

Secondly, AMRC aims to mathematically identify all kinds of management in which firms necessarily incur. So, there are two major implications that show up. On the one hand, AMRC clusters firms in more than two categories, which allows a more flexible study of their behaviour and also a more accurate comparison among them, since no element from the sample is excluded in the analysis. On the other hand, the use of mathematical procedures in the application of AMRC avoids using statistical methods which, in some cases, drops data to run the analysis. This means that the only limitation of this new methodology is the non-availability of financial information.

Thirdly, AMRC is based on accounting information reported by firms, which objective is drawing a representative picture of the economic and financial situation of a company, sector or even an economy within a region. Doing so, we are able to not only classify by kinds of management but also determine the optimal management.

Finally, the optimal management is achieved by the compliance of the Financial Sufficiency and the Liquidity on Transactions conditions. Within the financial structure of firms, the study of the composition of capital structure is important (Strange et al., 2009) in order to ensure the financial sufficiency. As well, the processes and the structure of resources of companies that make possible to meet the economic interests of shareholders, among others (Monks and Minnow, 1995; Keasey et al., 1997; Filatotchev et al., 2006), ensure the liquidity on transactions.

Therefore, this study aims to shed light on companies' management behaviour, as well as demonstrate the differences in capital structure and short-term economic structure among kinds of management determined by the AMRC.

In this paper, we use a sample consisting of Italian firms that are listed or have been once listed, with a total of 1,920 firm-year observations from 2007 to 2016. Italy is widely seen as "representative of contrasting models of European culture, economic and regulatory regimes" (Nobes and Parker, 2010).

The remainder of this paper is structured as follows. Section two exposes the sample employed in the study. In section three, the Accounting Methodology of Radar Charts (AMRC) is explained and presented. Section four deals with the techniques applied to obtain the results and the explanation of them. Finally, section five presents the conclusions and the implications of the study.

SAMPLE

Italian legal origin is characterised to have civil-law tradition. Furthermore, Italy has a less developed stock market, concentrated ownership, low level of investors' rights and weak legal enforcement, as pointed, for instance, by La Porta et al. (1998) or Elshandidy and Neri (2015). However, some of these features are for both listed and unlisted firms (Bianco and Casavola, 1999).

We concentrate the analysis on Italian firms that are or have been listed spanning 2007 to 2016, due to the fact that listed companies are usually the main driver of an economy and are the first adopters of regulatory changes as the IFRS in 2005 (Elshandidy and Neri, 2015), as well, they were newly required to disclose several indicators in order to be more transparent (Alegrini and Greco, 2013). Finally, we obtain a total amount of 1,920 firm-year observations. Table 1 summarizes the search strategy carried out from ORBIS database.

Table 1. Search strategy of Italian firms

Search steps	# firms
Companies that are active	172,048,793
Country: Italy	4,326,718
Listed companies or companies that were once listed on stock market	388
Companies whose data is available	**192**

METHODOLOGY

The need of new indicators is not a new concern in accounting and finance research, but it is still a topic of interest. Literature usually employs some proxies that do not always show exactly the characteristics that researchers want to obtain. Furthermore,

Rivero (1990) and Costa and Font (1992) alert that new indicators must show a deeper explanation of operative and financial leverage reported in financial statements.

The double-entry principle (ESA, 2010) establishes that in all commercial operation, the value of given assets and the value of assumed liabilities must agree with the monetary compensation (Figure 1). In the same way, the value of acquired assets and the value of given receivables must agree with the monetary compensation. In this sense, sales and purchases are the link between firm and goods market, and the financing with clients and suppliers is the link between firm and capital market. These relationships are represented by an economic flow (F_e) and a financial flow (F_f), respectively.

AMRC develops a radar chart (kind of management) according to the three basic areas related to the operative activity of firms, that is, sales area, treasury area and purchases area. The activity of each area exposed below is measured by the Average Period of Maturation (APM), which is the first indicator from financial statements. Table 2 shows that the sales area considers the APM of sales (Ps), treasury area uses the APM of collect (Pc) and purchases area employs the APM of payment (Pp). Every single area takes a variable from economic and financial flows (see Figure 1), a dynamic variable from financial statements (using the average balance of year) and a temporal measure (365 days).

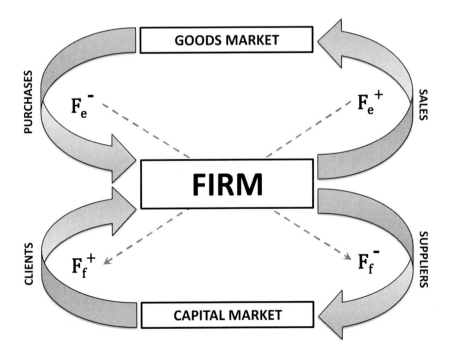

Figure 1. Double-entry principle diagram.

Table 2. Average Periods of Maturation

APM	F_e / F_f		Dynamic Variable		Time
Ps	Cost of Sales	[CS]	AInventory =	$\dfrac{Inventory_t + Inventory_{t-1}}{2}$	365
Pc	$\dfrac{Sales\cdot}{(1+VAT)}$	[S]	AReceivables =	$\dfrac{Receivables_t + Receivables_{t-1}}{2}$	365
Pp	$\dfrac{Purchases}{(1+VAT)}$	[P]	ASuppliers =	$\dfrac{Suppliers_t + Suppliers_{t-1}}{2}$	365

Ps=Sales Average Period of Maturation;
Pc=Collect Average Period of Maturation;
Pp=Payment Average Period of Maturation.

Thus we obtain each APM using the following expression:

$$P_i = \frac{Dynamic\ Variable_i \cdot 365}{F_{e_i}\ or\ F_{f_i}} \qquad (1)$$

where:

$$i= s(sales),\ c(collect),\ p(payment)$$

We may connect this expression (Eq. 2) with the rotation (r) of each area, which must comply in any case due to the assumption that Pi must be different from 0 value:

$$r_i \cdot P_i = 365 \qquad (2)$$

Radar Chart and Kinds of Management

Once we get the APM, next step is to create the "radiography" of firms, which consists of generating a radar chat of three axes, one for each APM. Then, joining the points, we can draw the situation of a firm in a year *t*. Figure 2 shows an example of the interpretation of APMs and rotations in the radar chart. We must be sure that the higher APM in a specific area the lower rotation (Eq. 2), that is, an inverse relationship between them.

Therefore, radar chart defines the Kind of Management (KM) that firm is adopting to perform its activity. Figure 3 shows that the KM depends on the magnitude of Perimeter Distances (PD), which means that the activity of a firm differs from the activity of others.

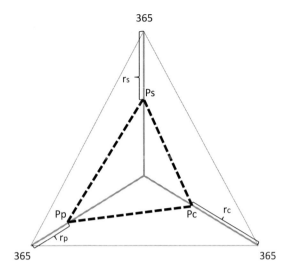

Figure 2. Radar chart representation of APMs and rotations.

Thus, KM is defined as a function of the radar chart's structure:

$$KM_k = f(PD1, PD2, PD3) \tag{3}$$

where:

k= A, B, C, D, E, F

1(sales area), 2(treasury area), 3(purchases area)

Moreover, modelling the KM of firms requires the application of *Cosine Theorem*, which is a generalization of Pythagoras Theorem according to the assumptions 12 and 13 of the Book II of the Euclid's Elements in 3th century BC. This generalization was completed by the mathematician Ghiyath al-Kashi in the 15th century.

$$PDk^2 = P_i^2 + P_j^2 - 2 \cdot \cos(120°) \cdot P_i \cdot P_j \tag{4}$$

where:

PDk = Perimeter Distance of area k
k = 1 (Sales Area); 2 (Treasury Area); 3 (Purchases Area)
P_i & P_j = *Average Period of Maturation*
$i \neq j; i = s$ *(sales); c (collect); p (payment)*

The Cosine Theorem (Eq. 4) is based on the constant value of angular coefficient between two axes (120°). In this sense, for each area considered in the radar chart, the APMs that determine it are used as sides of the triangle defined by them and the PD of the area. Therefore, we get the PD as the hypotenuse of triangles S, T and P (Figure 3). The structure defined by PD is not only a visual representation of firms' activity and the firms' KM, but the lineal combination (Eq. 5) of three distances is an indicator of firms' activity dynamism. It allows to determine how fast the company develops its ordinary activity: the lower the dynamism the more rotation of current assets.

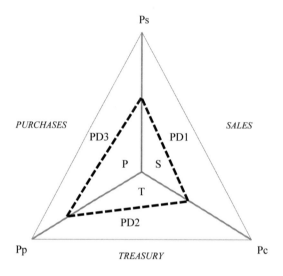

Figure 3. Radar Chart representation of Areas and Perimeter Distances according to APMs.

$$\sum PD = PD1 + PD2 + PD3 \qquad (5)$$

Table 3 shows the different KM regarding the relative position of PDs. Therefore, it is evident that one of the most important indicators of AMRC is the values of PDs and their implications on the firms' behaviour.

Table 3. Kinds of Management (KM) according to the compliance of Perimeter Distances' relative positions

Positives KMs		Negatives KMs	
A	PD2>PD3>PD1	D	PD1>PD3>PD2
B	PD3>PD2>PD1	E	PD1>PD2>PD3
C	PD3>PD1>PD2	F	PD2>PD1>PD3

PD1= Perimeter Distance for sales area; PD2= Perimeter Distance for treasury area; PD3= Perimeter Distance for purchases area.

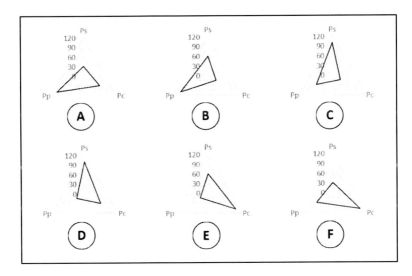

Figure 4. Standard Graphical Representation of Kinds of Management.

Figure 4 shows the graphical representations of radar charts related to every KM, which demonstrates the need of differentiating the firms' behaviour, since each KM implies that firms adapt its activity to several factors relative to culture, financial situation, and macroeconomic environment.

In the case of Positives KMs, the difference between sales area and purchases area is always positive in terms of dynamism. That is explained because one of the characteristics of firms that adopt these KMs is that Pc remains always lower than Pp, regardless the Ps. Conversely, negative KMs present always higher dynamism in purchases area than sales area, because Pp is always lower than Pc, regardless Ps. However, in both cases, depending on the time that firms manage to put their product or service on the market, the financial sufficiency and liquidity on transactions of firms' management will change. Therefore, treasury area will be more dynamic when Ps grows to the detriment of dynamism in sales and purchases areas. Nevertheless, the main idea that should be taken into consideration is that none of the KMs is harmful per se for firms, but is structured according to the requirements of their activity and other factors (culture, economy, among others).

Moreover, PDs tensions are necessary to explain the financial significance of: (i) credit supply granted by firms to their clients since the financing is granted by creditors to firms, for sales area analysis; (ii) liquidity from management of ordinary activity since they manage to put their product on the market, for treasury area analysis; and (iii) credit supply granted by creditors to the firms since the financing is granted by firms to their clients, for purchases area. Table 4 shows the Perimeter Differences (d) based on the linear combination of PDs of other two areas.

The main indicator obtained from the analysis of Perimeter Differences is that one related to Treasury area, which must accomplish the linear combination represented in Eq. 6.

$$d2 = d1 + d3 \qquad (6)$$

Table 4. Perimeter differences according to the Perimeter Distances

d1 = PD3 – PD2	(i) Financial significance of credit policy in Sales Area.
d2 = PD3 – PD1	(ii) Financial significance of liquidity from the firm ordinary activity.
d3 = PD2 – PD1	(iii) Financial significance of credit policy in Purchases Area.

PD1= Perimeter Distance for sales area; PD2= Perimeter Distance for treasury area; PD3= Perimeter Distance for purchases area.

Financial Sufficiency and Liquidity on Transactions Conditions

Once the KM of a firm has been obtained, it is time to define the indicators that allow to determine the Optimal Management (OM) in every considered area. In this sense, OM depends on the compliance of two characteristic of financial statements. On the one hand, firms must show Financial Sufficiency (SF) on their activity, that is, according to the firms' financial structure they are competent to develop their ordinary activity without deficiencies in the employment of their financial resources, regardless where they come from (Equity or external financing). On the other hand, firms must meet Liquidity on Transaction condition (LT) from their activity in every considered area. That means, to what extent it is worth to employ the resources in a specific area regarding the liquidity on transactions. Thus, firms have to manage the deficiencies detected in order to solve the possible problems related to lack of liquidity on transactions.

Therefore, both conditions (SF and LT) should be associated with the structure of radar chart. In this sense, and assuming that every area has 120 degrees as the value of the angular coefficient between the APMs, which form the triangles S, T and P (Figure 3), the sum of the remaining two angular coefficients must be up to 60 degrees. Moreover, these two angular coefficients will never be 30 degrees each at the same time for every area, because this would mean that firms would show the same value for all APMs, which is impossible regardless the KM adopted by company.

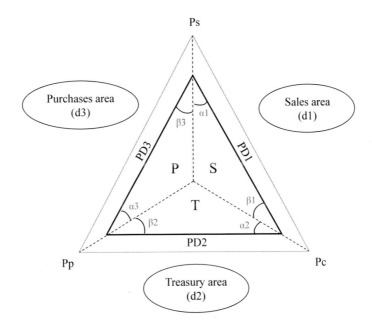

Figure 5. Radar Chart representation of angular coefficients by areas.

In this vein, angular coefficients show the relationship between APMs that delimit the triangle of every area (Figure 5). For instance, in the case of sales area, if α1 is wider (narrower) than 30 degrees means that Ps is lower (higher) than Pc, which implies, as well, a consequence in the others areas triggering more (less) dynamism for the area related to purchases than for the treasury area. That is different depending on the KMs adopted by firms.

Consequently, we need to apply other mathematical assumption from trigonometry: The *Sine Theorem*. The Sine Theorem is a generalization for all triangles, based on the solutions for triangles rectangles presented in Book IV of the mathematician Johann Müller "Regiomontanus," which demonstrates the proportionality of the triangles' sides whose vertices are in the circumference drawn using the circumcentre of them. Specially, in this case, it is very useful to determine the relation or proportion between two APMs of each area, due to there is an angle fixed in 120 degrees. Now, Sine Theorem (Eq. 7) allows to demonstrate that angular coefficients and their implications have a mathematical development from the APMs, which means that these indicators will be normalized, objective, independent and positive.

$$\frac{PDk}{\sin 120°} = \frac{Pi}{\sin \alpha k} = \frac{Pj}{\sin \beta k} \qquad (7)$$

where:

> *PDk = Perimeter Distance of area k*
> *k = 1 (Sales Area); 2 (Treasury Area); 3 (Purchases Area)*
> P_i & P_j *= Average Period of Maturation*
> *i ≠ j; i = s (sales); c (collect); p (payment)*

As having exposed above, triangles S, T and P are based on PD and two APMs as sides of them. So they have to accomplish the relation represented in Sine Theorem. Consequently, Table 5 shows that using the expression arcsine makes it possible to calculate the value of angular coefficients.

Therefore, angular coefficients must show specific values for each KM, due to the structure presented in radar chart. Panel A of Table 6 shows that every angular coefficient should be wider or narrower than 30 degrees depending on the KM displayed in radar chart according to its activity. Moreover, once the main indicators have been obtained from radar charts, it is possible to determine the financial significance of all areas, according to the compliance of two conditions: The Financial Sufficiency (FS), presented in Panel B, and the Liquidity on Transactions (LT) displayed on Panel C.

Determining both conditions is subject to the PDs' order stablished for every KM. Therefore, as we can see in Table 3, there are three combinations in order to compare one PDs to other one (PD3<>PD2; PD3<>PD1; PD2<>PD1). The mathematical development is expressed in Appendix (Table A1). However, the correct interpretation for each KM and area is displayed in Table 6.

Table 5. Angular Coefficients by area

Area	Angular Coefficients	
Sales	$\alpha 1 = \arcsin\left(\dfrac{Pc \cdot \sin 120°}{PD1}\right)$	$\beta 1 = \arcsin\left(\dfrac{Ps \cdot \sin 120°}{PD1}\right)$
Treasury	$\alpha 2 = \arcsin\left(\dfrac{Pp \cdot \sin 120°}{PD2}\right)$	$\beta 2 = \arcsin\left(\dfrac{Pc \cdot \sin 120°}{PD2}\right)$
Purchases	$\alpha 3 = \arcsin\left(\dfrac{Ps \cdot \sin 120°}{PD3}\right)$	$\beta 3 = \arcsin\left(\dfrac{Pp \cdot \sin 120°}{PD3}\right)$

PD1= Perimeter Distance for sales area; PD2= Perimeter Distance for treasury area; PD3= Perimeter Distance for purchases area.

Table 6. Necessary, Financial Sufficiency and Liquidity on Transactions conditions by Kinds of Management (KM) and areas (d)

Panel A: Necessary conditions

	Positives KM (+)			Negatives KM (-)		
	A	B	C	D	E	F
Angular Coefficients	PD2>PD3>PD1	PD3>PD2>PD1	PD3>PD1>PD2	PD1>PD3>PD2	PD1>PD2>PD3	PD2>PD1>PD3
$\alpha 1$	$\alpha 1 > 30$	$\alpha 1 < 30$	$\alpha 1 < 30$	$\alpha 1 < 30$	$\alpha 1 > 30$	$\alpha 1 > 30$
$\beta 1$	$\beta 1 < 30$	$\beta 1 > 30$	$\beta 1 > 30$	$\beta 1 > 30$	$\beta 1 < 30$	$\beta 1 < 30$
$\alpha 2$	$\alpha 2 > 30$	$\alpha 2 > 30$	$\alpha 2 > 30$	$\alpha 2 > 30$	$\alpha 2 < 30$	$\alpha 2 < 30$
$\beta 2$	$\beta 2 < 30$	$\beta 2 < 30$	$\beta 2 < 30$	$\beta 2 > 30$	$\beta 2 > 30$	$\beta 2 > 30$
$\alpha 3$	$\alpha 3 < 30$	$\alpha 3 < 30$	$\alpha 3 > 30$	$\alpha 3 > 30$	$\alpha 3 > 30$	$\alpha 3 < 30$
$\beta 3$	$\beta 3 > 30$	$\beta 3 > 30$	$\beta 3 < 30$	$\beta 3 < 30$	$\beta 3 < 30$	$\beta 3 > 30$

Panel B: Financial Sufficiency conditions (SF)

	A	B	C	D	E	F
Sales area (d1)	$\frac{\alpha 2}{\beta 3} < 1$	$\frac{\alpha 2}{\beta 3} > 1$	$\frac{\alpha 2}{\beta 3} > 1$	$\frac{\alpha 2}{\beta 3} > 1$	$\frac{\alpha 2}{\beta 3} < 1$	$\frac{\alpha 2}{\beta 3} < 1$
Treasury area (d2)	$\frac{\beta 1}{\alpha 3} > 1$	$\frac{\beta 1}{\alpha 3} > 1$	$\frac{\beta 1}{\alpha 3} > 1$	$\frac{\beta 1}{\alpha 3} < 1$	$\frac{\beta 1}{\alpha 3} < 1$	$\frac{\beta 1}{\alpha 3} < 1$
Purchases area (d3)	$\frac{\alpha 1}{\beta 2} > 1$	$\frac{\alpha 1}{\beta 2} > 1$	$\frac{\alpha 1}{\beta 2} < 1$	$\frac{\alpha 1}{\beta 2} < 1$	$\frac{\alpha 1}{\beta 2} < 1$	$\frac{\alpha 1}{\beta 2} > 1$

Panel C: Liquidity on Transactions conditions (LT)

	Positives KM (+)			Negatives KM (-)		
	A	B	C	D	E	F
	PD2>PD3>PD1	PD3>PD2>PD1	PD3>PD1>PD2	PD1>PD3>PD2	PD1>PD2>PD3	PD2>PD1>PD3
Sales area (d1)	$\frac{\beta 2}{\alpha 3} < \left(\frac{Rec}{Inv}\right)\cdot\left(\frac{CS}{S}\right)$	$\frac{\beta 2}{\alpha 3} > \left(\frac{Rec}{Inv}\right)\cdot\left(\frac{CS}{S}\right)$	$\frac{\beta 2}{\alpha 3} > \left(\frac{Rec}{Inv}\right)\cdot\left(\frac{CS}{S}\right)$	$\frac{\beta 2}{\alpha 3} > \left(\frac{Rec}{Inv}\right)\cdot\left(\frac{CS}{S}\right)$	$\frac{\beta 2}{\alpha 3} < \left(\frac{Rec}{Inv}\right)\cdot\left(\frac{CS}{S}\right)$	$\frac{\beta 2}{\alpha 3} < \left(\frac{Rec}{Inv}\right)\cdot\left(\frac{CS}{S}\right)$
Treasury area (d2)	$\frac{\alpha 1}{\beta 3} > \left(\frac{Rec}{Sup}\right)\cdot\left(\frac{P}{S}\right)$	$\frac{\alpha 1}{\beta 3} > \left(\frac{Rec}{Sup}\right)\cdot\left(\frac{P}{S}\right)$	$\frac{\alpha 1}{\beta 3} > \left(\frac{Rec}{Sup}\right)\cdot\left(\frac{P}{S}\right)$	$\frac{\alpha 1}{\beta 3} < \left(\frac{Rec}{Sup}\right)\cdot\left(\frac{P}{S}\right)$	$\frac{\alpha 1}{\beta 3} < \left(\frac{Rec}{Sup}\right)\cdot\left(\frac{P}{S}\right)$	$\frac{\alpha 1}{\beta 3} < \left(\frac{Rec}{Sup}\right)\cdot\left(\frac{P}{S}\right)$
Payment area (d3)	$\frac{\beta 1}{\alpha 2} > \left(\frac{Inv}{Sup}\right)\cdot\left(\frac{P}{CS}\right)$	$\frac{\beta 1}{\alpha 2} > \left(\frac{Inv}{Sup}\right)\cdot\left(\frac{P}{CS}\right)$	$\frac{\beta 1}{\alpha 2} < \left(\frac{Inv}{Sup}\right)\cdot\left(\frac{P}{CS}\right)$	$\frac{\beta 1}{\alpha 2} < \left(\frac{Inv}{Sup}\right)\cdot\left(\frac{P}{CS}\right)$	$\frac{\beta 1}{\alpha 2} < \left(\frac{Inv}{Sup}\right)\cdot\left(\frac{P}{CS}\right)$	$\frac{\beta 1}{\alpha 2} > \left(\frac{Inv}{Sup}\right)\cdot\left(\frac{P}{CS}\right)$

PD1=Perimeter Distance of sales area; PD2=Perimeter Distance of treasury area; PD3=Perimeter Distance of purchases area.

Ps=Sales Average Period of Maturation; Pc=Collect Average Period of Maturation; Pp=Payment Average Period of Maturation.

Rec=Average Receivables; In=Average Inventory; Sup=Average Suppliers.

S=Sales; CS=Cost of Sales; P=Purchases.

Financial Sufficiency is the way to corroborate the financial significance related to perimeter differences. In this sense, one observes whether firms properly employ financial resources according to their activity. Starting from the base of perimeter differences represented in Table 4, as well as using the Sine Theorem, it is possible to stablish the Financial Sufficiency conditions in accordance to mathematical development contrasting the ratios that contain the same APMs. Consequently, the indicator obtained is called Angular Relation, which indicates the adjustment of FS within its respective KM.

Liquidity on Transactions corroborates the optimal employment of resources to develop the firm's activity. In this sense, it is possible to analyse the specific management of every area to realise where the company fails or whether the resources are properly assigned. Starting from the base of perimeter differences represented in Table 4, as well as using the Sine Theorem, it is possible to stablish the Liquidity on Transaction condition in accordance to mathematical development contrasting the ratios that contain different APMs. Consequently, Angular Relation now indicates the adjustment of LT within its respective KM.

Optimal Management (OM)

Once all indicators from AMRC have been obtained, a company is properly performing its activity when it achieves an optimal management of the available resources and the financing (Equity or external debt). Eq. 8 expresses that OM is a function of good management in every area (sales, treasury and purchases). Thus, the OM for one area is determined according to the compliance of both conditions explained above (FS and LT). Consequently, when a company shows an OM, that going concern is granted for sure.

$$OM_k = f(FS_1 \cap LT_1 \cap FS_2 \cap LT_2 \cap FS_3 \cap LT_3) \tag{8}$$

where:

$k = A, B, C, D, E, F$
1(sales area), 2(treasury area), 3(purchases area)

RESULTS

We analyse the different elements related to the performance of Italian companies in order to demonstrate that the KMs define the firms' behaviour according to their capital structure (Short-Term Debt, Long-Term Debt and Equity), their short-term economic structure (Inventory, Receivable and Cash and cash equivalents), variables related to performance (ROA and ROE) and financial autonomy (FA), and finally, the number of employees (EMPLOYEES) and the market capitalization per share (MCSHARE) to control for the hiring policy and the interests of investors, respectively.

We focus our analysis in capital structure and short-term economic structure to observe the most representative firms' activity within the operational planification, since firms are able to change their KM depending on their needs. However, that is quite difficult in accordance with the existence of cultural factors among others.

Panel A in Table 7 shows that KMs classified as positive maintain on average a capital structure more focused on long-term debt than firms that adopt the negative KMs. As well, negative KMs are more dependent of equity than positive KMs. Additionally, short-term economic structure for both positive KMs and negative KMs is largely formed by receivables. However, we notice that positive KMs differs from negative KMs in the rest of current assets, that is, the former show higher level of cash and cash equivalent, but the latter have a higher value of inventory. That means that positive KMs' economic structure is more liquid. Panel B shows that there are no significant differences in capital structure according to the compliance of optimal management. It confirms that capital structure depends on the KM adopted by firm but not on the compliance of optimal management in the considered areas. Short-term economic structure differs between firms that get optimal management from those that do not. The former has more receivables and less cash and cash equivalents than the latter, regardless the KM. However, the value of inventory is higher for firms with optimal management when they adopt a positive KM, whereas the difference is in favour of firms that do not obtain the optimal management when they have a negative KM.

Moreover, profitability for positive KMs is higher than negative KMs taking Return on Equity, but there is no evidence about ROA. However, when we split the sample and analyse the differences between the compliance of optimal management or not, we observe a positive difference considering ROA for both positive and negative KMs. That means, regardless the KM, firms that achieve optimal management in their ordinary activity are more profitable than those failing in at least one of the considered areas. Yet, firms which adopt negative KMs show higher financial autonomy, so this confirms the significance of equity in these KMs.

Additionally, when we observe the employment and the capitalization of companies, we realise that firms with positive KMs have employed on average more human capital than negative KMs. In the same way, market capitalization is higher for companies that adopt positive KMs.

Table 7. Descriptive statistics

Panel A. Descriptive statistics considering kinds of management (KM)

	KM(+)			KM(-)			KM(+)- KM(-)	
	N	mean	median	N	mean	median	Diff. in mean	Diff in median
Short-Term debt	1,510	0.387	0.377	348	0.397	0.369	-0.010	0.008
Long-term debt	1,510	0.258	0.228	348	0.187	0.151	0.071 ***	0.077 ***
Equity	1,510	0.355	0.330	348	0.416	0.413	-0.061 ***	-0.083 ***
Inventory	1,555	0.235	0.192	350	0.388	0.399	-0.153 ***	-0.207 ***
Receivable	1,555	0.473	0.451	350	0.461	0.435	0.012	0.016
Cash and cash equivalents	1,555	0.292	0.237	350	0.151	0.090	0.142 ***	0.147 ***
ROA	1,560	0.030	0.040	352	0.027	0.027	0.004	0.013 *
ROE	1,560	0.094	0.131	352	-0.080	0.086	0.173 **	0.045 ***
FA	1,560	0.797	0.481	352	1.129	0.700	-0.858 ***	-0.219 ***
EMPLOYEES	1,428	4.801	1,326	306	1,403	379	3,398 ***	947 ***
MCSHARE	1,052	7.718	2.420	226	5.645	2.439	2.073 **	-0.019

Panel B. Descriptive statistics considering compliance with the optimal management (OM)

	OM			Non_OM			OM – Non_OM	
	N	mean	median	N	mean	median	Diff. in mean	Diff in median
Short-Term debt	1,117	0.389	0.377	393	0.379	0.377	0.010	-0.001
Long-term debt	1,117	0.256	0.231	393	0.266	0.218	-0.010	0.012
Equity	1,117	0.355	0.330	393	0.355	0.329	0.000	0.002
Inventory	1,148	0.236	0.185	407	0.231	0.201	0.005 ***	-0.016
Receivable	1,148	0.476	0.445	407	0.464	0.469	0.012 ***	-0.024
Cash and cash equivalents	1,148	0.288	0.235	407	0.305	0.244	-0.018 **	-0.010
ROA	1,151	0.035	0.042	409	0.017	0.037	0.018 ***	0.004 **
ROE	1,151	0.089	0.136	409	0.108	0.119	-0.020	0.017

Panel B. Descriptive statistics considering compliance with the optimal management (OM)

	KM(+) OM			KM(+) Non_OM			KM(+) OM – Non_OM		
	N	mean	median	N	mean	median	Diff. in mean		Diff in median
FA	1,151	0.829	0.482	409	0.703	0.476	0.126		0.006
EMPLOYEES	1,059	5,222	1,443	369	3,591	822	1,631	***	621 ***
MCSHARE	776	7.813	2.400	276	7.452	2.493	0.361		-0.093

	KM(-) OM			KM(-) Non_OM			KM(-) OM- Non_OM		
	N	mean	median	N	mean	median	Diff. in mean		Diff in median
Short-Term debt	220	0.399	0.359	128	0.394	0.382	0.005		-0.024
Long-term debt	220	0.190	0.149	128	0.182	0.157	0.008		-0.008
Equity	220	0.411	0.409	128	0.424	0.418	-0.013		-0.008
Inventory	220	0.365	0.396	130	0.428	0.401	-0.064	***	-0.004 *
Receivable	220	0.496	0.446	130	0.402	0.378	0.094	***	0.067 ***
Cash and cash equivalents	220	0.139	0.085	130	0.170	0.112	-0.031	**	-0.027
ROA	222	0.037	0.038	130	0.009	0.015	0.028	***	0.023 ***
ROE	222	-0.024	0.112	130	-0.173	0.039	0.149		0.073 ***
FA	222	1.122	0.685	130	1.139	0.709	-0.017		-0.024
EMPLOYEES	194	1,384	429	112	1,436	294	-54		135 ***
MCSHARE	142	5.059	2.376	84	6.636	2.782	-1.577		-0.406

KM is the Kind of Management adopted by firms; ST Debt is the short-term debt of the firm; LT Debt is the long-term debt of the firm; Equity is the equity of the firm; Inventory is the inventory of the firm; Receivables is the receivables of the firm; Cash is the cash and cash equivalents of the firm; ROA is the ratio between Net Income over total assets; ROE is the ratio between Net Income over equity; FA is the ratio defined by equity over total debt; EMPLOYEES is the number of employees of the firm; MCSHARE is the market capitalization per share of the firm. The statistical significance of the difference of means (medians) is based on the parametric t-test (the non-parametric Wilcoxon/Mann-Whitney test). ***, **, and * indicate statistical significance at the 1%, 5%, and 10% levels.

In this vein, a deeper analysis is required to discover how firms proceed according to the KM. The ternary diagram is a useful technique to describe which is the behaviour of companies taking into account three components that must sum up 100%. Therefore, both capital structure and short-term economic structure accomplish this assumption. This technique does not determine only the percentage of each component, but it allows us to stablish an area, according to some values of components, where the concentration of companies is higher and could differ from other KMs. As well, we can limit the area using both parallel limits (percentage of this component) and proportions between two components (in our case, short-term debt and long-term debt), because they form the external financing of firms, and depending on the proportion they can assume the debt with their short-term economic structure or not.

Figure 6 and Figure 7 demonstrate visually that, depending on the KM adopted by firms, the concentration of companies with a determined capital structure is different. Moreover, those KMs also trigger that companies are more or less likely to construct a wider (narrower) capital structure. That is similar for short-term economic structure.

Table 8 is linked to the Figure 6 and Figure 7, and represents the areas of larger concentration according to the limits stablished in Panel A. Therefore, as we can see for capital structure, firms with positive KMs (A, B, and C) shows bigger areas than negative KMs (D, E, and F), the minimum (maximum) level of ST Debt is higher (lower) for negative KM, as well as the proportion between LT Debt and ST Debt is narrower for negative KMs. In the case of short-term economic structure, the areas that contain a larger concentration are wider for positive KMs. The proportion of Receivables over Inventory is similar for same KMs, specially the KM "A" is like "F," "B" has a similar proportion to "E" and "C" seems to be linked with "D." However, negative KMs are concentrated in a level of Cash and cash equivalents lower than 30%, 20% and 15% for "D," "E" and "F," respectively. In a different way, positive KMs are not limited in this component such as "A" or they can reach higher level of cash and cash equivalents (50%) than negative KMs, such as "B" and "C."

Finally, Panel B in Table 8 displays the decile that could be considered as the "epicentre" of the concentration, that is, the point around which is grouped the more intense concentration. The point is drawn in Figure 6 and Figure 7 using a cross. Therefore, if we compare positive KM (A, B, C) and negative KMs (D, E, F) we realise that ST Debt has a very similar distribution for both groups, which confirms the lack of significance shown in descriptive statistics. LT Debt and Equity display different combinations confirming that "epicentre" in negative KMs will take higher values than "epicentre" in positive KMs. That is consistent with prior analysis. This consistency remains when we analyse the short-term economic structure, where "epicentre" of positive KMs could reach on average lower value than "epicentre" of negative KMs. Conversely, cash and cash equivalent amounts show higher values for the "epicentre" of positive KMs.

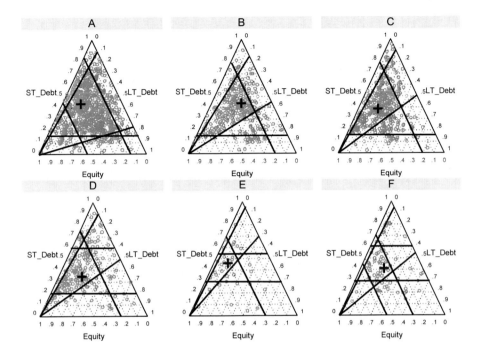

Figure 6. Ternary diagrams of capital structure by KM.

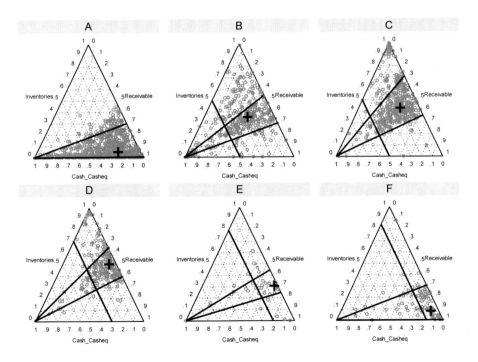

Figure 7. Ternary diagrams of short-term economic structure by KM.

Table 8. Limits for areas with more concentration and the "epicentre" by KM

Panel A. Levels of components that determine the area where there is higher firms' concentration

KM	Financial Structure			Short-Term Economical Structure		
	ST Debt	$\frac{\text{LT Debt}}{\text{ST Debt}}$	Equity	Inventory	$\frac{\text{Receivable}}{\text{Inventory}}$	Cash
A	15%<X	1/9<X<7.5/2.5	15%<X<55%	-	7/3<X<9.9/0.1	-
B	15%<X	1.5/8.5<X<5.5/4.5	20%<X	-	4.5/5.5<X<7/3	X<50%
C	15%<X	1/9<X<5/5	20%<X	-	3/7<X<6.5/3.5	X<50%
D	20%<X<60%	1/9<X<5.5/4.5	25%<X	-	3.5/6.5<X<6/4	X<30%
E	30%<X<55%	0.5/9.5<X<3/7	30%<X	-	5.5/4.5<X<7.5/2.5	X<20%
F	30%<X<60%	0.5/9.5<X<4.5/5.5	30%<X<55%	-	7/3<X<9.9/0.1	X<50%

Panel B. "Epicentre" area delimited by the deciles of components

KM	Financial Structure			Short-Term Economical Structure		
	ST Debt	LT Debt	Equity	Inventory	Receivable	Cash
A	40%<X<50%	10%<X<20%	30%<X<40%	0%<X<10%	70%<X<80%	20%<X<30%
B	40%<X<50%	20%<X<30%	20%<X<30%	30%<X<40%	30%<X<40%	20%<X<30%
C	30%<X<40%	10%<X<20%	40%<X<50%	40%<X<50%	30%<X<40%	10%<X<20%
D	30%<X<40%	20%<X<30%	40%<X<50%	50%<X<60%	40%<X<50%	0%<X<10%
E	40%<X<50%	10%<X<20%	40%<X<50%	30%<X<40%	60%<X<70%	0%<X<10%
F	40%<X<50%	20%<X<30%	30%<X<40%	0%<X<10%	80%<X<90%	0%<X<10%

KM is the Kind of Management adopted by the firm; ST Debt is the short-term debt of the firm; LT Debt is the long-term debt of the firm; Equity is the equity of the firm; Inventory is the inventory of the firm; Receivables is the receivables of the firm; Cash is the cash and cash equivalents of the firm.

CONCLUSION

The application of Accounting Methodology of Radar Charts (AMRC) on Italian companies analyses multi-effects of decision-making on areas represented on a radar chart, as well as defining the management behaviour of companies. Conditions of financial sufficiency and liquidity on transactions measure those multi-effects of decision-making in order to explain when a company meets the optimal management.

The manuscript describes the relationship between the financial structure of companies and the kind of management developed by them, as well as the economic position of current assets considering the position of treasury. Consequently, there is a visible relation between kinds of management and the economic and financial positions of companies with respect to their performance.

Our evidence from Italy demonstrates that capital structure and short-term economic structure depend on the kind of management adopted by companies. Firstly, positive kinds of management seem to maintain a capital structure more focused on long-term debt than negative kinds of management, which have, on average, higher Equity. Moreover, the short-term economic structure has higher (lower) cash and cash equivalents values (inventory) for positive kinds of management than for negative ones. Firms' profitability appears to be higher for positive and optimal management. Finally, positive kinds of management show more employees and higher market capitalization per share, which could be explained by a possible tendency of improving the human resources and value of firm, in contrast to preferences of negative kinds of management.

Although KMs are called positive/negative, they do not mean a good/bad management. A proper activity performance is determined by the optimal management in the considered areas.

Finally, KMs affect companies' performance and its employment policy and share price. In this sense, depending on the kind of management adopted, positive ones seem to prioritize the improvement of human capital and the value of firm, whereas negative ones could consider to distribute the profit to shareholders so as to attract investors.

The result of this research allows to apply the AMRC without adjusting the sectorial position of companies analysed, as well as tax policy, dividends policy, employment and other issues from Social Science that may be taken into consideration according to indicators' characteristics deducted from the application of AMRC, which could be future lines of research.

REFERENCES

Allegrini, M., & Greco, G. (2013). Corporate boards, audit committees and voluntary disclosure: Evidence from Italian listed companies. *Journal of Management & Governance, 17*(1), 187-216.

Bianco, M., & Casavola, P. (1999). Italian corporate governance: Effects on financial structure and firm performance, *European Economic Review, 43*(4), 1057-1069.

Birley, S., & Westhead, P. (1990). Growth and performance contrasts between 'types' of small firms. *Strategic management journal, 11*(7), 535-557.

Burgstahler, D., & Dichev, I. (1997). Earnings management to avoid earnings decreases and losses. *Journal of Accounting and Economics, 24*(1), 99-126.

Costa, L., & Font, M. (1992). Nuevos Instrumentos Financieros en la Estrategia Empresarial. [New Financial Instruments in the Business Strategy] *ESIC*, 112-121.

Elshandidy, T., & Neri, L. (2015). Corporate governance, risk disclosure practices, and market liquidity: comparative evidence from the UK and Italy. *Corporate Governance: An International Review, 23*(4), 331-356.

ESA (2010). Regulation (EU) No. 549/2013 of the European Parliament and of the Council, of 21 May 2013, on the European system of national and regional accounts in the European Union.

Filatotchev, I., Toms, S., & Wright, M. (2006). The firm's strategic dynamics andcorporate governance life cycle. *International Journal of Managerial Finance* 2(4), 256-279.

Keasey, K., Thompson, S. & Wright, M. (1997). *Introduction: the corporate governance problem competing diagnoses and solutions.* Oxford: Oxford University Press.

La Porta, R., Lopez-de-Silanes, F., Shleifer, A., & Vishny, R. (1998). Law and finance. *Journal of Political Economy, 106*(6), 1113-1155.

Mariadoss, B. J., Johnson, J. L., & Martin, K. D. (2014). Strategic intent and performance: The role of resource allocation decisions. *Journal of Business Research, 67*(11), 2393-2402.

Monks, R. A. & Minow, N. (1995). *Corporate governance.* Cambridge: Blackwell Business Ed.

Nobes, C. W., & Parker, R. H. (2010). *Comparative international accounting.* Harlow, Essex, UK: Pearson Education Limited.

Pérez, M. A., Porcuna, L., & Porcuna, R. (2017a). Los Mapas Contables de Gestión de las Empresas Cotizadas Chilenas: Análisis Cualitativo [The Management Accounting Maps of Chilean Listed Companies: Qualitative Analysis], *Información tecnológica, 28*(1), 161-170.

Pérez, M. A., Porcuna, L., & Porcuna, R. (2017b). Los Mapas de Gestión de las Empresas Cotizadas Chilenas. Análisis Cuantitativo, [The Management Accounting

Maps of Chilean Listed Companies: Qualitative Analysis] *Información tecnológica*, *28*(5), 03-14.

Rivero Romero, J. (1990). *Un análisis de estados financieros.* [An analysis of financial statements.] Ed. Trivim, Tema VII. 227-304.

Shefrin, H. (2002). *Beyond greed and fear: Understanding behavioral finance and the psychology of investing.* Oxford University Press on Demand.

Simon, H. A. (1978). Rationality as process and as product of thought, *The American economic review*, 1-16.

Strange, R., Filatotchev, I., Buck, T., & Wright, M. (2009). Corporate governance and international business, *Management International Review, 49*(4), 395-407.

APPENDIX

Table A1. Sine Theorem for each area and mathematical development of SF and LT conditions

SALES	TREASURY	PURCHASES
$\dfrac{PD1}{\sin 120}=\dfrac{Pc}{\sin \alpha 1}=\dfrac{Ps}{\sin \beta 1}$	$\dfrac{PD2}{\sin 120}=\dfrac{Pp}{\sin \alpha 2}=\dfrac{Pc}{\sin \beta 2}$	$\dfrac{PD3}{\sin 120}=\dfrac{Ps}{\sin \alpha 3}=\dfrac{Pp}{\sin \beta 3}$
Panel A. Mathematical development of Financial Sufficiency conditions		
SALES	TREASURY	PURCHASES
PD3<>PD2	PD3<>PD1	PD2<>PD1
$\dfrac{Pp}{\sin \beta 3}<>\dfrac{Pp}{\sin \alpha 2}$	$\dfrac{Ps}{\sin \alpha 3}<>\dfrac{Ps}{\sin \beta 1}$	$\dfrac{Pc}{\sin \beta 2}<>\dfrac{Pc}{\sin \alpha 1}$
$\dfrac{Pp}{\beta 3}<>\dfrac{Pp}{\alpha 2}$	$\dfrac{Ps}{\alpha 3}<>\dfrac{Ps}{\beta 1}$	$\dfrac{Pc}{\beta 2}<>\dfrac{Pc}{\alpha 1}$
$\dfrac{\alpha 2}{\beta 3}<>\dfrac{Pp}{Pp}$	$\dfrac{\beta 1}{\alpha 3}<>\dfrac{Ps}{Ps}$	$\dfrac{\alpha 1}{\beta 2}<>\dfrac{Pc}{Pc}$
$\dfrac{\alpha 2}{\beta 3}<>1$	$\dfrac{\beta 1}{\alpha 3}<>1$	$\dfrac{\alpha 1}{\beta 2}<>1$
Panel B. Mathematical development of Liquidity on Transaction conditions		
SALES	TREASURY	PURCHASES
PD3<>PD2	PD3<>PD1	PD2<>PD1
$\dfrac{Ps}{\sin \alpha 3}<>\dfrac{Pc}{\sin \beta 2}$	$\dfrac{Pp}{\sin \alpha 3}<>\dfrac{Pc}{\sin \alpha 1}$	$\dfrac{Pp}{\sin \alpha 2}<>\dfrac{Ps}{\sin \beta 1}$
$\dfrac{Ps}{\alpha 3}<>\dfrac{Pc}{\beta 2}$	$\dfrac{Pp}{\beta 3}<>\dfrac{Pc}{\alpha 1}$	$\dfrac{Pp}{\alpha 2}<>\dfrac{Ps}{\beta 1}$
$\dfrac{\beta 2}{\alpha 3}<>\dfrac{Pc}{Ps}$	$\dfrac{\alpha 1}{\beta 3}<>\dfrac{Pc}{Pp}$	$\dfrac{\beta 1}{\alpha 2}<>\dfrac{Ps}{Pp}$
$\dfrac{\beta 2}{\alpha 3}<>\dfrac{Rec/S}{Inv/CS}$	$\dfrac{\alpha 1}{\beta 3}<>\dfrac{Rec/S}{Sup/P}$	$\dfrac{\beta 1}{\alpha 2}<>\dfrac{Inv/CS}{Sup/P}$
$\dfrac{\beta 2}{\alpha 3}<>\left(\dfrac{Rec}{Inv}\right)\cdot\left(\dfrac{CS}{S}\right)$	$\dfrac{\alpha 1}{\beta 3}<>\left(\dfrac{Rec}{Sup}\right)\cdot\left(\dfrac{P}{S}\right)$	$\dfrac{\beta 1}{\alpha 2}<>\left(\dfrac{Inv}{Sup}\right)\cdot\left(\dfrac{P}{CS}\right)$

PD1=Perimeter Distance of sales area; PD2=Perimeter Distance of treasury area; PD3=Perimeter Distance of purchases area. Ps=Sales Average Period4 of Maturation; Ps=Treasury Average Period of Maturation; Ps=Purchases Average Period of Maturation. Rec=Average Receivables; Inv=Average Inventory; Sup=Average Suppliers. S=Sales; CS=Cost of Sales; P=Purchases.

INTRODUCTION

The diminishing of the geographical distance in the world leads to an increase of interconnection and interdependence of the world economy at the same time. The supporters of the globalization process, especially point out a growing amount of economic freedom, prosperity, innovations or technological expansion. In the financial system, we can see the strongest impacts of globalization. Financial globalization leads to the allocation of high amounts of capital to countries all over the world. Krugman (2009) points out that global capital flows added up to 2-6% of world GDP during 1980-1995. By 2006, the global capital flows were 7.2 trillion U.S. dollars, three times more than in 1995, and their total increase was about 15%. Another example given by Krugman is an increase of American assets and liabilities situated abroad. While in 1996 American assets located abroad were 52% and liabilities 57% of GDP, then in 2007, GDP reached 128% of assets and 145% GDP of liabilities. Flaring of the financial crisis in 2008, caused by the bursting of the housing bubble in 2007, may be seen as a proof of interconnection, dependence and in some sense even vulnerability of up-to-date financial markets. Consequently, it is not only the recent financial crisis we can label as a global crisis.

An analysis of potential causes of the financial crisis, culminating in 2008 and 2009, is quite long. The crisis pointed out not only a deficiency in the economy and threats of globalization, but also imperfections of economics as a scientific discipline. One of the factors often mentioned, is the unreliability of preconditions of econometric models. Such models based on current macroeconomic projections measure and alert to possible risks. Nowadays, from a retrospective point of view, these models may be considered as reliable. Therefore, a relatively young, interdisciplinary scientific field– behavioural economics became the centre of attention due to its followers pointing out the limits of econometric methods and models.

Consequently, the financial crisis gave rise to the shifting thoughts of many economists, including a wide range of central bankers, this can be proved by Yellen (2007) who assumes that people deal with issues like fairness and equity, succumb to money illusion and tend to follow rules of thumb. Moreover, Yellen (2007) also points out that work based on a behavioural basis, reach different impacts than ones built on standard theories bases. We can apply it not only for microeconomic behaviour, but also for research of macroeconomic variables development. In terms of inflation, behavioural research affirms the general conviction that inflation is costly, nevertheless, moderate inflation can prevent rigidity of nominal wages. Behavioural attitude and research provide theoretical foundations for policymakers, which in the case of monetary policy is as follows: monetary policy is supposed to make efforts to stabilize the real economy. However, it is also useful and thrilling for academics. It helps both groups to understand what they should focus on and improve within economic models.

The main objective of this paper is to evaluate whether it is possible to consider behavioural economics as a natural evolutionary development in economic theory. The result of the research is an enumeration of possible implications of behavioural economics for monetary theory and policy. In general, we can name a number of potential areas in which we can apply and use the findings of behavioural economics.

We have divided this chapter into three main chapters. The methodological-theoretical apparatus is a topic of the second and the third chapter. In the second chapter, the authors deal with some methodological notes, regarding a controversy about methods used in natural, and social sciences. We described specific theoretical papers and a genesis of opinions towards behavioural economics in the third chapter. The authors have explained the role of psychology and its disregard in economics for many years in the third chapter. Recently, the importance of research on the borderlines between psychology and economics becomes more and more significant. A substantial initiator of this trend is the financial crisis from 2008 and the following crises. Behavioural economics has a wide application in numerous economic disciplines. Nonetheless, in this paper, we focus on the implications of behavioural economics for monetary policy. Particularly, we focus on a new approach used by many central banks in the world economy, this so-called forward guidance, which is used by banks in order to communicate openly with the public. Thus, the way these central banks communicate, not only information about monetary policy, but also their intended steps in the future.

METHODS

In his article, concerning social and natural sciences, Von Mises (1942) concluded that an existing significant distinction is present between methods used in social and natural sciences. Social sciences tend to use certain methods to ensure that their growth and development comply with a specific character of their subject. Moreover, it must not use and adopt methodologies of natural sciences, as it would be incorrect to assume that mathematics would make the results of social sciences more precise. Research and work done in the area, quantified by mathematical and quantitative ways cannot ensure that results are more precise because people follow their human reasoning. Thus, any numeral statement is inexact either way.

Despite the above-mentioned statement, since the very birth of the classical political economy, it has been possible to observe an increasing need to quantify economic phenomena and relations. In 1871, these efforts culminated in a so-called marginal revolution, which was a revolution of methodology. Holman (2005) points out that economics had been a normative science up to that time, the marginal revolution brought evaluating judgements and transformation into a positive science. To sum up, the economists started to use mathematical methods within the marginal analysis.

In a current conception of economic science, as a social science, consists of two utterly different scientific disciplines – mathematics and the social branch. Economists of the mathematical branch admit using of a wide range of simplified preconditions, which the mathematical models are built on. Ultimately, these models may not be realistic in comparison with social life. These economists advert to the fact that, based only on mathematical evidence, we can ensure the verity, scientism and applicability of economic theories. Contrarily, the followers of the social branch of economics observe a complicated reality of economic life in a society, which is not possible to formulate by limited formulas (Macáková, 2003). Moreover, we must take into consideration particular spatial-temporal context, see Suchacek (2015).

From contemporary discussions of a scientific community, it is clear that a conflict over a mathematization of economics is still very topical and current. Although, the contribution of quantitative methods to economics is indisputable, the obsession of using these methods in the area of financial markets led to their evident overrating. We date an upswing of quantitative approach on the financial markets from the 80s of the 20th century. The so-called financial engineers, were creating progressively more complicated and derivative new products for their banks. They used these products as new and more sophisticated risk management methods and techniques. Large financial houses also focused on the employing of young mathematicians, statisticians and a general redirection of employing economists without knowledge of quantitative methods. The problems appeared particularly in situations when these mathematical engineers did not have sufficient knowledge of economic contexts. Nowadays, investors typically invest in complicated financial products without knowledge of their sophisticated mathematical mechanics. The financial engineers disconnected from reality and started to face various unanticipated market falls.

Nevertheless, even among them, we can find those who are critics of an incorrect application of mathematics on financial markets. One of them is a financial engineer Paul Wilmott, who is a researcher, consultant, lecturer and expert witness working in risk management, derivatives and in most things connected with quantitative finance. He has been called "cult derivatives lecturer" (Financial Times), "the smartest of the quants, he may be the only smart quant" (Portfolio magazine), "the finance industry's Mozart" (Sunday Business), "financial mathematics guru" (BBC) and "arguably the most influential quant today" (Newsweek). Paul Wilmott (2008) explains on his blog why he has always been critical towards quant modelling, especially their presumptions, construction of models as well as their final implementation, over the years. He claims that financial institutions such as banks employ staff workers, who deal with these models, without further knowledge and experience of financial markets. Thus, the results are inaccurate and politicians who do not understand, simply adopt them. Finally, the losses surprise not only the traders but also the people. Moreover, he compares salaries of the public and private sector, which are about ten times higher p.a. for instance Goldman Sachs, that in his opinion does not understand the game but has the power to set rules.

From the very beginning of the marginal revolution the controversy whether to use methods of social or natural sciences in economics or not started to be topical. Some economists, such as Ingthorsson (2013) perceive that the difference among them lies in the fact that the natural and human sciences must deal with dissimilar methodological problems and challenges connected with the specificity of their own subject of research. Thus, logically they can solve the problems in their own way sometimes, especially in their infancy they can learn from each other and have many things in common. Nevertheless, he believes that it is not verified that human sciences are stagnant in their methods and methodology and therefore do not have to adopt the natural sciences methods.

It is neither the purpose nor the ambition of the authors of this paper to infer a simple conclusion concerning this critical methodological dispute. Yet, we would like to bring to the fore that the financial crisis was a radical event that deserves self-reflection of the economic theory and methodology. Thus, we can see the behavioural economics as a natural development of economics, not as an attempt to destroy its foundations.

CHOSEN ASPECTS FROM THE THEORY AND METHODOLOGY OF BEHAVIOURAL ECONOMICS

During the studies of economic theory, we can find many definitions of economics. These definitions differ according to dissimilar approaches of economists. Nevertheless, all these definitions have something in common – Man. A Scotch economist Adam Smith (1776) introduced the following definition of economics: A discipline dealing with governing of countries, law making, incomes and livelihood of people. John Stuart Mill (1844) adds a social context in his definition: A science, which observes principles of human behaviour arising from interconnected activities of humankind, which acts in order to produce wealth unless people modify these activities to follow other aims. Alfred Marshall (1890) provides a definition extending economics on the microeconomic level. However, he does not omit a social level: Economics is a study of a changeless behaviour of man in an ordinary life. It researches how people gain their incomes and how they use them. On the one hand it is a study of wealth and on the other hand, more importantly, it is a study of man. Lionel Robbins (1932) is an author of the following definition: Economics is a science, which examines human behaviour as a relation among outputs and a limited number of inputs, which have alternative uses.

We have already mentioned all of these definitions that accent human behaviour. We can label everything concerning demeanour by the term behavioural. Psychology as a scientific discipline deals with human behaviour separately. Hence, an interconnection of economics and psychology is more than clear and apparent.

Classical economics of Adam Smith created a simplified model of man, i.e., "homo oeconomicus". Such a person acts entirely rationally, and his emotions do not influence him. According to the classics, this is the reason why all people naturally follow the economic rules but are also enough smart not to repeat the same mistakes again. Moreover, classical economics deals with a "ceteris paribus" rule - holding other things constant. So, economic theories based on this principle work only in the case that everything else remains unchanged and only a variable, which needs to be counted, changes.

In its models, the mainstream of economic thoughts did not pay much attention to psychological aspects. A certain contribution to psychological topics may be seen in the 40s of the 20th century, when an American economist Edward Chamberlin tested and experimented with the imperfections of market running and formulated his statements into a theory of monopolistic competition. Vernon Smith, the participant of these experiments and a subsequent professor of economics at the Arizona University, was also involved in the starting of many other experiments concerning the markets running. In the 50s, Heinz Sauermann dealt with the application of the prisoner´s dilemma to the other market structures of an imperfect competition market. Later, his colleague Reinhard Selten created a centre for research of theory of games and game experiments at a University in Bonn.

In the 40s of the 20th century, an American scientist, dealing with IT science, cognitive psychology, economics and philosophy, Herbert Simon worked towards a higher enforcement of psychology into economics. He is a laureate of Sveriges Riksbank Prize in Economic Sciences in Memory of Alfred Nobel from 1978 and an author of the term "bounded rationality ". According to Simon (1978), a human decision-making procedure consists of two systems. The first system using intuition is automatic and quick. While the second system is rational, logical and processes information slower. An example of this situation is when a man decides, according to the first system, a choice of the nicer of two bottles of perfume. The man uses the second system, for instance, during a calculation of a mathematical exercise. Since the second system remembers previous mistakes, it can moderate the intuitive system. However, if the rational system does not have enough information or experience, it can make a mistake either way.

In the 50s of the 20th century, Maurice Félix Charles Allais, who was a French economist, the 1988 winner of Sveriges Riksbank Prize in Economic Sciences in Memory of Alfred Nobel, was interested in psychology. As an economist, he made a wide range of contributions to decision theory, monetary policy and other areas. Based on a survey by questionnaire he opposed econometric models for not being realistic because they were not in accordance with human thought. At the same time, an American psychologist Ward Edwards was concerned with the penetration of psychology into economics. In his article from 1954, he pointed out that many social scientists (except psychologists) had dealt with the topic of human behaviour in their theories, but in comparison with a large number of theories, they had proved their theories by almost no experiments. Edwards (1954) concludes that mathematical theories about the human decision-making processes have been under development by economists and others for a long time. All they have in common is that they consider the subjective value or utility as a decisive determinant when more options are under consideration. We can also presume that humans act rationally; they make their decisions based on their transitive preferences and maximization of their utility. However, economists often question the transitivity of choices as a presumption. Research has shown that intransitive patterns of choices sometimes appear. Therefore, researchers developed stochastic models, which admit occasional intransitivity.

The founding fathers of behavioural economics, are considered to be two American psychologists, with an Israeli origin, Amos Tversky and Daniel Kahneman. They not only criticized a theory of expected utility, but also modified classical economics by a rational theory to correspond with a real human decision-making process. the so-called "Prospect theory", shows how people decide between alternatives that involve risk and uncertainty (e.g., % likelihood of gains or losses), and demonstrates that people think in terms of expected utility relative to a reference point (e.g., current wealth) rather than absolute outcomes. Kahneman and Tversky developed the prospect theory by framing risky choices, it indicates that people are loss-averse, and since individuals dislike losses more than an equivalent gain (see Figure 1), they are more willing to take risks, in order to avoid a loss (Kahneman and Tversky, 1979; Kahneman, 2011).

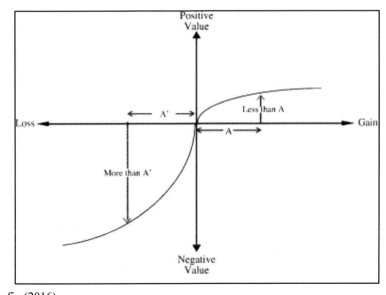

Source: Econfix (2016).

Figure 1. Prospect theory.

In the following years, an increase of interest of experimental economics started to be typical at numerous universities worldwide. The researchers practised various experiments at the intersection of psychology and economics, many results of these experiments were published in reputable economic journals. A separation of two directions, namely experimental economics and a behavioural economics, is typical for this period. While the centre of experimental economics is the studying of economic phenomena through a method of experiments, behavioural economics has ambitions to apply psychological findings into economics and verify new hypotheses. The difference between classical and behavioural economics lies in a point of view on human behaviour. Whilst classical economics consider economic phenomena and human behaviour to be rational and predictable, behavioural economics, then explain why the economic rules do not often work in practice.

In 2002, the Sveriges Riksbank awarded Daniel Kahneman and Vernon L. Smith with the Prize in Economic Sciences in Memory of Alfred Nobel (Nobelprize, 2016). Daniel Kahneman got the Prize "for having integrated insights from psychological research into economic science, especially concerning human judgment and decision-making under uncertainty" and Vernon L. Smith "for having established laboratory experiments as a tool in empirical economic analysis, especially in the study of alternative market mechanisms". Thus, 2002 may be seen as a turning year due to it being proved that behavioural economics has a rightful place among other sciences.

We can consider Richard Thaler, inspired by the work of Amos Tversky as a founding father of a newly created area – behavioural finance. Particularly, the findings of his colleagues fascinated him, in that people make predictable mistakes in their decisions. Thales explained some deviations in rational behaviour of investors and he proved that they were not random but systematic. A significant contribution of Thaler to behavioural economics is his "endowment effect", see Thales (1979).

IMPLICATION OF BEHAVIOURAL ECONOMICS FOR MONETARY POLICY

The traditional macroeconomic theory works with a hypothesis of rational expectations, formulated by J. F. Muth (1961). American economists Robert Lucas and Thomas Sargent made practical analyses of his hypothesis. A foundation of the so-called school of rational expectations is the work of these economists built on the following principles: a) people make decisions based on all available information, and b) do not make systematic mistakes and if so, then they learn a lesson and next time do not repeat them. T. Sargent and N. Wallace (1975) formulated a thesis about the ineffectiveness of economic policy. This hypothesis emphasized that people, who rationally estimate consequences of economic policy, adopt them and consequently economic policy is ineffective. Then the only effective policy is the one that is shocking or surprising. Nevertheless, such a sudden shock may lead towards destabilization of an economy. Therefore, they conclude their article with these following words: *"Operating under that rule, the loss is smaller, the more the monetary authority knows about the exogenous processes"*. As an example of a stable rule, for instance, inflation targeting, the monetary-policy regime which is nowadays used by a wide range of central banks.

In their work, Sargent and Wallace (1975) pointed out the so-called exogenous processes. These factors are those which are not under the control of central banks but can significantly influence the economic environment of a certain state (typical examples are worldwide prices of oil and food, but also governmental taxes). Contemporary economists point out not only exogenous but also unpredictable variables. According to Taleb (2016), most economists forget about these unpredictable events during the creation of their models of reality.

We live in a period in which many countries of the world economy, potential fiscal impulses are almost depleted or exceeded (for instance, in 2015 the government debt to GDP of Belgium was about 106%, Greece 177%, Italy 133%, Jamaica 130%, Japan 230%, USA about 104% etc. - see Trading economics, (2016)). Thus, the scientific community turns its attention to monetary policy makers. Nevertheless, Federico Favarettoa and Donato Masciandaro (2016) draw attention to the fact that central bankers are also people who are predisposed to fail. They are also just individuals who tend to be prone to enticement and emotions influencing their decisions while setting macroeconomic or interest rate targets. Therefore, the attention devoted to behavioural economics should be growing. Taleb (2016) is a big critic of a former boss of American Fed and especially criticises him for the above-mentioned areas. Bernanke uses tools based on facts and observation, but not empirically proved. Bernanke often compares the current economic crisis to the Great Depression of the 30s and he concludes that these crises are different and that this is the reason why it is not possible to use the same methods for their analysis. In this area, Taleb sees 99% risk in the current indebtedness and interconnection of the world economy ((see the beginning of this chapter and Krugman (2009)). The current expansive monetary policy affects many things, which Bernanke underestimates and does not take into consideration – these so-called "fat tails" (economic variables do not have to develop according to a standard probability curve of a normal distribution). Therefore, Taleb assumes that the biggest threat is a failure of the Fed itself.

However, not only monetary policy makers are predisposed towards failure and thus not only they can face the criticism from behavioural economists. Professor Sims (1998, 2003) formulated a thesis about a "rational inattention", which lies in the fact that agents cannot focus on every piece of information about new shocks. For instance, if a price-setter does not pay attention to a new shock then he cannot react, and his prices maintain rigidity. Matějka (2012) worked with this concept and he commented that monetary policy depends on a character of nominal rigidities. Thus, we typically model the nominal rigidities as sticky prices (Calvo-style models or Menu Cost models). So, Matějka introduced a new approach towards the grasping of nominal frictions, based on a pre-assumption that agents have problems with the processing of information. He gives an example of a situation when a price-setter finds out about a decrease of interest rate with delay. Prices then react slowly, and such a positive rigidity has temporary effects on economic output and unemployment in a certain economy.

So, a detailed evaluation of all the possible information becomes impossible, not only for ordinary people. Therefore, under pressure from a lack of time, people make decisions based on their intuition or common sense – heuristic. We also often become witnesses to a bandwagon effect typical on financial markets. Thus, it brings clear implications for monetary policy – central banks should try to communicate with the public as openly as possible. The so-called forward guidance is an example of such behaviour in practice. This is an unconventional strategy with behavioural elements. A central bank can carry out forward guidance in several ways:

- Verbal statements about an intended direction of monetary policy in the future (i.e., without announcement of exactly quantified monetary-policy interest rate);
- Verbal statements about an intended direction of monetary policy in the future, including announcing of the development of a base interest rate;
- A central bank gives an undertaking to some future level of its base interest rate as long as some certain conditions will be in effect (e.g., inflation expectations will not be changed);
- A central bank gives an undertaking to maintain its base interest rate at a certain level (or will not change it above some specific borderline) for a set period.

Table 1 states the particular FG´s carried out in countries with a reserve currency.

Table 1. FG´s in countries with a reserve currency

Country	Inflation targeting since	Present value of inflation target (%)	FG since	Monetary-policy rate	Value of monetary-policy rate	
					At the beginning (%)	Present value (%)
Euro Area	-	-	2013	Fixed Rate	0.50	0.00
Euro Area	-	-	2015-16	QE	60 bil. EUR/month	60 bil. EUR/month
Japan	2013	2	1999/2013	Overnight Call Rate	0.15/0.05	-0.10
UK	1992	2	2013	Bank Rate	0.50	0.25
USA	2012	2	2003/2008	Federal Funds Rate	1.00/0.00–0.25	1.00–1.25

Source: ECB (2017), BOJ (2017), BOE (2017), Federalreserve (2017), Komárek (2015).

CONCLUSION

In this chapter, the authors dealt with the topic of behavioural economics, it is a relatively new economic direction at the crossroad between psychology and economics. At the centre of attention of behavioural economics is the research of human irrationality. The human irrationality is the element of which economic theories are lacking, because of the pre-assumption that a human being thinks and acts rationally – homo oeconomicus. Nevertheless, many examples from real life indicate that people act heuristically and intuitively as in the case of the bandwagon effect on the financial markets.

With the beginning of a marginal revolution in the 70s of the 19th century, we can observe a big step towards mathematization of economics. A larger expansion of quantitative methods in economics is then typical for the 80s of the 20th century. The authors of this chapter found the biggest problem in the fact that econometric models do not reflect the irrational behaviours of people, which we can see in real life. Some economists even point out that *"unpredictable events", which are not integrated in the models, are oftentimes essential for a future development of economy.*

Surely, behavioural economics has a wide application in many economic areas (e.g., the influence of ownership on the value of goods). In this chapter, we focused on the implications for monetary policy. The main reason is that monetary policies are currently going through a period in which unconventional monetary-policy tools are used more and more often and a wide range of central banks in the world apply the monetary-policy regime of "inflation targeting". Within this regime, central bankers deal with inflation expectations. During the period of a raised uncertainty level on the financial market, it is more than desirable that central banks are successful in the creation of inflation expectations. Therefore, a space for unconventional approaches opens within this area. Central banks have become more open than they ever used to be before. They gradually add behavioural elements into a strategy of inflation targeting. One example of this is the area of communication with the public about the future value of key interest rates. We can call this tactic as "forward guidance".

At this point, we return to a thesis of J. F. Muth (1961) who claims that people do not make systematic mistakes and if they do so, they will learn a lesson and not repeat the same mistakes repeatedly. It was the economic crisis of 2008, which pointed out the fact that human factors are very important variables and therefore, economists should learn a lesson as well as deal with the topic of human decision-making processes much more. However, the result should not be a diversion from a basic paradigm in economics and an enforcement of only the behavioural approach. Mathematics can be a good servant but a bad master. Consequently, its combination and connection with economics can move economic theory ahead towards additional cognition.

Funding: This paper was supported within Operational Programme Education for Competitiveness – Project No. CZ.1.07/2.3.00/20.0296.

REFERENCES

BOE. (2017). *Bank of England.* [online] Available at: <http://www. bankofengland.co.uk/Pages/home.aspx> [Accessed 18 October 2017].

BOJ. (2017). *Bank of Japan.* [online] Available at: < https://www. boj.or.jp/ en/index.htm/> [Accessed 18 October 2017].

ECB. (2017). *European Central Bank.* [online] Available at: <http:// www.ecb.europa.eu/ home/html/index.en.html> [Accessed 18 October 2017].

ECONFIX. (2016). *Behavioral Economics: Prospect Theory.* [online] Available at: <https://econfix.wordpress.com/2013/03/27/behavioural-economics-propsect-theory/> [Accessed 2 December 2016].

Edwards, W. (1954). The theory of Decision Making. Psychological Bulletin, [online] Available at: *ScienceDirect* <http://www.sciencedirect.com/science/article/pii/S1572308916300985> [Accessed 2 December 2016].

Favarettoa, F. and Masciandaro, D. (2016). Doves, Hawks and Pigeons: Behavioral Monetary Policy and Interes Rate Inertia, *Journal of Financial Stability*, [online] Available at: <http://ac.els-cdn.com/S1572308916300985/1-s2.0-S1572308916300985-main.pdf?_tid=2bfa7a96-bbc0-11e6-8a11-00000aab0f02& acdnat=1481034652_8fa64e4cb9881a6ef0e2fc65c4584d2> [Accessed 2 December 2016].

Federalreserve. (2017). *Board of Governors of the Federal Reserve System.* [online] Available at: < https://www.federalreserve.gov/> [Accessed 18 October 2017].

Holman, R. (2005). *Dějiny ekonomického myšlení.* [History of Economic Thought.] Praha: C. H. Beck.

Ingthorsson, R. D. (2013). *The Natural vs. The Human Sciences: Myth, Methodology and Ontology,* [online] Available at: <http://www.scielo. org.co/pdf/difil/v14n22/v14n22a03.pdf> [Accessed 3 December 2016].

Kahneman, D. (2011*). Thinking, fast and slow.* London: Allen Lane.

Kahneman, D. and Tversky, A. (1979). *Prospect theory: An analysis of decision under risk. Econometrica,* 47(2), pp. 263-291.

Komárek, L. (2015). *Agresivita centrálních bank a nekonvenční měnová politika* [Central bank aggression and unconventional monetary policy], [online] Available at: <https://www.cnb.cz/miranda2/export/sites/www.cnb.cz/cs/verejnost/pro_media/ konference_projevy/vystoupeni_projevy/download/komarek_20150512_karvina.pdf> [Accessed 5 December 2016].

Krugman, P. (2009). *The Return of Depression Economics and the Crisis of 2008.* Praha: Nakladatelství Vyšehrad.

Macáková, L. (2010). *Microeconomics: Basic Course.* Slaný: Melandrium.

Matějka, F. (2012). *Information Frictions and Monetary Policy.* [online] Available at: <http://is.vsfs.cz/repo/3059/135_12_vsfs_acta_1-2012_matejka.pdf> [Accessed 5 December 2016].

Mill, J. S. (1844). *Essays on Some Unsettled Questions of Political Economy,* [online] Available at: <http://www.econlib.org/library/Mill/ mlUQP.html> [Accessed 5 December 2016].

Muth, J. F. (1961). *Rational Expectations and the Theory of Price Movements.* [online] Available at: <http://www.fep.up.pt/docentes/ pcosme/S-E-1/se1_trab_0910/se1.pdf> [Accessed 5 December 2016].

Nobelprize. (2016). *The Sveriges Riksbank Prize in Economic Sciences in Memory of Alfred Nobel 2002.* [online] Available at: <http://www. nobelprize.org/nobel_prizes/ economic-sciences/laureates/2002/> [Accessed 2 December 2016].

Robbins, L. (1932). *An Essay on the Nature and Significance of Economic Science.* London: Macmillan.

Sargent., T. J. and Wallace, N. (1975). *Rational Expectations, the Optimal Monetary Instument, and the Optimal Money Supply Rule,* [online] Available at: <http://www.fep.up.pt/docentes/pcosme/S-E-1/JPE-83-2-241.pdf> [Accessed 5 December 2016].

Simon, H. A. (1978). *Rational Decision-Making in Business Organizatins,* [online] Available at: <http://www.nobelprize.org/nobel_prizes/ economic-sciences/laureates/ 1978/simon-lecture.pdf> [Accessed 4 December 2016].

Sims, C. A. (1998). Stickiness. *Carnegie-Rochester Conference Series on Public Policy.* 49(1), pp. 317–356.

Sims, C. A. (2003). Implications of rational inattention. *Journal of Monetary Economics.* 50(3), pp. 665–690.

Smith, A. (1776). *An Inquiry into the Nature and Causes of the Wealth of Nations,* [online] Available at: <http://www.econlib.org/library/Smith/ smWN.html> [Accessed 7 December 2016].

Suchacek, J. (2015). Large Enterprise Branches: The Case of the Czech Republic. *Economics & Sociology.* 8(4), pp. 82-93.

Taleb, N. (2016). *Nassim Taleb: Život v nejistotě,* [Nassim Taleb: Life in Uncertainty,] [online]. Available at: <http://finmag.penize.cz/kaleidoskop/265047-nassim-taleb-zivot-v-nejistote> [Accessed 5 December 2016].

Thaler, R. (1979). *Toward a Positive Theory of Consumer Choice, Journal of Economic Behavior and Organization, [online].* Available at: <http://www.eief.it/butler/ files/2009/11/thaler80.pdf> [Accessed 2 December 2016].

Tradingeconomics. (2016). *Country List Government Debt to GDP,* [online] Available at: <http://www.tradingeconomics.com/country-list/government-debt-to-gdp> [Accessed 4 December 2016].

Von Mises, L. (1942). *Společenské vědy a přírodní vědy,* [Social Sciences and Natural Sciences] Terra Libera, [online] Available at: <http://www.libinst.cz/Files/KqLFy 4r2/profile/ 2579/tl_01_2005.pdf> [Accessed 1 December 2016].

Wilmott. (2008). *Terms of Membership*, [online] Available at: <https://forum.wilmott.com/ucp.php?mode=register> [Accessed 4 December 2016].

Yellen, J. L. (2007). *Implications of Behavioral Economics for Monetary Policy,* [online] Available at: <http://www.frbsf.org/our-district/ files/0928.pdf> [Accessed 1 December 2016].

In: Modeling Social Behavior and Its Applications   ISBN: 978-1-53613-666-1
Editors: L. A. Jódar Sánchez et al.   © 2018 Nova Science Publishers, Inc.

Chapter 11

A LITERATURE REVIEW AND MATHEMATICAL MODELING OF THE VALUE OF A BRAND: AN APPLICATION TO THE TECHNOLOGY SECTOR

Mª Ángeles Alcaide González, Elena de la Poza Plaza
and Natividad Guadalajara Olmeda
Universitat Politècnica de València, Center of Economic Engineering,
Faculty of Business and Management, Valencia, Spain

ABSTRACT

Although there are different interdisciplinary approaches to value a brand, no consensus has been about the most convenient methodology to be used in accordance with the purpose of the valuation. This fact has led international consultancy companies to have developed rankings to value brands using their own mixed methods, but these consultancy companies also diverge in their results. This chapter reviews the available approaches to brand valuations, especially recently published empirical works, and also develops mathematical models that explain the value of brand rankings in the new technologies sector based on economic-financial information.

The main results of this chapter suggest that the researchers who obtain a brand index only use qualitative factors, and the authors who obtain a quantitative brand value do not follow a particular method. However, the majority of authors agree about using a combination of quantitative and qualitative methods.

Our results also show that economic-financial information is useful for explaining the brand value of technological companies; specifically, the net results were the most significant driver in the three selected rankings. Their explanatory power oscillates within the interval [45.7%, 61.8%]. Furthermore, between 71.30% and 89% of the brand value is explained by economic-financial variables, while the remaining proportion [11%, 28.7%] is explained by the driver brand strength. Finally, this work shows how the consultancy company Millward Brown consistently values brands over others, while Brand Finance values are lower than the other two selected consultancy companies.

Keywords: brands, economic-financial, income approach, models, stocks, technology, rankings, valuation

INTRODUCTION

In the last half century, the business paradigm has undergone a change due to the growing value of intangible assets held by companies; more specifically, brands have become significantly relevant in the creation of the value of companies (Bonet, 2003). This change of paradigm has accelerated from the 1990s onward with the technological revolution affecting the whole society, and leading to the creation of numerous companies in the technological sector (Timoteo et al., 2015). This explains why numerous techniques have emerged in recent years to value intangibles such as brands.

According to the American Marketing Association, a brand is usually associated with a name, a term, a signal, a symbol, a design, or a combination of some of these, which identifies a company's products and services, and differentiates them from its competitors. A similar definition is used by Keller (2007), who states that whenever a marketer creates a new name, logo or symbol for a new product, a brand has been created. Due to a brand's immateriality and subjectivity contributions, no consensus has been reached about the valuation method. As a result, numerous valuation methods have been developed.

When analyzing the international literature, the techniques for assessing brands are classified according to the perspective or the purpose of the valuation. In this way, valuation methods of brands can be grouped into two main categories:

1) Marketing perspective or consumer perception: these models provide an index of the value of a brand using qualitatives variables.
2) Economic-financial perspective: it provides a quantitative value of the brand through economic-financial variables.

This chapter is based on the study and analysis of brand valuation methods with an economic-financial purpose. Furthermore as part of the economic-financial approach to brand valuations, there are three: one types based on costs, one on the market and another on results. However, the vast majority of researchers do not use a pure method, (Majerova & Kliestik, 2015; Salinas & Ambler, 2009), but a combination of them as a consensus about methodologies is lacking.

Thus the mixed methods are those that combine qualitative and quantitative variables. These facts have led international consultancy companies, such as Interbrand, Brand Finance and Millward Brown, to develop rankings that value brands by mixed methods. However, these companies only publish the top 100 brands of their rankings. At the same time, their annual rankings offer divergent results since the position of a brand in each ranking differs according to the methodology used by each consultancy company, but also to the different variables considered to be influential for determining the value of a brand.

The aim of this chapter is to analyze the valuation methods of brands used more recently in the scientific literature, especially those methods with an economic-financial purpose. Then mathematical models were built by employing economic-financial and stock market information to explain the value of brand rankings in the new technologies sector for the 2000-2016 period.

METHODS

This chapter applies different methods. In the first place, a literature review about the valuation of brands was performed to identify and classify the valuation methods found in previous studies. Second, mathematical models were built by employing a Multivariate Regression Analysis to explain the value of the brand in rankings with the economic-financial information, and also stock market information, in the new technologies sector for the 2000-2016 period.

Analysis of the Methods through the Literature Review

A brief review on brand valuation was performed to analyze the main contribution of each approach:

1) Methods based on marketing or consumer perception

In recent years, brands have acquired much importance, especially from the marketing perspective (Lambin, 1995). This fact explains why companies wish to create powerful brands in an attempt to differentiate their products from those of their competitors (Kapferer & Thoenig 1991). In this way, brands act as a strategic asset for companies, and it is necessary to assess them to manage them properly. From this perspective, it is important to take into account the relationship of trust created between the brand and the consumer. This trend is defined as "marketing or consumer-focused," whose central idea is based on the fact that brand confers the product added value. This perspective was adopted by Kamakura and Russell (1993), Keller (1993), Erdem and Swait (1998) or Nielsen (2004). Other authors have also attempted to measure consumers' behaviors and perceptions by associating brand capital with brand strength. For this reason, it is convenient to remark the set of attributes related to consumer perception and the attitudes generated toward the brand. The purpose of these methods is not to obtain the monetary value of the brand, but index trending.

2) Methods based on economic-financial information or the economic-financial perspective:

A myriad of valuation methods have been developed from the economic-financial perspective by both specialized companies and experts in this field. They employ the company's economic-financial information to estimate a quantitative brand value. In general, there are three main approaches to classify economic-financial brand valuation methods, depending on their basis:

- *Market*: it uses transactions that involve brands in similar markets to determine the market value by comparing with other brands (Salinas & Ambler, 2009). This approach is very useful when someone wishes to sell the brand (Abratt & Bick, 2003). However, a marketer is required to determine the brand's fair market value by comparing it with similar brands on the market (Virvilaitè & Jucaitytè, 2008). Market methods are based on stock price movements and their goal is to estimate the price of shares. In this field it is relevant to highlight the studies by Simon & Sullivan (1993), or by Damodaran (1996).
- *Costs*: it accumulates the costs that have actually been, or will be, incurred on a particular intellectual property product (Abratt & Bick, 2003). This approach uses four different costs based on calculations: considering the costs incurred to set the brand (historical creation cost); considering the costs that derive when replacing the brand; the costs incurred in creating a replica of the

  mark (cost of reproduction); or the development costs attributable to the brand. These methodologies are characterized by their difficulty for calculating them. For example, historical costs models have the disadvantage of determining which costs should be included, and others, such as the replacement cost, which is one of the most difficult models to calculate.
- *Incomes*: it focuses on the revenues generated by the brand in the future, the brand's ability to generate profits, or exclusively on its cash flows. This approach consists in discounting the future values to the present by applying a discount rate. In this approach, several brand valuation models emerge depending on the employed economic information. These models can be grouped into three

categories: based on the income generated by the brand in the future; based on the benefits to be generated; based on cash flows. Table 1 classifies them according to these three financial methodologies.

However, most of these income-based methods are mixed models as they do not use only quantitative variables (pure model), but they also use qualitative variables based on consumer perceptions of the brand. However, they provide an economic value of the brand and are, therefore, classified from the economic-financial perspective.

- *Mixed methods*: This approach includes all the models that are not based on a single technique (market, cost, income), but determine the brand value by combining two different approaches or more. This category embraces models such as the Value Sales Ratio (Damodaran, 1994) and the Brand Finance Method (Haigh, 1996). The latter combines a market approach (royalty-based methods) with brand strength associated with the marketing approach.

Table 1. Classification of economic-financial methods according to the income approach

Methodology	Model	Type of model	Author/Consultant company
Incomes	Equity map	Mixed	Srinivasan, V., Park, C. & Chang, D. (2001)
	Millward Brown Optimor	Mixed	Millward Brown (2002)
Benefits	Multiple method	Mixed	Interbrand (1998)
	Price premium	Pure	Aaker (1991)
	Global brand equity	Mixed	Montameni, R., & Sharohrokhi, M. (1998)
	Advanced brand valuation	Mixed	GFK, PWC, & Sattler (2002)
	Hirose model	Pure	Hirose, Y. (2002)
Cash flows	Houlihan Advisors	Pure	Houlihan Valuation Advisors (1986)
	Flows discounts	Mixed	Interbrand (1993)
	Future Brand	Mixed	Future Brand (1999)

Source: The Authors (2017).

The importance of providing a monetary value to a brand leads international consultancy companies to develop their own methods (not completely public) to value brands by performing annual rankings that are recognized worldwide. These rankings are used by authors as the basis to build their own brand valuation models. The best known consultancy companies are the British Interbrand, which uses a mixed model of discounted cash flows, along with marketing methods; US Millward Brown, which publishes the ranking Brand Z, and uses a mixed model between marketing variables and Millward Brown Optimor; British Brand Finance, which has already been explained.

The Most Recent Contributions from the Economic-Financial Perspective

After analyzing the most recent contributions of brand valuation from the economic-financial perspective, we find that three research works have used the brand value provided by Interbrand, and all three used mixed methods by combining the market approach with the marketing methodology.

The first research work was conducted by Chehab, Liu and Xiao (2016) in the United States. They analyzed the relationship between the brand value provided by Interbrand, and short and long-run stock performance. They tested if a relationship existed between financial markets and consumers' reaction to Interbrand's recognition of a product. Their sample was composed of 439 North American non financial companies, considered by Interbrand as the most valuable global brands to earn abnormal returns (cumulative abnormal returns, CARs) from 2001 to 2012. The regression results showed that the companies' brand value and their capitalization were a significant contribuion to CARs, while consumers' reaction to brand ranking was positive, but not significant.

The second study was carried out by Johansson, Dimofte and Mazvancheryl (2012). These authors used the top 100 brand ranking of Interbrand in September 2008. They applied a popular consumer-based method, the Fama-French model, to a sample of 50 brands from different industries. This research analyzed how some of the strongest brands on the US market fared in financial performance terms during the fall 2008 stock market downturn. The consumer-based measures showed a significant incremental effect on stock performance. These positive effects also applied to stock volatility and the firm betas. None of these effects held for the financially-based measure.

The third research, based on the Interbrand model, was conducted by Ratnatunga and Ewing (2009). It was applied to a leading Australian service company (IT and telephony systems solutions firm). They used a hybrid approach into which they incorporated tangible and intangible assets to value brand capability.

Recently, Rubio and Pérez-Hernández (2016) used a mixed method, based on the market approach, with royalties from franchises. This study was based on Spanish franchises that belonged to three different industries: food, health-beauty and fashion. The sample was composed of 149 food firms, 105 health-beauty, and 67 fashion. They found that higher royalties correlated positively with a firm market position and its economic profit, measured by number of establishments and EBITDA margin. The authors concluded by stating that it was not possible to use the same model for all the sectors e.g., in the food and fashion sector, royalties are explained positively by other productivity variables, such as employee productivity and ROA. Thus the behavior and the relevance of the exogenous variables differ depending on the industry.

Baquero (2015) also analyzed the value of international brands with franchises in three rankings (Interbrand, Brand Finance and Millard Brown) of the textile, hotel and food sectors. She used the econometric method to estimate the value of rankings based on economic-financial variables. Depending on the sector, sales or profits were the variables that explained the value of brands.

Two studies used the Hirose model based on the income approach. In 2012, Wang, Yu and Ye (2012) explored the factors that contributed to the brand values of Taiwan's banking service companies to measure the relevance of their brand value. These authors used a sample of 124 firm-year observations over the 2002-2010 period. Variables were collected from the Taiwan Economic Journal and from the companies' annual reports. The OLS Regression results (least squares and quantile regression) showed that advertising expenditure in banking firms had positive significant effects on brand valuation, but also that the brand equity of banking firms related positively to their market value. The second study was conducted by Majerova and Kliestik (2015) on national brands of the Slovak Republic to identify the most appropiate valuation method. To do this, they applied to a sample of 384 national brands methods of valuing brands based on incomes, and assigned them an indicator of the method's performance (1 to 10) and importance (1 to 100%), depending on each method's main advantages and disadvantages (PEST analysis). The results showed that the Hirose model is currently the most convenient model for brand valuations in the Slovak Republic.

Next Reyneke, Abratt and Bick (2014) calculated the corporate brand value of the South African Gold Coin Exchange by different methods, which all based on the cost approach and the investment approach (seven different brand values were estimated). The authors built a mathematical model for each valuation approach, as did Abratt and Bick (2003) who employed financial reports and management accounts dating back to 5 years. The results showed that each brand valuation method provided a different brand equity value. Therefore, an organization would select a brand valuation approach model by considering its objectives. This would explain why there is considerable discrepancy to select only one brand valuation model.

Finally, Gupta, Czinkota and Melewar (2013) presented a mixed model to integrate the sustainability concept with branding by analyzing the three sustainability dimensions (social, nvironmental and economic aspects) about the brand value. Their study introduced the social and environmental aspects based on consumers' perceptions, and the economic part was measured by the income approach. Surveys were carried out with 236 respondents (using a random sampling method) to obtain data on consumers' perceptions. Their results recommended embedding sustainability into brand value to create a differenciation for the brand in a competitive market.

Mathematical Modeling of the Brand Value in the New Technologies Sector from the Economic-Financial Perspective

Once the different methods followed to value brands were known, especially those based on the economic-financial perspective, following Baquero (2015), this chapter focused on building mathematical models to explain the value of the brand rankings published by the three aforementioned international consultancy firms: Interbrand, Millward Brown and Brand Finance. These models were based only on the economic-financial information of the brands that belonged to the new technologies sector.

The technology sector was selected because is the most incipient in the economy, and it is revolutionizing markets and society around the world. This sector is the fastest growing one in terms of both turnover and number of companies.

For this porpose, data were obtained from secondary sources of information, particularly from the annual rankings of the brands estimated by these three consultancy firms during from 2000 to 2016, but also from the annual income statements of the brand's companies. The study population consisted of those brands that had been ranked in the top ranking 100 of at least two of the three consultancy firms (Interbrand, Millward Brown and Brand Finance). Moreover, the companies had to belong to the technology sector. The economic-financial information of the selected companies was obtained from the firms' publicly reported income statements for the 2000-2016 period.

With these requirements, the study sample was composed of 13 technology brands, which are shown in Table 2: Apple, Cisco, Google, HP, IBM, Intel, Microsoft, Oracle, Samsung, SAP, Sony, Accenture and Facebook.

Table 2. Selected technology brands and number of years in which each consultant included each brand in the top 100 of its ranking

	APPLE	CISCO	GOOGLE	HP	IBM	INTEL	MICROSOFT	ORACLE	SAMSUNG	SAP	SONY	ACCENTURE	FACEBOOK
INTERBRAND [2000-2016]			2005 2016					2001 2016			2002 2016		2012 2016
BRAND FINANCE [2007-2016]									2008 2012 2013 2014		NO DATA		2015 2016
MILLWARD BROWN [2006-2016]													2010 2016

Source: The Authors (2017).

Table 2 shows the number of years in which each consultancy company included each brand in the top 100 of its ranking. For example, Interbrand included in the top 100 of its ranking all the companies over the 2000-2016 period, except for Google, which belonged to the ranking since 2005, and Oracle since 2001, Accenture since 2002, and Facebook since 2012. Brand Finances values have been built since 2007 for all the brands, except Sap, which was in the ranking in 2008, 2012, 2013 and 2014, while Accenture was not ranked in the top 100 during the study period, and Facebook has been since 2015. Finally, the ranking values of Millward Brown were collected since 2006 for all the brands, except for Facebook since 2010.

To characterize the value of the selected sample, Figure 1 shows the evolution of the total value of the 13 technology brands for each considered ranking.

The three consultancy firms agreed that the brand values of the technological companies sample have constantly grown since 2007. Figure 1 also shows that the company Millward Brown estimated the highest brand values, while Brand Finance estimated the lowest ones.

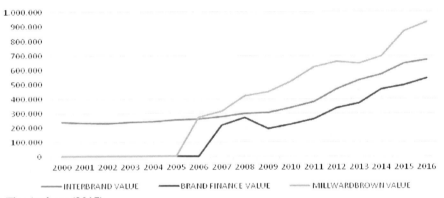

Source: The Authors (2017).

Figure 1. Magnitude of the brands' total values in the sample (thousands of US$).

In this study, the Multivariate Linear Regression Analysis was the methodology used to explain the brand ranking value. The mathematical expression is shown:

$$Y = a + b_1 X_1 + b_2 X_2 + \ldots\ldots + b_n X_n + \varepsilon$$

where:

Y: Dependent variable
a: Constant term
b_i: Coefficients of the explanatory variables (estimated by Ordinary Least Squares)
X_i: Explanatory variables
ε: Random disturbance term.

However, to satisfy the normality, heterogeneity, and linearity hypotheses, the dependent variable was transformed into a logarithmic form, and the model can be expressed as follows:

$$\text{Ln } Y = a + b_1 X_1 + b_2 X_2 + \ldots\ldots + b_n X_n + \varepsilon$$

Dependent variables are the value of the brands estimated by the three selected consultancy firms. According to these criteria, eight models were built, where the dependent variables in each model were:

Model 1 and 2 → V_{Imn}: Interbrand value (\$) of brand m during period n

Model 3 and 4 → V_{Bmn}: Brand Finance value (\$) of brand m during period n

Model 5 and 6 → V_{Mmn}: Millward Brown value (\$) of brand m during period n

Model 7 and 8 → V_{mn}: Value (added) of the three firms (\$) of brand m during period n

In all, 17 explanatory variables were taken into account to express the companies' economic-financial information. These variables were: account receivables, capital, current assets, current liabilities, dividends, dividends per share, financial expenses, net equity, net result, number of employees, number of shares, operating income, R&D, sales, tax rate, total assets and total liabilities.

The Regression Analysis results are offered in Table 3.

Table 3. The models obtained by Regression Analysis for each ranking

	Dependent Variables					
	Ln VImn		Ln VBmn		Ln VMmn	
Explanatory Variables	Model 1	Model 2	Model 3	Model 4	Model 5	Model 6
Constant	9.475	9.014	9.523	9.095	9.712	9.777
Net Result	7.12	9.104	5.243	2.698	6.778	2.562
R&D		7.951				-5.545
Employees		1.24		3.267		3.932
Financial Expenses		-1.525		-1.293		-2.919
DVND. Per Share		-0.04				-0.04
Account Receivables		1.837		3.053		4.231
Num. Shares				1.264		
Total Liabilities						-7.645
N	201		104		137	
Adjusted R2	58.80%	89.00%	61.80%	79.00%	45.70%	71.30%
F	234.687	190.508	154.907	60.702	103.748	38.885

Source: The Authors (2017).

As Table 3 shows, the goodness of fit of Models 1, 3 and 5 varies within the interval [45.7%, 61.80%]; for these models, *net results* was the only explanatory variable. However, Models 2, 4 and 6 obtained a better goodness of fit by including additional explanatory variables, which led to a higher goodness of fit. Thus the Interbrand values reached 89% explanatory power, while that of Brand Finance was 79% and that of Millward Brown was 71.30%.

Model 2 gave the best goodness of fit (89%), as explained by the quantitative variables. The remaining percentage, 11% was explained by the qualitative variables or brand strength.

Table 4 shows the results of Models 7 and 8, where the dependent variables are the values of the three rankings jointly in a logarithmic form from period 2007 to 2016. In this case, the number of observations is 312. Moreover, the dummy variables of the three rankings were introduced into these two models.

Model 7 was explained only by *net results*, where its goodness of fit was 51.10%. However, model 8 was explained by quantitative variables (see Table 3). Model 8 proved better than model 7 because its goodness of fit was 74.50%.

Therefore, Brand Finance added less value than the Interbrand and Millward Brown valuations. In particular, Millward Brown increased values by approximately 51% *versus* Brand Finance, and Interbrand did so by 23.70%.

Table 4. Models generated by Regression Analysis jointly for the three rankings

	Dependent Variable: Ln Vmn		
Explanatory Variables	Model 7	Model 8	
Constant	9,.15	9.212	
Net Result	6.085	1.858	
Current Assets		3.162	
Employees		4.166	
Num. Shares		9.838	
Account Receivables		3.04	
Total Liabilities		-4.156	
Financial Expenses		-18	
D. Interbrand		0.213	Δ +23.70%
D. Millward Brown		0.412	Δ +50.98%
N	312		
Adjusted R2	51.10%	74.50%	
F	383.083	94.911	

Source: The Authors (2017).

CONCLUSION

This chapter shows the diversity of the methods followed to estimate a brand value. The literature reveals that most authors agree about using mixed methods, and about combining behavioural and economic approaches. That is to say, on the one hand, these models are dedicated to value the brand from the customer's point of view and use qualitative variables to identify consumers' perceptions, especially brand strength; on the other hand, they use financial and economics asset factors. However, all the methods provide an economic value of the brand. In the economic-financial methods, the most commonly used one is the method that focuses on both the market and income. In contrast, the cost-based methods are the least employed ones because of their difficulty to calculate them.

Much research into the market approach has used the brand value provided by Interbrand, while others have been based on the royalties paid to franchises. However, the income-based ones have used the Hirosi model. This evidences that pure economic methods are scarcely used, while mixed techniques are often used.

Furthermore, the literature review shows that pure marketing methods are the subject of many studies. However, they do not provide an economic value of the brand, but only an index brand value, so they were not taken into account in this chapter.

The main conclusion drawn from the proposed models is that the economic-financial information is useful for estimating the brand value of technological companies. Specifically, the results show that the net result is the most significant driver in the three rankings, and its explanatory power ranges within the interval [45.7%, 61.8%]. This coincides with Baquero (2015), who demonstrated that the net result was one of the most influential variables.

Other common significant quantitative variables are financial expenses, number of employees and account receivables, because they are all common in all the proposed models. In addition, between 71.30% and 89% of the brand value is explained by economic-financial variables, while the remaining 11-28.7% is accounted for by brand strength.

Lastly, our analysis results indicate that some consultancy companies value higher than others as Millward Brown's values are higher, while those of Brand Finance are lower than the other two companies' values.

REFERENCES

Aaker, DA. (1991). *Managing brand equity. Capitalizing on the value of a brand name.* Editorial the Free Press.

Abratt, R. & Bick, G. (2003). Valuing brands and brand equity: Pitfalls and processes. *Journal of Applied Management and Entrepreneurship*, 8, 21-39.

Baquero, P. (2015). *Valuation of intangible assets in the financial statements: Application to the international brands of the textile, hotel and food sectors.* Tesis. Valencia: Polytechnic University of Valencia.

Bonet, J. (2003). The importance of brands for the company. Valuation criteria. *Judicial Studies,* 49, 305.

Chehab, A., Liu, J. & Xiao, Y. (2016). More on intangibles: Do stockholders benefit from brand values?. *Global Finance Journal*, 30, 1-9.

Damodaran, A. (1994). *Damodaran on valuation.* John Wiley and Sons. New York.

Damodaran, A. (1996*). Investment valuation.* John Wiley and Sons. New York.

Erdem, T. & Swait, J. (1998). Brand equity as a Signaling Phenomenom. *Journal of Consumer Psychology*, 7(2), p. 131-157.

Fernández, P. (2005). Valuation of companies: How to measure and manage the creation of value. *Editions Management 2000.*

Gupta, S., Czinkota, M. & Melewar, T. C. (2013). Embedding knowledge and value of a brand into sustainability for differentiation. *Journal of World Busines*, 29, 287-296.

Haigh, D. (1996). Founder and CEO, Brand Finance [Online] http://brandfinance.com/who-we-are/our-people/person/david-haigh/ (Consulted on 20-12-2016)

Hirose, Y. (2002). *The report of the committee on brand valuation. Ministry of Economy, Trade and Industry*, The Government of Japan, Tokyo.

Johansson, J. K, Dimofte, C. V., & Mazvancheryl, S. K. (2012). The performance of global brands in the 2008 financial crisis: A test of two brand value measure. *International Journal of Research in Marketing*, 29, 235-245.

Kamakura, W. A. & Russell, G. J. (1993). Measuring brand value with scanner data. *International Journal of Research Marketing*, 10, 9-22.

Kapferer, J. N. & Thoenig, J. C. (1991). *The brand: engine of competitiveness of the companies and growth of the economies.* McGraw-Hill Editions.

Keller, K. L. (1993). Conceptualizing, measuring and managing customer-based brand equity. *Journal of Marketing*, 57, 1-22.

Keller, K. L. (2007). *Strategic Brand Management.* Praha: Grada Publishing, 796.

Lambin, J. (1995). *Strategic marketing.* McGraw-Hill Editions.

Majerova, J. & Kliestik, T. (2015). Brand valuation as immanent component of brand value building and managing. *4th World Conference on Business, Economics and Management, WCBWM*, 26, 546-552.

Montameni, R., & Sharohrokhi, M. (1998). Brand equity valuation: a global perspective. *Journal of product & brand management,* 4, 7, 275-290.

Ratnatunga, J. & Ewing, M. T. (2009). An ex-ante approach to brand capability valuation. *Journal of Business Research*, 62(3), 323-331.

Reyneke, J., Abratt, R. & Bick, G. (2014). What is your corporate brand worth? A guide to brand valuation approaches. *South African Journal of Business Management*, 45 (4), 1-10.

Rubio, G., Manuel, C. M. & Pérez-Hernández, F. (2016). Valuing brands under royalty relief methodology according to international accounting and valuation standards. *European Journal of Management and Business Economics*, 25, 76-87.

Salinas, G. & Ambler, T. (2009). A taxonomy of brand valuation practice: Methodologies and purposes. *Journal of Brand Management*, September, 17(1), 39-61.

Simon, J. & Sullivan, M. (1993). The measurement and determinants of brad equity: A financial approach. *Marketing Science*, 1(12), 28-52

Srinivasan, V., Park, C. & Chang, D (2001). Equitymap: Measurement, analysis, and prediction of brand equity and its sources. *Research Paper Series*, 1685.

Timoteo, J., Matías, G., Buxaderas, E. & Ferruz, S. (2015). *Intangibles in the value of companies. The business of Faust*. Editions Díaz de Santos.

Virvilaitè, R. & Jucaytè, I. (2008). Brand valuation: viewpoint of costumer and company. *Engineering Economics,* 56, 111-119.

Wang, D.H. M., Yu, T. H. K. & Ye, F. R. (2012). *The value relevance of brand equity in the financial services industry: an empirical analysis using quantile regression*. Springer-Verlag, 6, 459-471.

In: Modeling Social Behavior and Its Applications
Editors: L. A. Jódar Sánchez et al.

ISBN: 978-1-53613-666-1
© 2018 Nova Science Publishers, Inc.

Chapter 12

EXPLORING THE DETERMINANTS OF FIRMS' TWITTER ADOPTION, USE INTENSITY AND ONLINE INFLUENCE

Robert Selles, Desamparados Blazquez
and Josep Domenech[*]
Department of Economics and Social Sciences,
Universitat Politècnica de València, València, Spain

ABSTRACT

This chapter explores which business structural characteristics (size, age, productivity, technology level and area) affect the adoption of Twitter by companies, as well as their use intensity and online influence. Data regarding 405 manufacturing firms were collected from their financial statements and Twitter accounts and, three regressions were proposed to explain Twitter adoption, use intensity and online influence. The results suggest that the determinants of these three aspects differ. Young firms are likely to use Twitter more intensively despite not translating this into greater online influence, which is mainly affected by labor productivity.

Keywords: social media, Twitter, online influence, technology adoption, SNS intensity

[*] Corresponding Author E-mail: jdomenech@upvnet.upv.es.

INTRODUCTION

Before the inception of the Internet, companies were able to control the information available about them through strategically placed press announcements and good public relations managers (Kaplan and Haenlein, 2010). However, Web 2.0 totally changed their control over this information (Mangold and Faulds, 2009), particularly because of the arising of social networking sites (SNS) and their potential to provide 'user-generated communication'. Now, customers post their experiences and thoughts about any product on SNS, with companies having limited ability to alter them. Hence, customers are no longer merely passive recipients in the marketing process but participants on social media with a tremendous impact in firms' reputation and potential gains (Kietzmann et al., 2011). In this context, Twitter is the leading microblogging SNS. It is the most popular and regularly visited web site in the world[1] with about 284 million users who are active monthly and send on average 500 million tweets per day.

Despite its popularity and widespread adoption by individuals, companies face important barriers to include Twitter and other SNS in their corporate strategy. One of these barriers could be related to the ICT component of social media, which combined with a lack of staff familiarity and technical skills may prevent firms from effectively adopting them (Michaelidou et al., 2011).

When using SNS, the main objective of companies is to connect their brand to customers, increase their engagement by making them feel part of a community (Cetina et al., 2014). However, the mere presence of a company on SNS is not enough, as an active management of firm's online activities is required to spread information on its products and services. In this regard, the effective use of SNS has demonstrated to involve increased returns and efficiencies in marketing activities (Kim and Ko, 2010), although effective metrics for measuring their returns are still to be developed (Thoring, 2011).

Previous research on the corporate use of Twitter focused on surveying the intentions and practices of businesses on SNS (Baird and Parasnis, 2011; Michaelidou et al., 2011; Wamba and Carter, 2013). However, little is known about the actual adoption of corporate Twitter and the structural determinants of its use intensity. This chapter attempts to fill this gap by analyzing three aspects of the real use of Twitter by 405 manufacturing firms. Particularly, it addresses which firms' structural characteristics contribute to the adoption of Twitter, usage intensity and their relation with greater business' online influence.

---

[1] Source: alexa.com.

THEORETICAL BACKGROUND

Research on the determinants of SNS usage is still at an embryonic stage, given its recent explosion. However, its adoption could resemble the adoption of other ICT-related innovations.

Size

Firm size has shown to be positively related to the use of technology and the adoption of innovative technologies (Aguila-Obra and Padilla-Meléndez, 2006). This is due to the fact that large firms have the budget, expertise and economies of scale to adopt new ICTs (Meske and Stieglitz, 2013). However, in the particular case of SNS, Michaelidou et al. (2011) found no relation between size and usage.

Age

Oldest firms tend to show lower innovative probabilities (Huergo and Jaumandreu, 2004), as with increasing age comes bureaucratic procedures that often constrain innovation (Van de Ven et al., 1999). Futhermore, firms born in the digital era and with younger managers are expected to adopt ICT-based innovations quicker.

Labor Productivity

Labor productivity as well as the level of training of the workforce are usually associated with the innovation capacity of companies. In particular, they are positively related to higher adoption of ICTs (Giunta and Trivieri, 2007). Thus, the same relation is expected to be found in the specific case of SNS.

Industry Technology Level

High technology firms are usually related to more innovative practices (Heavey and Simsek, 2013), so the adoption of innovations by them are expected to be faster. However, for the particular case of ICTs, Kaplan and Haenlein (2010) found that the company sector does not influence the adoption of technology. Therefore, the impact of the industry technology level on the adoption of SNS is unknown a priori.

Area

Although the environment in which a firm is located may bolster or undermine the innovation process, previous research studies are inconclusive about the influence of firm location on the adoption of ICTs. On the one hand, there are several studies which showed that businesses in rural areas are more likely to adopt Internet-related technologies because this is a way to overcome the disadvantages of being far from most customers (Domenech et al., 2014; Forman et al., 2005). On the other hand, Wamba and Carter (2013) found that, in the particular case of Twitter, firms in urban areas are more likely to adopt it.

The present study aims at exploring how the described variables affect the adoption and use intensity of Twitter by companies, as well as the online influence earned with this activity. With this exploration, similarities and differences in the adoption of other ICTs can be found.

DATA

The sample for this study, which consists of 405 manufacturing firms (mainly SMEs) within the Region of Valencia (Spain), was randomly retrieved from SABI[2]. The following firms' structural and financial variables were retrieved from SABI and INE[3] databases:

- SIZE: Continuous variable measured as the logarithm of the number of employees in a firm.
- AGE: Continuous variable measured as the number of years since a firm's founding.
- LP: Continuous variable, representing firm's labor productivity, measured as the value added per employee.
- HIGHTECH: Dichotomous variable that takes a value of 1 when a company belongs to a High or Medium-High Technology industry, and 0 otherwise. It is based on the NACE Rev. 2 at 2-digit level classification for the technological intensity of manufacturing firms (Eurostat, 2014).
- URBAN: Dichotomous variable that takes a value of 1 when a firm's headquarters are located in an urban municipalty, and 0 when they are in a rural area according to the OECD definition.

---

[2] SABI: Sistema de Análisis de Balances Ibéricos. It is published by Bureau Van Dijk and includes information on the financial statements of more than 1.2 million of Spanish firms.
[3] INE: National Statistics Institute in Spain.

This information was complemented with information about the use of Twitter by companies. To do so, we manually searched for and analyzed each firm's Twitter account. Specifically, we gathered the following variables:

- TW_ACCOUNT: Dichotomous variable that takes a value of 1 when a firm has a Twitter account. This represents the adoption of Twitter by a company.
- TWEETS: Count variable that measures the number of tweets which were posted on a firm's Twitter account within the last month. It is related to the use intensity.
- FOLLOWERS: Count variable that measures the number of followers that a company has on Twitter. It is related to a company's online influence.

Table 1 exhibits some descriptive statistics for the whole dataset, for Twitter and non-Twitter users. It shows that the Twitter adoption is still low across manufacturing firms, as only 13% of them have an active Twitter account. It can also be observed that, on average, companies which engaged with Twitter are larger, older and slightly more productive. Regarding location, both subsets of firms are mainly located in urban areas.

ANALYSIS AND RESULTS

To study the determinants of companies' adoption and usage of Twitter, as well as of their influence in this social network, three regression models were proposed.

Table 1. Descriptive statistics

	All firms		Twitter users		Non-Twitter users	
	Mean	SD	Mean	SD	Mean	SD
SIZE	2.26	1.14	2.70	1.13	2.20	1.13
AGE	20.43	10.95	22.92	12.63	20.04	10.63
LP	36.79	32.63	37.31	20.62	36.71	34.16
URBAN	0.80	0.40	0.80	0.41	0.80	0.40
TW_ACCOUNT	0.13	0.02	1	0	0	0
TWEETS	-	-	11.33	3.60	-	-
FOLLOWERS	-	-	383.76	154.11	-	-

Model 1 seeks to explain the adoption of Twitter by companies:

$$TW\_ACCOUNT = f(AGE, SIZE, LP, HIGHTECH, URBAN) \qquad (1)$$

Model 2 examines the determinants of Twitter use intensity:

$$\text{TWEETS} = f(\text{AGE, SIZE, LP, HIGHTECH, URBAN}) \qquad (2)$$

Lastly, Model 3 studies the online influence achieved by companies:

$$\text{FOLLOWERS} = f(\text{AGE, SIZE, LP, HIGHTECH, URBAN}) \qquad (3)$$

Model 1 is based on a logistic regression due to the binary nature of the dependent variable. For Models 2 and 3, two negative binomial regressions were used, since the dependent variable is a count and the data showed overdispersion (Ryan, 2009).

Table 2 shows the results for the estimation of the proposed models. The estimation results for Model 1 indicate that, despite being free of charge, the adoption of Twitter is positively affected by firm size. That is, the larger a firm is the more likely it is to adopt Twitter. This is in line with previous works that found a positive relation between firm size and ICTs adoption and use (Aguila-Obra and Padilla-Meléndez, 2006; Meske and Stieglitz, 2013) and particularly, between size and Twitter adoption (Thoring, 2011). However, the area in which a company is located does not seem to influence the adoption of SNS, unlike what Wamba and Carter (2013) found.

Regarding Model 2, the estimation results exhibit that firm size is not only related to the adoption of Twitter, but also contributes to a more frequent use. Younger companies also tend to be more active on Twitter although results for Model 1 evidenced that they do not present a higher adoption. While opening a Twitter account is immediate, being active requires posting and interacting with customers continuously, activity which older firms do not seem to maintain. This could be due to the increased interest of younger firms to increase market share, or to the generally lower predisposition for ICTs of the older workforce, which could be an important part of older SMEs staff (Van de Ven et al., 1999; Meyer, 2011).

Table 2. Estimates of the effect of the firm characteristics on Twitter adoption and use

Model	(1)	(2)	(3)
Dependent variable	TW_ACCOUNT	TWEETS	FOLLOWERS
AGE	0.011	-0.057**	-0.022
	(0.013)	(0.027)	(0.019)
SIZE	0.398***	0.684**	0.598***
	(0.143)	(0.324)	(0.222)
LP	-0.001	0.019	0.032***
	(0.006)	(0.016)	(0.011)
HIGHTECH	-0.525	0.085	-0.140
	(0.410)	(0.912)	(0.627)
URBAN	-0.102	0.162	-0.977*
	(0.371)	(0.807)	(0.556)
(Constant)	-2.837***	0.574	3.796***
	(0.520)	(1.062)	(0.725)

Standard errors in parentheses: $^{*}p \leq 0.1$, $^{**}p \leq 0.05$, $^{***}p \leq 0.01$.

Finally, results for Model 3 evidence that larger and more productive firms usually have an increased online influence, regardless of the age of a company. This result suggests that firms that use their workforce efficiently also manage to use Twitter more efficiently.

Estimation results also show that the adoption, use intensity and online influence are independent from the sector technology level in which the firm operates. This could be related to the fact that benefits from adopting Twitter are equally applicable across sectors and to the relatively low complexity of adopting SNS.

CONCLUSION

This chapter explored the actual adoption and use of corporate Twitter by manufacturing firms. The analyses revealed that the adoption and use of Twitter by firms have different structural determinants. While firm size is positively related to each of the three considered aspects of Twitter, firm age only has a negative effect on Twitter use intensity, and firm labor productivity only has a positive effect on online influence. This research represents a new point of view that complements other studies in the related literature, which are mainly based on surveys about managers' intentions.

This work is a first step to understanding how companies actually adopt and use Twitter. Future research should explore further how labor productivity is translated into online influence and check whether there exists a feedback effect, in which online influence improves a firm's efficiency.

ACKNOWLEDGMENTS

This work has been partially supported by the Spanish Ministry of Economy and Competitiveness under grant TIN2013-43913-R.

REFERENCES

Aguila-Obra, A. R. D., Padilla-Meléndez, A. (2006) Organizational factors affecting internet technology adoption, *Internet Research* 16, pp. 94-110.

Cetina, I., Dumitrescu L., Vinerean S. (2014). Exploring Consumer Engagement in an E-Setting: A Qualitative Research of Marketing Executives. *Economic Computation & Economic Cybernetics Studies & Research* 48, 2.

Domenech, J., Martinez-Gomez, V., Mas-Verdú, F. (2014) Location and adoption of ICT innovations in the agri-food industry, *Applied Economics Letters* 21, pp. 421-424.

Eurostat (2016) High-tech aggregation by NACE rev. 2, *Eurostat indicators of High-tech industry and knowledge - intensive services*.

Forman, C., Goldfarb, A., Greenstein, S. (2005) How did location affect adoption of the commercial Internet? Global village vs. urban leadership, *Journal of Urban Economics* 58, pp. 389-420.

Giunta, A., Trivieri, F. (2007) Understanding the determinants of information technology adoption: Evidence from Italian manufacturing firms, *Applied Economics* 39, pp. 1325-1334.

Heavey, C., Simsek, Z. (2013) Top management compositional effects on corporate entrepreneurship: The moderating role of perceived technological uncertainty, *Journal of Product Innovation Management* 30, pp. 837-855.

Huergo, E., Jaumandreu, J. (2004), How does probability of innovation change with firm age? *Small Business Economics* 22, pp. 193-207.

Kaplan, A. M., Haenlein, M. (2010) Users of the world, unite! The challenges and opportunities of social media, *Business Horizons* 53, pp. 59-68.

Kietzmann, J. H., Hermkens, K., McCarthy, I. P., Silvestre, B. S. (2011) Social media? Get serious! Understanding the functional building blocks of social media, *Business Horizons* 54, pp. 241-251.

Kim, A. J., Ko, E. (2010) Impacts of luxury fashion brand's social media marketing on customer relationship and purchase intention, *Journal of Global Fashion Marketing* 1, pp. 164-171.

Mangold, W. G., Faulds, D. J. (2009) Social media: The new hybrid element of the promotion mix, *Business Horizons* 52, pp. 357-365.

Meske, C., Stieglitz, S. (2013) Adoption and Use of Social Media in Small and Medium-Sized Enterprises, *Lecture Notes in Business Information Processing* 151, pp. 61-75.

Meyer, J. (2011) Workforce age and technology adoption in small and medium-sized service firms, *Small Business Economics* 37, pp. 305-324.

Michaelidou, N., Siamagka, N. T., Christodoulides, G. (2011) Usage, barriers and measurement of social media marketing: An exploratory investigation of small and medium B2B brands, *Industrial Marketing Management* 40, pp. 1153-1159.

Ryan, T. (2009) *Modern regression methods*, 2nd Ed., Wiley, Hoboken, NJ.

Thoring, A. (2011) Corporate tweeting: Analysing the use of twitter as a marketing tool by UK trade publishers, *Publishing Research Quarterly* 27, pp. 141-158.

Van de Ven, A. H., Polley, D. E., Garud, R., Venkataraman, S. (1999) *The Innovation Journey*, 1st Ed., Oxford University Press, New York.

Wamba, S. F., Carter, L. (2013) Twitter adoption and use by SMEs: An empirical study, in *4 Hawaii International Conference on System Sciences*, pp. 2042-2049.

In: Modeling Social Behavior and Its Applications
Editors: L. A. Jódar Sánchez et al.

ISBN: 978-1-53613-666-1
© 2018 Nova Science Publishers, Inc.

Chapter 13

A MATHEMATICAL MODEL STRUCTURED BY AGE GROUPS AND VARYING THE POPULATION SIZE TO PREDICT THE USERS OF E-COMMERCE OVER THE NEXT FEW YEARS

C. Burgos[1,*]*, J.-C. Cortés*[1,†]*, I.-C. Lombana*[2,‡]*,*
D. Martínez-Rodríguez[1,§] *and Rafael-J. Villanueva*[1,¶]
[1]Instituto Universitario de Matemática Multidisciplinar,
Universitat Politècnica de València, Spain
[2]Facultad de Ingeniería Civil - Campus Ibagué
Universidad Cooperativa de Colombia,
Ed. Urrutia, Ibagué - Colombia

Abstract

The electronic commerce (e-commerce) is an economic activity which volume has increased over the last few years. The possibility of purchasing the desired product anywhere and anytime, and receive it at home is an attractive service. Also, the price of the goods can be compared in several shops easily.

Then, it is expected that e-commerce will keep increasing over the next years. The estimation of this growth could be useful to find out how the shopping may change over the next years.

In this chapter, we propose an age-structured diffusion model with varying population size to study the use of e-commerce as a habit susceptible to be transmitted among peers. Then, using data from the Spanish Statistics Institute (INE) we find the model parameters that make the model to fit the data. With these parameters, we can estimate the users of e-commerce in Spain over the next years.

---
[*]E-mail address: clabursi@posgrado.upv.es.
[†]E-mail address: jccortes@imm.upv.es.
[‡]E-mail address: ivan.lombana@campusucc.edu.com.
[§]E-mail address: damarro3@etsii.upv.es.
[¶]E-mail address: rjvillan@imm.upv.es.

Keywords: electronic commerce, diffusion mathematical model, nonlinear system of difference equations

AMS Subject Classification: 39A60, 37N40

1. Introduction

Electronic commerce (e-commerce) is increasing every day. It makes shopping easier because we can purchase goods from foreign countries or compare prices without moving from home. Therefore, e-commerce is becoming an important economic opportunity to offer a wide range of products.

Here, in this chapter, we are going to observe the phenomenon of e-commerce diffusion with the aim to model its dynamics assuming that the use of e-commerce is due to personal decision or by "contagion" between peers, that is, because individuals in the environment convince others to use e-commerce. Models related with the diffusion of new technologies have been presented in [1], [4] and [9], however, they have not considered age as a factor that influence the use of new technologies.

This way, we are going to consider two age-groups, $15 - 44$ and $45 - 74$ because data from [7], [8] about users of e-commerce report significant differences between them. Using demographic data, we will stablish a varying size demographic model and from it we build a dynamic model that will allow us to determine the evolution of e-commerce users over the time.

The chapter is organized as follows. In Section 2 the model is built and scaled. Then, in Section 3, using data of the use of e-commerce retrieved from the Spanish Statistics Institute (INE) [7, 8], we determine the model parameters that make the model as close as possible to the available data. With the obtained model parameters, we will predict the evolution of the e-commerce over the next few years. Finally, in Section 3 some conclusions are presented.

2. Model Building

The aim of this section is to twofold. First, we will construct a demographic model (Subsection 2.1), and second we will propose a mathematical model to describe the dynamic of e-commerce in Spain, (Subsection 2.2). This later model will be scaled.

2.1. Demographical Model

Taking into account the official data from INE [7], a consistent age-structured demographic model with population varying size is required to integrate demographic information into the diffusion of the e-commerce model. This age-structured model considers two different age groups due to the significant differences between both groups with respect to their attitude about e-commerce. These groups are:

- Group 1 ($G_1(t)$): Population between 15 and 44 years old at the time instant t (in months).

- Group 2 ($G_2(t)$): Population between 45 and 74 years old at the time instant t (in months).

The following system of difference equations [2] describes the demographic evolution in each t in months for the two different groups of ages.

$$
\begin{aligned}
G_1(t+1) &= \mu - c_1 G_1(t) - d_1 G_1(t), \\
G_2(t+1) &= \quad\ c_1 G_1(t) - d_2 G_2(t).
\end{aligned}
\tag{1}
$$

where μ is the monthly birth rate (assuming that almost nobody dies between 0 and 14 years), c_1 is the monthly growth rate from G_1 to G_2, d_1 is the monthly death rate in the first group, d_2 is the rate of people coming out from people aged between 45-74 years old, by death or because they are older than 74. Is important to remark that studying the available data from [7] and in order to guarantee our parameters represent the reality as much as possible, the value of μ has to be close to the interval $[7.5125 \cdot 10^{-4}, 9.0475 \cdot 10^{-4}]$, d_1 close to $[3.73 \cdot 10^{-5}, 5.97 \cdot 10^{-5}]$ and d_2 close to $[3.3849 \cdot 10^{-3}, 4.12 \cdot 10^{-3}]$.

We are going to consider that the size of population in the demographic model varies over the time. Techniques for handling this kind of models in continuous versions have been presented in [5] and [6]. We are going to adapt these techniques to discrete models.

2.2. Electronic Commerce Model

In this section, we propose a discrete model which describes the dynamics of the e-commerce users. This model is built on the proposed demographic model. In Table 1,

Table 1. E-commerce data from Spanish population divided into the two age groups from 2007 to 2015, source: [8]

Using of e-commerce	First Group of age (15-44 years)		Second Group of age (45-74 years)	
	No	Yes	No	Yes
$t_1 = $ Dec 2007 ($j = 1$)	0.4255	0.1416	0.3824	0.0400
$t_2 = $ Dec 2008 ($j = 2$)	0.3955	0.1790	0.3822	0.0431
$t_3 = $ Dec 2009 ($j = 3$)	0.3652	0.2039	0.3755	0.0551
$t_4 = $ Dec 2010 ($j = 4$)	0.3425	0.2158	0.3781	0.0607
$t_5 = $ Dec 2011 ($j = 5$)	0.3242	0.2284	0.3730	0.0742
$t_6 = $ Dec 2012 ($j = 6$)	0.2891	0.2546	0.3716	0.0845
$t_7 = $ Dec 2013 ($j = 7$)	0.2668	0.2661	0.3718	0.0951
$t_8 = $ Dec 2014 ($j = 8$)	0.2258	0.2958	0.3568	0.1214
$t_9 = $ Dec 2015 ($j = 9$)	0.1891	0.3230	0.3459	0.1417

we can find data retrieved from INE [8] about the users and non-users of the e-commerce, per age-group, from 2007 and 2015 in Spain. In that survey, non-users have been defined as those who have not used e-commerce, at least, in the last 6 months. The available data lead us to define the following subgroups:

- $N_1(t)$, $N_2(t)$, the amount of people who have not used e-commerce in the last 6 months at the time instant t, for age groups $G_1(t)$ and $G_2(t)$ respectively.

- $Y_1(t)$, $Y_2(t)$ the amount of people who have used e-commerce in the last 6 months, in the time instant t, for age groups $G_1(t)$ and $G_2(t)$, respectively.

We are going to consider that an individual uses e-commerce because:

1. He/she decides it by himself (innovator).

2. He/she is influenced by his/her peers to use it (imitator).

The diffusion of the technology will be represented by the transition of an individual from the population $N_i(t)$ to $Y_i(t)$ ($i = 1, 2$) through the coefficients of innovation or imitation described by:

- p_1, p_2 are the coefficients of innovation for the age groups G_1 and G_2, respectively.

- α_1, α_2 are the e-commerce influence coefficients of individuals in N_1 by individuals in Y_1 and Y_2 respectively. And α_3, α_4 are the e-commerce influence coefficients of individuals in N_2 by individuals in Y_1 and Y_2, respectively.

If an individual who has already bought by the Internet does not buy anymore in six months, he/she moves to $N_1(t)$ or $N_2(t)$ depending on his/her age. This behavior will be described in the model by the coefficients γ_1, γ_2. Specifically γ_1 and γ_2 are related to people aged between 15-44 and 45-65 respectively.

Furthermore, we will consider the following assumptions:

- The time step is defined as one month.

- Each individual can contact with any other, i.e., we assume that there is homogeneous population mixing [2].

- The number of deaths of people aged under 14 is negligible. Moreover we assume that such individuals still have not bought by the Internet. With this assumption we can establish that people with 15 years old come into $N_1(t)$ at rate μ, where μ is the monthly birth rate.

- The total population $P_T(t) := N_1(t) + Y_1(t) + N_2(t) + Y_2(t)$ is variable over the time.

Under the above assumptions, our age-structured mathematical diffusion model describing the use of e-commerce in Spain with varying population size is based on the following nonlinear system of ordinary difference equations.

$$N_1(t+1) = (1 - d_1) N_1(t) + \gamma_1 Y_1(t) - c_1 N_1(t) - N_1(t) \frac{\alpha_1 Y_1(t) + \alpha_2 Y_2(t)}{P_T(t)} - p_1 N_1(t) + \mu P_T(t),$$
(2)

$$Y_1(t+1) = (1 - d_1) Y_1(t) - \gamma_1 Y_1(t) - c_1 Y_1(t) + N_1(t) \frac{\alpha_1 Y_1(t) + \alpha_2 Y_2(t)}{P_T(t)} + p_1 N_1(t),$$
(3)

$$N_2(t+1) = (1 - d_2) N_2(t) + \gamma_2 Y_2(t) + c_1 N_1(t) - N_2(t) \frac{\alpha_3 Y_1(t) + \alpha_4 Y_2(t)}{P_T(t)} - p_2 N_2(t),$$
(4)

$$Y_2(t+1) = (1 - d_2) N_2(t) - \gamma_2 Y_2(t) + c_1 Y_1(t) + N_2(t) \frac{\alpha_3 Y_1(t) + \alpha_4 Y_2(t)}{P_T(t)} + p_2 N_2(t).$$
(5)

A graphical representation of the above model can be seen in the Figure 1.

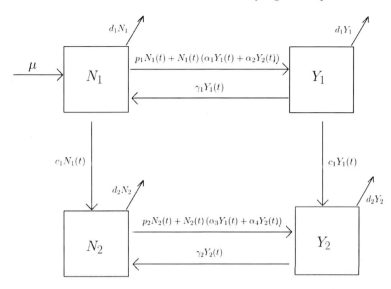

Figure 1. Compartmental model. The boxes represent the populations and the arrows the transitions between subpopulations.

2.3. Model Scaling

As we can see in Table 1 our data is given in percentages, therefore it is necessary to scale the model. First of all, in order to establish a relationship between $P_T(t)$ and $P_T(t+1)$, we will sum up Eqs. (2) to (5) obtaining

$$P_T(t+1) = P_T(t) + \mu P_T(t) - d_1(N_1(t) + Y_1(t)) - d_2(N_2(t) + Y_2(t)). \tag{6}$$

If we denote by

$$n_1(t) := \frac{N_1(t)}{P_T(t)}, \qquad y_1(t) := \frac{Y_1(t)}{P_T(t)}, \qquad n_2(t) := \frac{N_2(t)}{P_T(t)}, \qquad y_2(t) := \frac{Y_2(t)}{P_T(t)}, \tag{7}$$

and we divide Eq. (2) by $P_T(t+1)$ we obtain the following expression

$$\frac{N_1(t+1)}{P_T(t+1)} = \frac{\mu P_T(t) + N_1(t) - d_1 N_1(t) + \gamma_1 Y_1(t) - c_1 N_1(t) - N_1(t)\frac{\alpha_1 Y_1(t) + \alpha_2 Y_2(t)}{P_T(t)} - p_1 N_1(t)}{P_T(t) + \mu P_T(t) - d_1(N_1(t) + Y_1(t)) - d_2(N_2(t) + Y_2(t))}. \tag{8}$$

Then multiplying and dividing Eq. (8) by $P_T(t)$ we obtain:

$$n_1(t+1) = \frac{n_1(t) + \mu - d_1 n_1(t) + \gamma_1 y_1(t) - n_1(t)(\alpha_1 y_1(t) + \alpha_2 y_2(t)) - c_1 n_1(t) - p_1 n_1(t)}{1 + \mu - d_1(n_1(t) + y_1(t)) - d_2(n_2(t) + y_2(t))}. \tag{9}$$

Applying the same technique in Eqs. (3) to (5), we obtain the scaled system of difference equations given by

$$n_1(t+1) = \frac{n_1(t) + \mu - d_1 n_1(t) + \gamma_1 y_1(t) - n_1(t)\left(\alpha_1 y_1(t) + \alpha_2 y_2(t)\right) - c_1 n_1(t) - p_1 n_1(t)}{1 + \mu - d_1(n_1(t) + y_1(t)) - d_2(n_2(t) + y_2(t))},$$
(10)

$$y_1(t+1) = \frac{y_1(t) - d_1 y_1(t) - \gamma_1 y_1(t) + n_1(t)\left(\alpha_1 y_1(t) + \alpha_2 y_2(t)\right) - c_1 y_1(t) + p_1 n_1(t)}{1 + \mu - d_1(n_1(t) + y_1(t)) - d_2(n_2(t) + y_2(t))},$$
(11)

$$n_2(t+1) = \frac{n_2(t) - d_2 n_2(t) + \gamma_2 y_2(t) - n_2(t)\left(\alpha_3 y_1(t) + \alpha_4 y_2(t)\right) + c_1 n_1(t) - p_2 n_2(t)}{1 + \mu - d_1(n_1(t) + y_1(t)) - d_2(n_2(t) + y_2(t))},$$
(12)

$$y_2(t+1) = \frac{y_2(t) - d_2 y_2(t) - \gamma_2 y_2(t) + n_2(t)\left(\alpha_3 y_1(t) + \alpha_4 y_2(t)\right) + c_1 y_1(t) - p_2 n_2(t)}{1 + \mu - d_1(n_1(t) + y_1(t)) - d_2(n_2(t) + y_2(t))}.$$
(13)

3.　Fitting the Scaled Model with the Real Data

Once we have scaled the model, we can find the parameters

$$X = (\mu, d_1, c_1, d_2, p_1, \alpha_1, \alpha_2, \gamma_1, p_2, \alpha_3, \alpha_4, \gamma_2)$$

that best fit our data given in Table 1.

On the one hand, let us denote by $n_1^*(t_j)$, $y_1^*(t_j)$, $n_2^*(t_j)$ and $y_2^*(t_j)$ $j = 1, \ldots, 9$, the first, the second, the third, and the fourth columns in Table 1, respectively. On the other hand, let us denote by $n_1(t_j, X)$, $y_1(t_j, X)$, $n_2(t_j, X)$ and $y_2(t_j, X)$, the model evaluated using the set of parameters X in each time instant t_j, (j=1, ...,9). Note that the initial conditions of the model are given by the first row of the Table 1, so $n_1(t_1, X) = n_1^*(t_1)$, $y_1(t_1, X) = y_1^*(t_1)$, $n_2(t_1, X) = n_2^*(t_1)$ and $y_2(t_1, X) = y_2^*(t_1)$.

The error function is defined by

$$\text{Error}(X) = \sum_{j=2}^{9} |n_1^*(t_j) - n_1(t_j, X)| + \sum_{j=2}^{9} |y_1^*(t_j) - y_1(t_j, X)|$$

$$+ \sum_{j=2}^{9} |n_2^*(t_j) - n_2(t_j, X)| + \sum_{j=2}^{9} |y_2^*(t_j) - y_2(t_j, X)|.$$
(14)

Thus, applying the random particle swarm optimization (rPSO) algorithm [3] to minimize Eq. (14), we obtain that the set of parameters, X, that best fit our data are given in Table 2

Table 2. Parameters that best fit the model with data in Table 1

μ	$7.2650 \cdot 10^{-4}$	γ_1	0.001553	γ_2	0.901928
d_1	$5.0333 \cdot 10^{-5}$	α_1	0.030568	α_3	0.598622
d_2	$6.2792 \cdot 10^{-5}$	α_2	0.011360	α_4	0.286072
c_1	$1.8602 \cdot 10^{-3}$	p_1	0.000106	p_2	0.022511

In Fig. 2 we have drawn the model evaluated according to the parameters in Table 2. The red points represent the data in Table 1. Moreover the predictions for the next 4 years shown in Table 3 have been plotted in the same Figure.

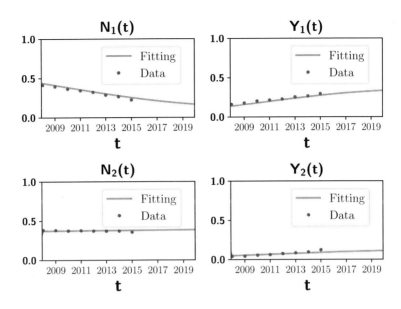

Figure 2. Result of the model fitting. Red points correspond real the data collected in Table 2, green lines are, the model outputs. Also, we have drawn predictions from 2016 to 2019.

Table 3. Prediction for E-commerce using from 2016 to 2019

	First Group of age (15-44 years)		Second Group of age (45-74 years)	
Using e-commerce	No	Yes	No	Yes
Dec 2016 ($j = 1$)	0.21548733	0.30405321	0.38181143	0.09864803
Dec 2017 ($j = 2$)	0.19761239	0.31633172	0.38333545	0.10272044
Dec 2018 ($j = 3$)	0.18170888	0.32681106	0.38510538	0.10637468
Dec 2019 ($j = 4$)	0.16770487	0.33555746	0.38711248	0.10962519

Conclusion

In this chapter we have proposed a discrete diffusion model in order to study the dynamics of e-commerce in Spain. Besides having two different age groups, the model considers variable population along the time. Using the data available from INE (Spanish Statistics Institute), we have fitted the e-commerce scaled model. Then, we have made predictions for the next 4 years. The prediction shows a substantial increasing of the use of electronic commerce, more likely in the first group of age than in the second one.

Acknowledgments

This work has been partially supported by the Ministerio de Economía y Competitividad grant MTM2013-41765-P.

References

[1] R. T. Frambach, An integrated model of organizational adoption and diffusion of innovations. *European Journal of Marketing* 27 (1993) 22-41.

[2] H. W. Hethcote, The Mathematics Of Infectious Diseases. *Society For Industrial and Applied Mathematics* 42 (2000) 599-653.

[3] C. Jacob, N. Khemka, Particle Swarm Optimization in *Mathematica*. An exploration kit for evolutionary optimization, IMS'04, *Proc.* Sixth International Mathematica Symposium, Banff, Canada, 2004.

[4] V. Mahajan, E. Mullerm F. M. Bass, New product diffusion models in marketing: A review and directions for research. *The Journal of Marketing* 54 (1990) 1-26.

[5] M. Martcheva, C. Castillo-Chavez, Diseased with chronic stage in a population with varying size, *Mathematical Biosciences* 182 (2003) 1-25.

[6] J. Mena-Lorca, H. W. Hethcote, Dynamic models of infectious diseases as regulators of population sizes. *Journal of Mathematical Biology* 30 (1992) 693 - 716.

[7] National Statistics Institute `http://www.ine.es/dyngs/INEbase/es/operacion.htm?c=Estadistica_C&cid=1254736177003&menu=resultados&idp=1254735573002`.

[8] National Statistics Institute `http://www.ine.es/dyngs/INEbase/es/operacion.htm?c=Estadistica_C&cid=1254736176741&menu=resultados&idp=1254735576692`.

[9] D. Zhang, A. Ntoko, Mathematical model of technology diffusion in developing countries. *Computational methods in decision-making, economics and finance* (2002) 526-539.

In: Modeling Social Behavior and Its Applications
Editors: L. A. Jódar Sánchez et al.

ISBN: 978-1-53613-666-1
© 2018 Nova Science Publishers, Inc.

Chapter 14

A METHOD TO DETERMINE PROBABILISTICALLY PROFITING POSITIONS WITH INVESTMENT SPECULATIVE STRATEGIES BASED ON SPREAD DERIVATIVES: THEORY AND APPLICATIONS

C. Burgos[*], *J.-C. Cortés*[†], *D. Martínez-Rodríguez*[‡]
and R.-J. Villanueva[§]
Instituto Universitario de Matemática Multidisciplinar,
Universitat Politècnica de València, Valencia, Spain

Abstract

This chapter presents a method that permits determining Bull Call spread strategies so that they provide profits at the expiration date with a prefixed probability. To this end, the underlying is assumed to follow a Geometric Brownian Motion. The analysis can straightforwardly be extended to another type of synthetic derivatives such as Bull Put Spread and Bear Call/Put Spread. The theoretical results are applied to real data of REPSOL SA asset traded in the Spanish stock market IBEX-35.

Keywords: Geometric Brownian Motion, Black-Scholes formula, Bull Call/Put Spread, Bear Call/Put Spread

1. Introduction

Financial derivatives are synthetic expressions of underlying prices of financial securities or asset investments. They are contracts that mimic or *summarize* the economics of the underlying asset classes. They permit investors to express their views and trade quickly and efficiently, at lower cost than if they were trading cash securities. The demand for financial derivatives is increasing worldwide. The key drivers for this growth are globalization of

[*]E-mail address: clabursi@posgrado.upv.es.
[†]E-mail address: jccortes@imm.upv.es.
[‡]E-mail address: damarro3@etsii.upv.es.
[§]E-mail address: rjvillan@imm.upv.es.

finance, regulatory modernization and technological advances which facilitate the access to information of this type of investments. Traded derivatives have become a universal tool for expressing market views, hedging (risk transfer), active portfolio management and arbitrage. Derivatives help increase liquidity in the cash market and attract foreign investor interest. These financial products emerge when markets become more sophisticated and liquid, and in turn they contribute to stimulate liquidity and attract more sophisticated investing and foreign investors to the cash market. Basic financial securities derivatives are *Options*. Options allow us to make money whether the stock market is going up, down or sideways because, just as the name suggests, Options give us the option to buy or sell a security (stocks, exchange-traded funds, indices, commodities, etc.) at some point in the future. Options are divided into two categories: Calls and Puts. Calls increase in value when the underlying security is going up, and they decrease in value when the underlying security declines in price. The value of a Put Option increases when the underlying security decreases, while its value decreases when the underlying increases. So depending on what you anticipate happening in the market, we can buy a Call or a Put and profit from that movement [1]. In important class of synthetic investment consisting of mixing two or more Calls and/or Puts Options together are *Spread Options*. Throughout this chapter we will consider this class of Options only.

In this chapter we propose a methodology to determine a suitable investment on Spread Options so that profits at the expiration time can be achieved with a prefixed probability, assuming a Geometric Brownian Motion for the underlying asset. Our theoretical findings will be applied to Repsol SA assets traded in the Spanish stock market.

This chapter is organized as follows. Section 2 is divided into several parts where the main financial and mathematical tools required to conduct our analysis are presented. In Subsection 2.1 we summarize the main concepts related to Spread Options including its benefits/losses function at expiration date. In Subsections 2.2 and 2.3 we recall, respectively, the main results concerning the mathematical model assumed to the dynamics of the underlying assets (Geometric Brownian Motion) and the celebrated Black-Scholes formula that allows us to compute the premium of a Call and Put European Options. As we will apply our results to one share of the REPSOL SA company traded in the Spanish stock market IBEX-35, Section 3 is devoted to calibrate model parameters (drift and volatility) involved in the Geometric Brownian Motion from historical quotations of this asset. In this section, goodness-of-fit measures of such a calibration are calculated in validated model parameters estimates. Assuming the dynamic of the underlying asset is modelled via a Geometric Brownian Motion, a methodology to define a Bull Call Spread strategy that generates a profit with a prefixed probability at the expiration date is presented in Section 4. Conclusions are drawn in Section 4.

2.   Financials and Mathematical Tools

In this section we summarize the main concepts, definitions and results about Finance and Mathematics that will be require throughout our subsequent analysis. Hereinafter, European Call and Puts Options will be the basic financial derivatives that we will consider to construct other more complex investment (synthetic derivatives). It is worth remembering that an option is European when it can only be exercised at its expiration time.

2.1. Mathematical Description of *Bull* and *Bear Spreads*

A *Spread* is a transaction in which an investor simultaneously buys one Option and sells another Option, both on the same underlying asset, but with different terms (strike price and/or maturity). Henceforth, we will restrict ourself to the case where only strike is different. A *Call Spread* involves the purchase and sale of Calls, and similarly for a *Put Spread*. The main idea behind Spreads is that one Option is used to hedge the risk of the other Option. Obviously, there exist many combinations of Calls and Puts producing a number of different classes of Spreads. In the subsequent analysis, we will focus on Bull Call Spreads, although our results can straightforwardly be extended to Bull Put Spreads and Bear Call/Put Spreads. This is why down below we only introduce Bull/Bear Call Spreads [2].

In a *Bull Call Spread*, the investor buys a Call (long position) at a certain strike price, say K_1, and sells (short position) another Call at a higher strike price K_2 (hence $K_2 > K_1$), with the same expiration or maturity date. While in a *Bear Spread*, the investor buys a Call at a certain strike price, say K_1, and sells another Call at a lower strike price K_2 (hence $K_2 < K_1$), with the same expiration or maturity date.

If S_T denotes the value of the underlying asset at the expiration date T, and C_1 and C_2 are the premiums of the two Calls involved in a Bull Call Spread strategy, then as the Benefits/Losses of one long Call or long position, $(B/P)(S_T)_{LC}$, and one short Call (short position), $(B/P)(S_T)_{SC}$, are given by

$$(B/P)(S_T)_{LC} = \begin{cases} -C_1 & \text{if } 0 \le S_T \le K_1, \\ S_T - (C_1 + K_1) & \text{if } S_T \ge K_1, \end{cases} \tag{1}$$

and

$$(B/P)(S_T)_{SC} = \begin{cases} C_2 & \text{if } 0 \le S_T \le K_2, \\ (C_2 + K_2) - S_T & \text{if } S_T \ge K_2, \end{cases} \tag{2}$$

respectively, then the Benefits/Losses of a Bull Call Spread at the expiration time T is given by

$$(B/P)(S_T) = \begin{cases} -C_1 + C_2 & \text{if } 0 \le S_T \le K_1, \\ S_T - (C_1 + K_1) + C_2 & \text{if } K_1 \le S_T \le K_2, \\ (C_2 - C_1) + (K_2 - K_1) & \text{if } S_T \ge K_2. \end{cases} \tag{3}$$

As $K_2 > K_1$, it should be noticed that $C_2 < C_1$ since both the premium and the strike are paid by the owner of the Call option, so they compensate. Observe that the initial cost of this position is then a debit ($-C_1 + C_2 < 0$). In Figure 1, we can derive the main investment features of this synthetic strategy. The Bull Call Spread profits if the stock price moves higher. The maximum loss is very limited. The worst that can happen is for the stock to be below the lower strike price K_1 at expiration. In that case, both Call Options expire worthless, the loss incurred is simply the initial outlay for the position (the net debit). The maximum gain is capped at expiration, should the stock price do even better than hoped and exceed the higher strike price. If the stock price is at or above the higher (short Call) strike at expiration, in theory, the investor would exercise the long Call component and presumably would be assigned on the short Call. As a result, the stock is bought at the lower (long Call strike) price and simultaneously sold at the higher (short Call strike) price. The maximum profit then is the difference between the two strike prices $K_2 - K_1 > 0$, less the initial outlay $C_2 - C_1 < 0$ (the debit) paid to establish the Spread. Therefore, investors of Bull Call Spreads have an optimistic view of underlying asset at its maturity.

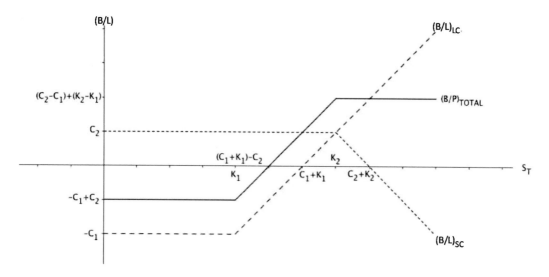

Figure 1. Benefits/Losses function, given by (3), of a Bull Call Spread (B/L_{TOTAL}) at the expiration date. $(B/P)(S_T)_{LC}$ and $(B/P)(S_T)_{SC}$ denote Benefits/Losses functions, given by (1) and (2), to Long Call and Short Call Options, respectively.

2.2. Geometric Brownian Motion

The Geometric Brownian Motion (GBM), $S(t)$, is the continuous time stochastic process most widely used to model stock market prices because it is everywhere positive (with probability 1) and it is a natural generalization of its deterministic counterpart for pricing bonds [1, 2, 3]. The GBM $S(t)$ is the solution of the following stochastic differential equation

$$\left.\begin{array}{rcl} \mathrm{d}S(t) & = & \mu S(t)\,\mathrm{d}t + \sigma S(t)\,\mathrm{d}W(t), \\ S(0) & = & s_0, \end{array}\right\} \qquad \mu \in \mathbb{R}, \sigma > 0, \tag{4}$$

where s_0 denotes the value of the underlying at the starting date, $t = 0$, $\mu \in \mathbb{R}$ and $\sigma > 0$ are parameters, usually referred to as, the drift and the diffusion, respectively, and $W(t)$ is the standard Wiener process. Using the so-called Itô calculus, it can be shown that the solution of stochastic differential equation (4) is given by [4]

$$\begin{aligned} S(t) & = s_0 \exp\left(\left(\mu - \frac{1}{2}\sigma^2\right)t + \sigma W(t)\right) \\[2mm] & = s_0 \exp\left(\left(\mu - \frac{1}{2}\sigma^2\right)t + \sigma\sqrt{\Delta t}Z\right), \end{aligned} \tag{5}$$

where in the last step we have used that $W(t) \overset{\mathrm{d}}{=} \sqrt{\Delta t}Z$, $Z \sim \mathrm{N}(0; 1)$.

2.3. Black-Scholes Formula

As we are interested in determining a suitable strategy based on financial derivatives based upon European Call Options that provides benefits at its expiration date with a prefixed probability, we will require the application of the celebrated Black-Scholes (and Merton) formula that allows us to calculate the premium of an European Call and Put Options [3]. Although this formula is established under a number of idealized hypotheses, in many practical cases it provides a good estimation of the premium of an Option. Such hypotheses are: (a) no dividends are paid out during the life of the Option; (b) markets are efficient (i.e., market movements cannot be predicted); (c) there are no transaction costs (negligible costs) in buying the Option; (d) the risk-free rate and volatility of the underlying are known and constant; (e) the returns on the underlying are normally distributed. A criticism to these assumptions can be checked in [2].

For an European Call Option, its premium C is given by

$$C = s_0 \Phi(d_1) - K \exp(-rT)\Phi(d_2), \quad \begin{cases} d_1 &= \dfrac{\log\left(\frac{S_0}{K}\right) + \left(r + \frac{\sigma^2}{2}\right)T}{\sigma\sqrt{T}}, \\[2mm] d_2 &= d_1 - \sigma\sqrt{T}, \end{cases} \tag{6}$$

where s_0 is the initial price of the underlying or stock, T stands for the time until option is expired (expiration date or maturity), r is the risk-free interest rate (usually identified with the value of a bond) and $\Phi(\cdot)$ is the cumulative standard Gaussian distribution

$$\Phi(x) = \frac{1}{\sqrt{2\pi}} \int_{-\infty}^{x} \exp\left(-\frac{z^2}{2}\right)\, dz. \tag{7}$$

For an European Put Option on the same written underlying, strike and expiration time, its premium can be calculated by applying the so-called Put-Call parity formula

$$P = C - s_0 + K \exp(-rT).$$

3. Model Calibration and Validation of Geometric Brownian Motion Model

As announced in the Section 1, we will work with Repsol SA stock during the period August 01 to October 31, 2016. The quotations of this share are collected in Table 7 in the Appendix Section. In Figure 2 we show its historical dynamics during the period referred to.

Now, we will estimate the model parameters $\mu \in \mathbb{R}$ and $\sigma > 0$ of the GBM (5). Let us denote by $\{s_0, s_1, \ldots, s_N\}$ the real observed quotations of the asset to be modelled by the stochastic process $S(t)$, at the respective uniformly distributed times $t_i = i\,\Delta t$, for $i = 0, 1, \ldots, N$, where $\Delta t = T/N$. Thus, if the model is accurate, it is expected that $S(t_i) \approx s_i$, $i = 0, 1, \ldots, N$. In our case, these quotations are sampled daily. Therefore, the problem is to find estimates of parameters μ and σ given the $N + 1 = 66$ quotations. Hereinafter, we will consider a likelihood-type method to achieve this goal. Let $f(t_k, s_k | t_{k-1}, s_{k-1}; \mu, \sigma)$

Repsol SA Stock

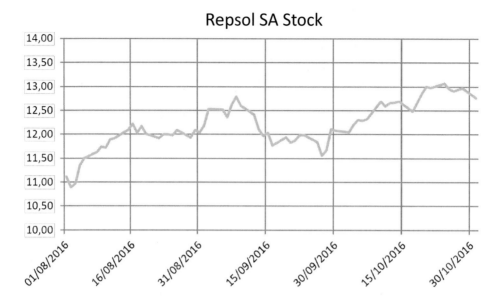

Figure 2. Stock prices of REPSOL SA from August 01 to October 31, 2016. Quotations are collected in Table 7.

be the transition probability density function of (t_k, s_k) starting from (t_{k-1}, s_{k-1}) given the parameters μ and σ. We will denote by $f_0(s_0; \mu, \sigma)$ the probability density function of initial state s_0. According to the maximum likelihood estimation method of (μ, σ), the joint density function is given by

$$D(\mu, \sigma) = f_0(s_0; \mu, \sigma) \prod_{k=1}^{N} f(t_k, s_k | t_{k-1}, s_{k-1}; \mu, \sigma)$$

where $(\mu, \sigma) \in \mathbb{R} \times]0, \infty[$, [5]. However, to avoid small numbers on a computer, it is more convenient to minimize the log-likelihood function $L(\mu, \sigma) = -\ln(D(\mu, \sigma))$ which has the following expression

$$L(\mu, \sigma) = -\ln(f_0(s_0; \mu, \sigma)) - \sum_{k=1}^{N} \ln\left(f(t_k, s_k | t_{k-1}, s_{k-1}; \mu, \sigma)\right). \tag{8}$$

One difficult to find the optimal value $(\hat{\mu}, \hat{\sigma})$ that maximizes $D(\mu, \sigma)$ is that the transition densities are not generally known. At this crucial point we need to apply some kind of strategy to overcome this drawback in a rigorous manner. With this aim, we will consider the Euler-Maruyama scheme to the stochastic differential equation (4), [6]. Let us denote $S(t_{k-1}) = S_{k-1}$ at $t = t_{k-1}$, then

$$S(t_k) \approx S_{k-1} + \mu S_{k-1} \Delta t + \sigma S_{k-1} \sqrt{\Delta t} \eta_k,$$

where we have used that $W(t) \overset{\mathrm{d}}{=} \sqrt{\Delta t} \eta_k$, $\eta_k \sim \mathrm{N}(0; 1)$. Here the symbol d means that identity must be interpreted in the probabilistic distribution sense. This implies

$$f(t_k, S_k | t_{k-1}, S_{k-1}; \mu, \sigma) \approx \frac{1}{\sqrt{2\pi\sigma_k^2}} \exp\left(-\frac{(S_k - \mu_k)^2}{2\sigma_k^2}\right), \quad \begin{cases} \mu_k &= S_{k-1}(1 + +\mu\Delta t), \\ \sigma_k &= \sigma S_{k-1}\sqrt{\Delta t}. \end{cases}$$

Substituting this expression in (8), simplifying the resulting expression and considering the approximation $S(t_i) \approx s_i$, $i = 0, 1, \ldots, N$, one obtains the

$$\min_{(\mu,\sigma)\in\mathbb{R}\times]0,\infty[} L(\mu,\sigma) = -\frac{N}{2}\ln(2\pi) - \frac{N}{2}\ln(\Delta t) - N\ln(\sigma)$$

$$-\sum_{k=1}^{N}\ln(s_{k-1}) + \frac{1}{2\sigma^2\Delta t}\sum_{k=1}^{N}\left(\frac{s_k}{s_{k-1}} - 1 - \mu\Delta t\right)^2.$$

Applying classical optimization arguments, one can prove that

$$\hat{\mu} = \frac{1}{N\Delta t}\sum_{k=1}^{N}\left(\frac{s_k}{s_{k-1}} - 1\right), \quad \hat{\sigma}^2 = \frac{1}{N\Delta t}\sum_{k=1}^{N}\left(\frac{s_k}{s_{k-1}} - 1 - \hat{\mu}\Delta t\right)^2. \tag{9}$$

In Table 1, we show the values of estimates for model parameters.

Table 1. Model parameter estimation to the Geometric Brownian Motion model (5) using maximum likelihood estimates given by (9) from quotations of REPSOL SA collected in Table 7

Parameter Estimate	Maximum Likelihood Method
$\hat{\mu}$	0.56335707
$\hat{\sigma}$	0.21283936

To validate model parameters estimates shown in Table 1, we have computed several measures of goodness-of-fit, namely, RMSE (Root Mean Square Error) and MAPE (Mean Absolute Percentage Error) defined by

$$\text{MAPE} = 100 \times \frac{1}{N}\sum_{i=1}^{N}\frac{|s_i - S_i|}{s_i}, \quad \text{RMSE} = \sqrt{\frac{1}{N}\sum_{i=1}^{N}(s_i - S_i)^2},$$

where s_i and S_i denote the real value (collected in Table 7) and theoretical value (obtained by expression (5) with estimates $\hat{\mu}$ and $\hat{\sigma}$ collected in Table 1) of REPSOL SA stock, respectively.

4. Determining an Investment Bull Call Spread Strategy with Benefits

Let us observe that according to (3), if the stock's price at expiration date, S_T, is greater than $K_1 + C_1 - C_2$, then the Bull Call Spread will generate a profit. As we have assumed

Table 2. MAPE and RMSE of Geometric Brownian Model with parameter estimates given in Table 1

MAPE	RMSE
2.93910%	0.17826

that the underlying is governed by the Geometric Brownian Motion (5), this will happen with a probability that can be determined as

$$
\begin{aligned}
P_{\text{Bull Call Spread}}^{\text{Benefit}} &= \mathbb{P}[S_T > K_1 + C_1 - C_2] \\
&= \mathbb{P}\left[s_0 \exp\left(\left(\mu - \frac{1}{2}\sigma^2\right)T + \sigma\sqrt{T}Z\right) > K_1 + C_1 - C_2\right] \\
&= \mathbb{P}\left[\exp\left(\left(\mu - \frac{1}{2}\sigma^2\right)T + \sigma\sqrt{T}Z\right) > \frac{K_1 + C_1 - C_2}{s_0}\right] \\
&= \mathbb{P}\left[\left(\mu - \frac{1}{2}\sigma^2\right)T + \sigma\sqrt{T}Z > \ln\left(\frac{K_1 + C_1 - C_2}{s_0}\right)\right] \\
&= \mathbb{P}\left[\sigma\sqrt{T}Z > \ln\left(\frac{K_1 + C_1 - C_2}{s_0}\right) - \left(\mu - \frac{1}{2}\sigma^2\right)T\right] \\
&= \mathbb{P}\left[Z > \frac{1}{\sigma\sqrt{T}}\left(\ln\left(\frac{K_1 + C_1 - C_2}{s_0}\right) - \left(\mu - \frac{1}{2}\sigma^2\right)T\right)\right] \\
&= 1 - \Phi\left(\frac{1}{\sigma\sqrt{T}}\left(\ln\left(\frac{K_1 + C_1 - C_2}{s_0}\right) - \left(\mu - \frac{1}{2}\sigma^2\right)T\right)\right),
\end{aligned}
\tag{10}
$$

where $\Phi(\cdot)$ is defined in (7). Therefore, fixed a probability, say $p^* \in]0, 1[$, and taking into account that estimates $\hat{\mu}$ and $\hat{\sigma}$ of the two parameters of the Geometric Brownian Model for the underlying are already known (see Table 1), expression (10) provides a useful relationship among the key quantities (K_1, C_1, C_2) of a Bull Call Spread in order to establish a benefit strategy. Indeed, if we assume that $p^* = 0.5$, for example, then according to (10)

$$
\begin{aligned}
P_{\text{Bull Call Spread}}^{\text{Benefit}} > 0.5 \quad &\leftrightarrow \quad \frac{1}{\sigma\sqrt{T}}\left(\ln\left(\frac{K_1 + C_1 - C_2}{s_0}\right) - \left(\mu - \frac{1}{2}\sigma^2\right)T\right) < 0 \\
&\leftrightarrow \quad \ln\left(\frac{K_1 + C_1 - C_2}{s_0}\right) - \left(\mu - \frac{1}{2}\sigma^2\right)T \\
&\leftrightarrow \quad \ln\left(\frac{K_1 + C_1 - C_2}{s_0}\right) < \left(\mu - \frac{1}{2}\sigma^2\right)T \\
&\leftrightarrow \quad \frac{K_1 + C_1 - C_2}{s_0} < \exp\left(\left(\mu - \frac{1}{2}\sigma^2\right)T\right) \\
&\leftrightarrow \quad K_1 + C_1 - C_2 < s_0\exp\left(\left(\mu - \frac{1}{2}\sigma^2\right)T\right).
\end{aligned}
\tag{11}
$$

Notice that, for a Bull Call Spread with expiration date $T = 0.25$ (three months) written on the REPSOL SA stock previously described, we known that $s_0 = 11.11€$, $\mu \approx \hat{\mu} = 0.56335707$ and $\sigma \approx \hat{\sigma} = 0.21283936$. This means that the right-hand term in the last inequality is just a known quantity. On the one hand, the premiums C_1 and C_2 of long and short Calls can be obtained using the Black-Scholes formula (6), once we have fixed its corresponding strikes K_1 and K_2, respectively, provided $K_2 > K_1$. For the free-risk interest rate r involved in the Black-Scholes formula (6), we will take a ten-year Spanish government bond $r = 1.02\%$, [7]. This approach allows us to construct different investment scenarios in order to get benefits, with a prefixed probability $p^* = 0.5$, using a Bull Call Spread. To perform our analysis, we will put $K_1 = K_2 - \Delta K$, $\Delta K > 0$ (hence $K_2 > K_1$) and we choose different values of K_2 and ΔK. Depending on the values of K_2, the scenarios will be termed bearish, average and optimistic. It is important to notice that, in practice, the value of K_2 is fixed at the beginning of the contract ($t = 0$). In Tables 3–5, we report the figures obtained in our analysis. In all the scenarios we have taken $\Delta K = 0.50€$.

- Bearish scenario: We have taken $K_2 = 10.89€$ (the minimum value of REPSOL SA stock in the period August 01- October 31, 2016). In Table 3 we show all the parameters and figures obtained in this case. According to (11), since

$$K_1 + C_1 - C_2 = 10.71221€ < 12.71805€ = s_0 \exp\left(\left(\mu - \frac{1}{2}\sigma^2\right)T\right),$$

this strategy will provide us benefits at the expiration date with 50% of probability.

- Average scenario: We have taken $K_2 = 12.18€$ (the average value of REPSOL SA stock in the period August 01- October 31, 2016). In Table 4 we show all the parameters and figures obtained in this case. According to (11), since

$$K_1 + C_1 - C_2 = 11.80466€ < 12.71805€ = s_0 \exp\left(\left(\mu - \frac{1}{2}\sigma^2\right)T\right),$$

again this strategy will provide us benefits at the expiration date with 50% of probability.

- Optimistic scenario: We have taken $K_2 = 13.07€$ (the maximum value of REPSOL SA stock in the period August 01- October 31, 2016). In Table 5 we show all the parameters and figures obtained in this case. According to (11), since

$$K_1 + C_1 - C_2 = 12.612851€ < 12.71805€ = s_0 \exp\left(\left(\mu - \frac{1}{2}\sigma^2\right)T\right),$$

this strategy will provide us benefits at the expiration date with 50% of probability.

Although in all the scenarios (bearish, average and optimistic) reported previously, the Bull Call Strategy gives profits with 50% of probability, the proposed approach can be applied to calculate the threshold value that delineates investment strategies having losses

Table 3. Values of the Bull Call Spread investment in the bearish scenario

BULL CALL SPREAD (Bearish scenario)	Long Call	Short Call
s_0	11.11€	11.11€
strike (K_i)	10.39€	10.89€
yearly risk-free interest rate (r)	1.02%	1.02%
volatility or diffusion (σ)	0.21283936	0.21283936
drift (μ)	0.56335707	0.56335707
initial date (t_0) August 1, 2016	0	0
maturity date (T in year scale) October 31, 2016	0.25	0.25
d_1	0.706771278	0.265113003
d_2	0.600351599	0.158693324
$\Phi(d_1)$	0.760145687	0.604538795
$\Phi(d_2)$	0.725864031	0.563044751
Call premium (C_i)	0.92270€	0.60048€

Table 4. Values of the Bull Call Spread investment in the average scenario

BULL CALL SPREAD (Average scenario)	Long Call	Short Call
s_0	11.11€	11.11€
strike (K_i)	11.93333€	12.18€
yearly risk-free interest rate (r)	1.02%	1.02%
volatility or diffusion (σ)	0.21283936	0.21283936
drift (μ)	0.56335707	0.56335707
initial date (t_0) August 1, 2016	0	0
maturity date (T in year scale) October 31, 2016	0.25	0.25
d_1	−0.594602686	−0.789428426
d_2	−0.701022365	−0.895848105
$\Phi(d_1)$	0.276054542	0.214930824
$\Phi(d_2)$	0.241644529	0.185166947
Call premium (C_i)	0.19069€	0.13768€

and profits. Below we show an investment which does not provide benefits with 50% of probability. Notice that in this case $\Delta K = 0.39€$.

$$K_1 + C_1 - C_2 = 12.71985€ > 12.71805€ = s_0 \exp\left(\left(\mu - \frac{1}{2}\sigma^2\right)T\right),$$

In Table 6 are specified all the values and parameters of such position.

Conclusion

In this chapter we have provided a methodology to construct Bull Call Spreads investment that gives benefits with a prefixed probability assuming that the dynamics of the underlying

Table 5. Values of the Bull Call Spread investment in the optimistic scenario

BULL CALL SPREAD (Bearish scenario)	Long Call	Short Call
s_0	11.11€	11.11€
strike (K_i)	12.57€	13.07€
yearly risk-free interest rate (r)	1.02%	1.02%
volatility or diffusion (σ)	0.21283936	0.21283936
drift (μ)	0.56335707	0.56335707
initial date (t_0) August 1, 2016	0	0
maturity date (T in year scale) October 31, 2016	0.25	0.25
d_1	-1.083021917	-1.449556616
d_2	-1.1894415967	-1.555976295
$\Phi(d_1)$	0.139399348	0.073591101
$\Phi(d_2)$	0.11713297	0.059856865
Call premium (C_i)	0.08012€	0.03726€

Table 6. Values of the Bull Call Spread investment that will give losses with 50% of probability

BULL CALL SPREAD	Long Call	Short Call
s_0	11.11€	11.11€
strike (K_i)	12.68€	13.07€
yearly risk-free interest rate (r)	1.02%	1.02%
volatility or diffusion (σ)	0.21283936	0.21283936
drift (μ)	0.56335707	0.56335707
initial date (t_0) August 1, 2016	0	0
maturity date (T in year scale) October 31, 2016	0.25	0.25
d_1	-1.16489518	-1.449556616
d_2	-1.271314859	-1.555976295
$\Phi(d_1)$	0.122030712	0.073591101
$\Phi(d_2)$	0.101808329	0.059856865
Call premium (C_i)	0.06812€	0.03726€

stock follows a Geometric Brownian Motion. The proposed analysis can straightforwardly be generalized to Bull Put Spreads and to Bear Call/Put Spreads. Even, if the mathematical model of the underlying is described by other stochastic differential equations different from the classical Log-Normal model, for instance, introducing jumps via Poisson or Lèvy processes, the methodology could easily be adapted, although numerical schemes would probably be needed.

Appendix

Table 7. Values of Repsol SA asset during the period August 01–October 31, 2016

Date	Price	Date	Price
Aug 01, 2016	11.11	Sep 15, 2016	12.03
Aug 02, 2016	10.89	Sep 16, 2016	11, 77
Aug 03, 2016	10.97	Sep 19, 2016	11.94
Aug 04, 2016	11.35	Sep 20, 2016	11.83
Aug 05, 2016	11.50	Sep 21, 2016	11.87
Aug 08, 2016	11.63	Sep 22, 2016	11.98
Aug 09, 2016	11.74	Sep 23, 2016	11.99
Aug 10, 2016	11.72	Sep 26, 2016	11.84
Aug 11, 2016	11.89	Sep 27, 2016	11.56
Aug 12, 2016	11.92	Sep 28, 2016	11.67
Aug 15, 2016	12.09	Sep 29, 2016	12.11
Aug 16, 2016	12.22	Sep 30, 2016	12.08
Aug 17, 2016	12.03	Oct 03, 2016	12.05
Aug 18, 2016	12.17	Oct 04, 2016	12.20
Aug 19, 2016	12.01	Oct 05, 2016	12.30
Aug 22, 2016	11.92	Oct 06, 2016	12.29
Aug 23, 2016	12.00	Oct 07, 2016	12.32
Aug 24, 2016	12.00	Oct 10, 2016	12.69
Aug 25, 2016	11.98	Oct 11, 2016	12.59
Aug 26, 2016	12.09	Oct 12, 2016	12.66
Aug 29, 2016	11.93	Oct 13, 2016	12.67
Aug 30, 2016	12.09	Oct 14, 2016	12.69
Aug 31 , 2016	12.04	Oct 17, 2016	12.48
Sep 01, 2016	12.18	Oct 18, 2016	12.67
Sep 02, 2016	12.53	Oct 19, 2016	12.85
Sep 05, 2016	12.52	Oct 20, 2016	13.00
Sep 06, 2016	12.36	Oct 21, 2016	12.98
Sep 07, 2016	12.62	Oct 24, 2016	13.07
Sep 08, 2016	12.79	Oct 25, 2016	12.95
Sep 09, 2016	12.60	Oct 26, 2016	12.91
Sep 12, 2016	12.41	Oct 27, 2016	12.94
Sep 13, 2016	12.11	Oct 28, 2016	12.97
Sep 14, 2016	11.97	Oct 31, 2016	12.77

References

[1] J. C. Hull, *Options, Futures, and Other Derivatives*, Pearson Education India, 2016.

[2] S. Roman, Options, Introduction to the Mathematics of Finance: Arbitrage and Option Pricing, *Series Undergraduate Texts in Mathematics*, Springer-Verlag New York, 2012.

[3] P. Wilmott, S. Howison and J. Dewynne, Options, The Mathematics of Financial Derivatives: A Student Introduction, Cambridge University Press, UK, 1995.

[4] B. Øksendal, *Options, Stochastic Differential Equations An Introduction with Applications*, Series Universitext, Springer-Verlag Berlin Heidelberg, 2003.

[5] E. Allen, Modelling with Itô Stochastic Differential Equations, Springer, *Series Mathematical Modelling: Theory and Applications*, 2007.

[6] P. E. Kloeden, E. Platen, Numerical Solution of Stochastic Differential Equations, Springer, *Series Applications of Mathematics: Stochastic Modelling and Applied Probability* 23, 1992.

[7] http://www.datosmacro.com/bono/espana?dr=2016-08 (Accessed 20 December 2017).

In: Modeling Social Behavior and Its Applications
Editors: L. A. Jódar Sánchez et al.

ISBN: 978-1-53613-666-1
© 2018 Nova Science Publishers, Inc.

Chapter 15

THE SCENARIOS AND NEEDS FOR SPECIALIST PHYSICIANS IN A EUROPEAN REGION

Isabel Barrachina Martínez[1] and David Vivas Consuelo[*]

[1]Center of Economic Engineering,
Universitat Politècnica de València, Valencia, Spain

ABSTRACT

Background: In recent years, the market and needs for specialist physicians have changed in most European countries. Shortage of doctors in some district hospitals is a well-established problem. The aims of this work are to analyse surpluses and deficiencies and to identify the future shortage of specialists.

Method: A semi-structured interview to analyse and interpret the present-day needs to train specialised doctors in Spain. This study focuses on 14 previously selected medical specialties. The interviews covered hospitals in terms of their size, complexity and geography. A total of 45 experts, 4 hospital directors and 41 specialised doctors of all the selected specialties who have undergone human resources (HR) training were interviewed.

Results: The demand for specialists has increased in recent years, particularly in certain medical specialties. The problems involved are multidimensional, and are especially more noticeable in local hospitals which often contract foreign doctors. The main causes are inadequate planning, lack of incentive policies, demographic factors in the medical community and the increasing demands of today's population.

* Corresponding Author address
   Email:ibarrach@upvnet.upv.es

Conclusion: Training quality is the result of housemen's and tutors' vocation and attitudes, there being high technology available in the public sector, interaction between various specialties; teamwork and collaboration, and the opportunity of undertaking practices.

Keywords: resident housemen, human resource planning in healthcare, quality of training programmes, specialists' needs

INTRODUCTION

The world health report 2006 ("WHO | The World Health Report 2006 - Working Together for Health") indicates that most of the world's countries are undergoing a crisis in terms of qualified health human resources, which will potentially intensify over forthcoming years.

One suggestion is that the global supply of physicians will be roughly in balance with demand ("WHO | Forecasting the Global Shortage of Physicians: An Economic- and Needs-Based Approach"). Moreover, professional mobility is a determining factor to estimate doctors' and the general heathcare staff's needs.

In the United States there are now more physicians than there have been for at least 50 years, the Council on Graduate Medical Education (COGME) recently predicted a 10% shortfall of physicians by 2020. Public concern about access to care, reports of difficulties in recruiting physicians in many specialties, and discussion of the looming collapse of primary care all contribute to the sense of crisis. Physician supply varies dramatically per region in each country (Goodman DC et al., 2008).

In Spain, the forecast surplus of specialists gradually left to work in other countries, leading to costs in terms of their training, for the system, and their emigration, for the families of such professionals.

The lack of physicians is more acute in district hospitals and in more remote areas, especially islands, which do not cover posts because the salaries paid are the same as those in other more accessible areas, so there is little incentive to work in more isolated hospitals (González López-Valcárcel B et al., 2008).

Some authors González López-Valcarcel (2006) and Garcia-Prado (2006) analyse, among other aspects, the negative consequences associated with such a dualist practice which have a direct impact on specialist needs, such as: absenteeism at work, the shirking of public sector duties and the selection of those patients to be channelled towards the public or private sectors.

Other studies (Alonso Magdaleno, MI, 2003) have established the need to implement short-term actions that involve urgent solutions, and which use long-term prediction techniques.

This study focuses on the Valencian Community (CV) (east Spain), and specifically analyses 14 of the 40 specialties as an initial approach to be supplemented by subsequent work.

The specific aim is to clarify the following issues for the VC and the selected specialties:

1. Those specialties with a deficit or surplus of doctors.
2. The quality of specialist training currently being received: strengths, weaknesses and proposed improvements.
3. The most likely scenarios per specialty.

METHODS

The study took place in the Valencian Community (VC) in the year 2006. Given the large number of specialties established in Spain, the study focuses on a selection made in advance with the help of a group of specialists working in administration at public hospitals, which was ultimately narrowed down to 14 of the 40 medical specialties which currently exist, selected in accordance with the following criteria: some were medical and others surgical, while some were apparently subject to deficits, and others not. The specialties ultimately chosen were as follows: 1) Anaesthesia; 2). General Surgery; 3) Gynaecology and Obstetrics, 4) Orthopaedic Surgery 5) Ophthalmology; 6) Internal Medicine 7) Cardiology; 8) Neurology: 9). Paediatrics; 10) Psychiatry; 11). Radiodiagnosis; 12). Oncology; 13). Rheumatology and 14). Intensive Medicine.

A semi-structured interview was selected as the methodological tool. This type of methodology offers an understanding of and perspective on the process of building such important meanings and social realities as we find in the development of human resources in the health sciences. The methodological strategy employed allows for the interpretation and analysis of the current problems involved in training needs for specialist physicians in the VC. The semi-structured interviews constitute a qualitative method presenting various processes from a comprehensive viewpoint, while also providing for a participatory approach involving the key players in the phenomenon, in this case hospital administrators and representatives of the medical and surgical specialties at the various hospitals of the VC. The main methodological characteristics of these semi-structured interviews are:

1. It is the most reliable method for gathering information about complex issues, while also allowing related opinions and comments to be collated.
2. It is one of the methodological strategies offering the greatest quality of data in the information sought, as it accesses the source of information directly.

3. It allows for the usage and combination of other methods of research, such as for example the combination of surveys of specialist doctors undergoing training and the exploitation of numerical data, which in this case enrich and supplement the research.

4. The experts are visited at their place of work or at a location chosen by the interviewee, in order to guarantee a high quality interview.

5. It requires the prior preparation of a script of issues and questions, thereby guaranteeing the inclusion of those data and issues we wish to explore.

6. The sample required is not statistical, but rather as it has a theoretical saturation point, in other words the point at which the responses and opinions are repeated, it becomes a structured sample.

A script of questions is drawn up in order to guide the experts through the interview dialogue process. The general content of the issues dealt with in the interviews was threefold:

- The current state of specialist training
- The future of medical specialties
- The personal reflections, positions and recommendations of each expert with a view to the future.

A total of 45 experts were interviewed, 31 men and 14 women. 4 of them are administrators, and the remaining 41 specialists representing the medical and surgical specialties chosen for the study. The interviewees belong to hospitals of varying sizes and location within the Autonomous Region of Valencia.

The teaching committees in accordance with the following criteria selected the experts interviewed:

a. They are medical professionals responsible for RH training in one of the specialties covered by the study, ensuring that there were representatives of each of these.

b. They belong to hospitals of differing size and complexity.

c. They practise at hospitals in different geographical regions, thereby guaranteeing that all three provinces of the Valencian Community were represented, while also ensuring that some hospitals were located in provincial capitals, and others in outlying parts of the region.

d. The gender of the interviewees was taken into account, in order to obtain the positions of both men and women.

RESULTS

Overall View of Medical Specialties

Undergraduate Education
    a.   Quality of the undergraduate programme

Although there is a consensus that the length of the degree course (6 years) is sufficient to provide comprehensive training, two conflicting positions emerge as to the quality of the undergraduate programme. One of the groups believes that a thorough review of the quality of medical subjects is required (Sánchez Gómez, Suárez Nieto & Cobeta Marco 2009), while the other group agrees with the way it currently stands. This review would necessarily involve having to rethink the current structure in terms of the teaching staff's number and profile in order to accompany and support students and guarantee the quality of their learning.

    b.   The number of medical students

Once again we find two different positions regarding the number of students studying Medicine:

- There are those who believe that the numerus clausus quota at medical faculties should be increased as one of the strategies to alleviate the deficit of specialist physicians.
- There are those who feel that it would be better to maintain the number of places currently offered at medical faculties, and to limit student dropout rates as much as possible. This would be combined with the application of new teaching methodologies so that the number of students who successfully complete the medical course increases.

Some of the experts consulted claim there is a need to closely scrutinise the training received by medical students, and they believe efforts also have to be made to make the course more attractive and better aligned with new educational methods.

One study undertaken in Germany (Janus et al. 2007) in response to increased dropout rates in medical courses indicates dissatisfaction with financial and non-financial incentives during practical training. The conclusion drawn from this study is that it is necessary to improve certain non-financial incentives in order to recruit and retain doctors.

c. Specialisation

A mismatch between the needs for specialists and the specialists available has been uncovered as a result of the following factors: 1) insufficient number of recognised centres at hospitals to train interns in certain specialties; 2) concentration of physicians retiring in forthcoming years, especially in certain specialties, and 3) lack of incentives to retain recently trained specialist physicians.

Changes in Medical Practice
a. Feminisation process

Medicine records a significant and unchecked process with a proportion of women at Medical Faculties that is now in excess of 70%. Evidence reveals that women tend to prefer certain specialties (Amaya Pombo, C. & García Pérez, M.A, 2005).

In the light of this demographic process of feminisation of the medical profession, the experts adopt two different positions:

*   There are those who view that it is particularly important to strike a balance between doctors' professional and personal spheres.
*   There are those who feel that the same working and administrative structure established to date should be maintained.

b. Participation of foreign doctors

More than 50% of the interns at some district hospitals are foreign doctors who arrive in search of better living conditions and improved job opportunities.

The experts see two different perspectives on the phenomenon:

*   The positive aspects may be summarised as an opportunity to observe and compare other experiences from other schools, and to benefit from the knowledge exchange.
*   The negative aspects include the lack of Spanish language skills and familiarity with the Spanish health system of those foreign doctors who are not native speakers.

The USA is examining the consequences of the influx of foreign doctors into its system where they make up a large and growing proportion of the medical workforce Mullan (1995), Akl (2007) and Mick (2000). The figures reveal that this sector grew by a factor of 2.4 between 1978 and 2004, and that it continues to increase.

c.   Socio-demographic changes on the demand side

In addition to the ageing population, the most significant socio-demographic change in terms of demand is the expanding immigrant population.

Because of the expanding immigrant population, there are certain critical areas, which are subject to more pressure than others, such as Intensive Medicine, Psychiatry, Orthopaedic Surgery, Gynaecology and Obstetrics and Clinical Laboratories.

The ageing population is one factor evidenced for a considerable time now, and the specific pathologies involved are very familiar. However, the specific needs in terms of specialists have not been properly planned. The percentage of those aged over 65 varies across the VC according to districts, with figures ranging from between 15% and a peak of 26%, according to the population information system data of February 2007.

d.   Technical changes in medical practice

Spain is one of the countries with the largest number of medical specialties. Currently, the scientific associations and competent bodies with access via the HR system to medical qualifications acknowledge more specialities. Thus, there is a need to adapt the health system itself and training to this new context.

THE MAIN STRENGTHS OF SPECIALISTS' TRAINING IN THE VALENCIAN COMMUNITY

Those specialists consulted believe that the fact that hospitals provide HR training is in itself a guarantee of quality medical care, up to a point, as the specialists working there are obliged and need to constantly update their skills.

Therefore, quality training is a result of the aptitude and attitude of all those who are responsible for raising and maintaining the prestige of training programmes. The hours dedicated to teaching and the time given to study result in excellent training programmes with a fine national reputation.

THE MAIN WEAKNESSES OF SPECIALISTS' TRAINING IN THE VALENCIAN COMMUNITY

The chief problem in the public health training system is based on an excessive burden of care and the lack of time available for training. In the experts' opinion, the weaknesses of the medical specialist training programmes are the following:

1. A learning system that is not formal enough.

There is no assessment system for interns, which means that no-one fails training. This inevitably leads to a sense of believing that a specialty can be obtained quite easily.

2. Some training periods are not adequately oriented.

The 4 or 5 years that specialist training lasts are ultimately inadequate as a result of the pressure of health care demands.

3. There is an evident lack of support for research.

The third weakness is the genuine lack of support for research. This is viewed as the great shortcoming within training programmes.

4. The time dedicated by tutors and interns to the teaching-learning process is highly limited.

In many cases, the excess burden of care currently experienced at all the public hospitals makes it impossible for tutors to provide their HR systems with the appropriate guidance.

Furthermore, the Anaesthetics and Reanimation, General and Digestive System Surgery, Gynaecology and Obstetrics, Neurology, Paediatrics, Radiodiagnosis, Oncology and Rheumatology specialties recommend increasing training by one year (from 4 to 5 years).

5. Lack of healthcare guidelines and protocols.

Both the absence of healthcare guidelines and protocols and the lack of standardisation across training programmes are also the result of the limited time dedicated to such training programs.

6. Lack of recognition of the guidance, education and teaching of interns.

The last weakness in specialists' training is the lack of both incentive policies and the time dedicated to teaching as part of the HR training programmes. The interviewees highlight two different aspects of this issue:

•   The applicable regulations: The interviewees do not wish to do away with the regulations, but feel that they ought to be updated.

- Professional development is not stimulated, meaning that specialist tutors can often find themselves "stagnating" professionally.

THE MOST LIKELY SCENARIOS

The most probable scenarios focus on three major aspects:

a. Branched core themes as a training strategy

The experts refer to the unfortunate emergence of excessively "fragmented" healthcare because it is often necessary to call on a range of specialists to deal with one patient, a situation which increases the cost of care.

There are two very clear positions in terms of the development of core content:
There are those who believe that the six-year medical degree training is more than adequate and, for most of those interviewed, a branched core element in specialist training would guarantee better quality training.

b. Occupational mobility

Occupational mobility has no conceptual basis in Spain. Nonetheless, four major forms of mobility have been identified:
The first involves the public and private sectors. The mobility rate between these two sectors is very limited. Nonetheless, private insurers in the health field expect considerable progress as a result of the purchasing power of new generations of doctors, which is much lower than that of previous generations, which leads them to seek out alternative sources of employment to supplement their income.
The second form of mobility takes place among the various hospitals of the Valencian Community. The region's specialist physicians reveal a marked propensity to gravitate towards major towns and cities for their personal and professional development.
The third form of occupational mobility identified involves working overseas. The most popular choices of country are Portugal, France and England.
The fourth form of mobility is not occupational but academic. The general profile of the migrant physician is, on the whole, a single, male doctor with no family seeking employment opportunities and professional development.

c. Incentive Policy

The interviewees propose a number of strategies for recognition purposes:

1) Professionalising the teaching with specialists, which involves sole and exclusive dedication to teaching and research activities, free of all health care responsibilities, which occurs in many establishments in the United States and in a number of European countries.

2) Implementation of the incentive policies for the entire centre or department where the intern is being trained in recognition of the work performed by all those individuals who are involved in training.

3) The following proposals are made to develop the quality of specialists' training, to an extent: teamwork involving all the hospitals of the Valencian Community to deal with issues such as increasing the loyalty of Human Resources; rotation of interns around various centres across the region, allocation of bursaries for research in Spain and abroad by means of written agreements, and ongoing and continuous education.

Shortage of Specialists Forecast

In general, all the experts we consulted agree that there is an acute need to plan human resources in accordance with needs by covering such aspects as creation of new hospitals, forthcoming retirements, exemptions from duty shifts for those aged over 55, maternity and holiday leave covers.

The forecast of future shortage scenarios across the 14 selected specialties was in accordance with the opinion of the 44 experts interviewed within the 14 cited specialties. The shortage of specialists affects some specialities more than others. The table below presents the scarcity of specialists, in the order of greater to lesser.

Table 1. Scarcity of specialists

Marked deficit	Anaesthesia
	General Surgery
	Gynaecology and Obstetrics
	Paediatrics
	Radiodiagnosis
Deficit	Psychiatry
	Oncology
	Rheumatology
Slight deficit	Orthopaedic Surgery
	Cardiology
	Neurology
No deficit	Internal Medicine
	Intensive Medicine
Slight surplus	Ophthalmology

CONCLUSION

The training of students at medical faculties requires a thorough and painstaking review of the content of subject matters and the teaching methodology employed. Regarding the number of students, it is essential to consider needs in accordance with the places allocated in each region in order to alleviate the current shortage of doctors.

There is currently no incentives policy designed to retain the human resources presently working at hospitals, to prevent them from migrating to other institutions in Spain or abroad, or to recognise the teaching work undertaken at hospitals.

The changes seen in the medical practice focus on three aspects: the feminisation process of the profession, immigration and new medical practices. The increasing feminisation process of the medical profession makes us to reconsider our approach to policies with a view to consolidating the personal and professional life of female doctors. Immigration affects two major areas of the healthcare system: medical provision for foreign patients and the integration of overseas doctors with the health system.

The quality of teaching delivered to resident housemen is of high quality, and is comparable with that of other countries such as the USA and other EU countries.

Meanwhile, the most striking weakness is based on some tutors,' and also some interns', lack of academic commitment. The main factor lies in the lack of time dedicated to teaching as a result of the excessive healthcare workloads to which they are subject.

We must acknowledge value and incentivise all those directly and indirectly involved in intern training programmes by means of an incentive policy, and also introduce a system to assess the quality of these programmes to ensure that we maintain the prestige and quality achieved to date.

In the opinion of the managers interviewed, the issue of human resources and the quality of internal training programmes vary from hospital to hospital in accordance with their complexity and geographical location. This means that it is essential to establish a structural evaluation system that considers the intrinsic and external variables of each hospital.

ACKNOWLEDGMENTS

The authors wish to thank the Directorate-General for Health Administration, Evaluation and Research of the Valencian Regional Government for its funding and methodological assistance in the selection of experts and specialties.

We would like to thank the R&D+I Linguistic Assistance Office, Universidad Politécnica de Valencia (Spain), for translating this paper.

REFERENCES

Akl E. A., Mustafa R., Bdair F., Schünemann H. J. The United States physician workforce and international medical graduates: trends and characteristics. *J Gen Intern Med.* 2007 Feb; 22(2):264-8

Alonso Magdaleno, M. I. (2003). Dynamic analysis of the call process for specialized medical training posts in Spain. *ICE* 804: 57-73

Alonso Magdaleno, M. I. (2003) Managing the number of medical specialists in Spain. Dynamic analysis of some alternatives for improvement. *ICADE: Journal of the Faculties of Law and Economic and Business Studies.* No. 59: 193-202

Amaya, Pombo, C., & García Pérez, M. A., (2005): *Demografía médica en España. Mirando al futuro, Madrid, Fundación CESM. [Medical demographics in Spain. Looking to the future. Madrid, Fundación CESM].*

García-Prado, A. & González, P. (2006). Moonlighting physicians: analysis of its causes and consequences. *Gac Sant.* 20 (Supl2): 29-40

González López-Valcárcel, B. & Barber Pérez, P. (2008). Difficulties, pitfalls and stereotypes in physician workforce planning. *Gac Sanit.* 22(5):393-5.

González López-Valcárcel, B. & Barber, P. (2006). Human resources and their mitigating unbalances. *Gac Sanit.* 20 (Supl 1): 103-9.

Goodman, D. C. & Fisher, E. S. (2008). Physician workforce crisis? Wrong diagnosis, wrong prescription. *N Engl J Med.* 358(16):1658-61.

Janus, K., Amelung, V. E., Gaitanides, M. and Schwartz, F. W. (2007) 'German physicians "on strike"—Shedding light on the roots of physician dissatisfaction', *Health Policy.* Elsevier, 82(3), pp. 357–365.

Mick S. S, Lee S.Y., Wodchis W.P. (2000) Variations in geographical distribution of foreign and domestically trained physicians in the United States: 'safety nets' or 'surplus exacerbation'?. *Soc Sci Med.* 50 (2):185-202

Mullan F., Politzer R. M., Davis C. H. (1995) Medical migration and the physician workforce. International medical graduates and American medicine. *JAMA.* 17; 273(19):1521-7

Sánchez Gómez, S., Suárez Nieto, C. and Cobeta Marco, I. (2009). "Demand and Supply of Otolaryngology Specialists Based on Evidence: What Is the Required Number of Specialists That Should Be Trained?" *Acta Otorrinolaringologica* (English Edition) 60 (6). Elsevier: 443–50.

WHO | *Forecasting the global shortage of physicians: an economic- and needs-based approach'* (2011) WHO. World Health Organization.

WHO | HRH | *Powered by the Global Health Atlas (no date).* Available at: http://apps.who.int/globalatlas/default.asp

In: Modeling Social Behavior and Its Applications   ISBN: 978-1-53613-666-1
Editors: L. A. Jódar Sánchez et al.   © 2018 Nova Science Publishers, Inc.

Chapter 16

MODELING SPATIAL VARIABILITY OF TYPE 2 DIABETES MELLITUS MEDICATION: ITS USE AND COST IN THE VALENCIAN COMMUNITY

Javier Díaz-Carnicero, David Vivas-Consuelo*,
Natividad Guadalajara-Olmeda
and Vicent Caballer-Tarazona
INECO, Research Centre for Economics Engineering,
Group of Health Economics and Management,
Universitat Politècnica de València, Valencia, Spain

ABSTRACT

A spatial analysis of the prevalence and the total pharmaceutical cost of type 2 diabetes was carried out, using clustered information from primary health centres. The results show a spatial dependence for both variables, which was more significant for the cost. The prevalence could be explained according to comorbidity but not the cost, which shows a spatial variability in the treatment not justified by clinical reasons.

Keywords: pharmaceutical costs, diabetes, spatial distribution

---

* Corresponding Author: dvivas@upv.es.

INTRODUCTION

Diabetes is a well-known metabolic pathology that affects glucose levels due to problems associated with insulin. The different types depend on the origin of the disease: in Type 1 there has been a complete destruction of the ß cells in the pancreas, causing the absence of insulin, while Type 2 (T2D) is related to a deficit or resistance to this hormone. We can also find other minor types, such as LADA or gestational diabetes.

To provide a context for diabetes in Spain, we take the results of the 'di@bet.es' study of patients affected with T2D as reference. This presents alarming data indicating that this pathology affects 13.8% of the population older than 18, with 43% of these people (nearly 2.3 million) not having been diagnosed. The population distribution of the prevalence for this disease varies with age and gender, so no demographic models of evolution can be established. In addition, 12.6% of the population presents glucose intolerance, a previous stage that can lead to the presence of T2D [1].

This data shows the importance and great impact of the disease on the Spanish National Health Service, both at present and for the future. Therefore, it is significantly important to take into account the consumption of resources associated with T2D, seeking to maximize efficiency as health care quality improves.

One of the main factors in the health care of diabetic patients is the pharmaceutical treatment. Following the recommendations provided by the American Diabetes Association (ADA) there are four different stages in the treatment, starting with the use of metformine, a drug with moderate cost, which can then be combined with one or several second-generation compounds, and ending up on the higher therapy level where the use of injected insulin is required [2]. The importance of this classification goes beyond patient care, given the cost of the treatment also rises as we move on to the different stages. The correct choice of therapy will involve both the correct patient care and the rational use of resources [3].

The main goal of this study is to analyse and model the spatial distribution and variation of pharmaceutical treatment for T2D in the Valencian Community (an eastern Spanish region).

METHODS

We used a database containing the prescriptions dispensed in the primary healthcare centres (n = 50) and hospitals in the different health districts in the Valencian Community in 2015. The Valencian Community is made up of three provinces (Castellón in the north, Valencia in the middle and Alicante in the south), with a total of five million inhabitants.

Firstly, we clustered the initial information of the patient data according to primary health centre. With these aggregated data and the population affiliated to each health centre, we calculated both the prevalence and the average cost per patient by health centre. Finally, the spatial mapping was carried out using these variables, and the linear regression model was proposed

To explore the spatial dependence [4-6] of the variables (X) we used Moran's index (I), the equation for which is given below (1), and which offers a value between 0 and 1, with 1 being complete spatial correlation and values close to 0 corresponding to a random spatial distribution. To generate the weights matrix required (w_{ij}), a threshold distance was established, warranting the existence of at least one neighbour for each node.

$$I = \frac{N}{\sum_i \sum_j w_{ij}} \frac{\sum_i \sum_j w_{ij}(X_i - \bar{X})(X_j - \bar{X})}{\sum_i (X_i - \bar{X})^2} \qquad (1)$$

We plotted the result using the LISA (Local Indicator of Spatial Association) maps, which cluster areas of high and low values, as well as the distribution outliers.

OLS linear regression models (2) were designed using demographic, clinical and socio-economic variables. As clinical variable we used the Clinical Risk Groups (CRG) index of morbidity [7, 8]. In the regression residuals we distinguished one part as corresponding to the spatial dependence of the variable, which, as mentioned, is estimated using Moran's I index.

$$Y = \beta_0 + \beta_1 X_1 + \beta_2 X_2 + \ldots + \varepsilon_s + \varepsilon \qquad (2)$$

where Y is the dependent variable (the prevalence and the pharmaceutical cost), X_{jn} are the different explanatory variables, β_{jn} the corresponding parameters, ε_s the part of the residuals attributed to the spatial distribution, and ε the general residuals.

RESULTS

Prevalence of Type 2 Diabetes

The value of Moran's I, as explained, was 0.2941, showing that while there is a certain spatial dependence in the prevalence results, the correlation is not high (Figure 1).

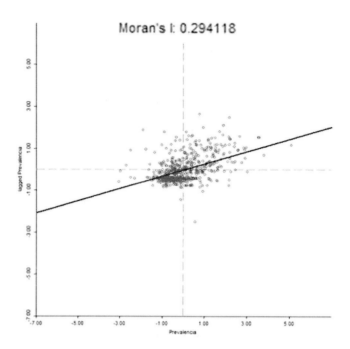

Figure 1. Moran's I test for the prevalence.

Analysing the LISA maps (Figure 2), we can see that half of the health centres present significant values which can be divided into two different cluster types: on the one hand, the metropolitan zones of the capitals of each province, together with the greater part of the Alicante region, where there are low value clusters; and on the other hand, the interior zones of Valencia and Castellon, the southern coast of Valencia and small interior areas of Alicante, which present high values. In addition, we find significant outliers, principally in the capitals, where some health centres rise above the values expected for the location.

As the nature of the disease is that it often occurs in relation with others, when trying to generate a valid regression model to explain the prevalence values, we decided to add a well-known comorbidity index that has been studied, the CRG values [7]. If we represent the spatial distribution of the average CRG value of the primary health centers, we can find a mapping similar to that for prevalence, with general matching of the clusters (Figure 3).

We obtained a regression model for the prevalence in each primary health centre. This model showed a strong relation with the state of health quantified in the CRG values, as well as with the average patient age of the health centre (R^2 value of 0.6401) (Table 1).

If we take into account the spatial dependence reflected in Moran's I, we could consider that the majority of the variability in prevalence values can be explained by comorbidity and average age.

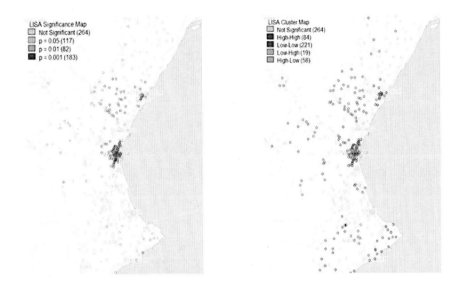

Figure 2. LISA maps of statistical significance (left) and clustering (right) for the prevalence.

Figure 3. LISA clustering map of the average value of CRG.

Table 1. Regression model for T2D in each health centre

Variable	Coefficient	Std. Error
Constant	-0.01902	0.00347
CRG - Weight	0.00109	0.00005
Average age	0.00094	0.00009

Total Pharmaceutical Expenditure of Type 2 Diabetes

Regarding pharmaceutical expenditure, we start the study with Moran's I test (Figure 4) giving a high value of 0.6825. This result is indicative of the presence of a high spatial dependence in the total pharmaceutical cost.

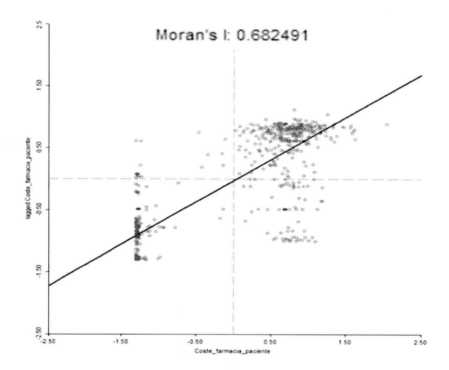

Figure 4. Moran's I test for the pharmaceutical cost.

The results of the LISA maps (Figure 5) show a clear spatial dependence in most health centres as well as Moran's I. We found high values in the southern half of the community, especially in Alicante province, as well as in the northern part of Castellon. By contrast, we found Valencia province and the southern part of Castellon clustering with low values. The outliers can be found mainly in the capital, Valencia city, where some centres present higher values when compared to the neighbouring cluster.

In the regression model, we found that variables which we had initially assumed to be explicative, such as the prevalence itself previously studied or the state of health measured in the comorbidity index, were not statistically significant for the model. As Moran's I showed in advance, the pharmaceutical cost presents a spatial dependence stronger than any of the variables studied, which are not able to explain the distribution satisfactorily.

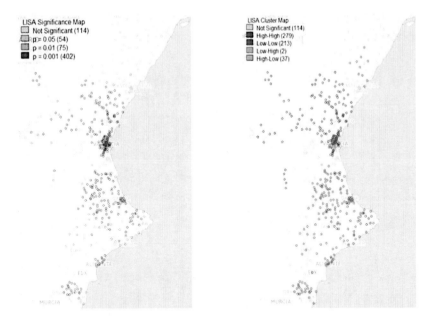

Figure 5. LISA maps of statistical significance (left) and clustering (right) for the total pharmaceutical cost.

CONCLUSION

A spatial dependence in the variables studied was observed, which is significantly higher for the pharmaceutical cost than for the prevalence. This is an indicator of a high variability in the use of pharmaceutical resources, which is not related to patient clinical characteristics.

The development and implementation of clinical guidelines of clinical evidence and cost-effectiveness could be a great tool in correcting this variability.

REFERENCES

[1]   International Diabetes Federation Guideline Development Group, *Global guideline for type 2 diabetes*, vol. 104, no. 1. 2014.

[2]   Inzucchi S. E., Bergenstal R. M., Buse J. B., Diamant M., Ferrannini E., Nauck M., Peters A. L., Tsapas A., Wender R., and Matthews D. R., "Management of Hyperglycemia in Type 2 Diabetes, 2015: A Patient-Centered Approach: Update to a position statement of the american diabetes association and the european association for the study of diabetes," *Diabetes Care*, vol. 38, no. 1, pp. 140-149, 2015.

[3]   Sancho-Mestre C., Vivas-Consuelo D., Alvis-Estrada L., Romero M., Usó-

Talamantes R., and Caballer-Tarazona V., "Pharmaceutical cost and multimorbidity with type 2 diabetes mellitus using electronic health record data," *BMC Health Serv. Res.*, vol. 16, no. 1, pp. 1-8, 2016.

[4]   Lawson A. B., *Statistical methods in spatial epidemiology*. Wiley, 2013.

[5]   Dijkstra A., Janssen F., De Bakker M., Bos J., Lub R., Van Wissen L. J. G., Hak E., and Timmer A., "Using Spatial Analysis to Predict Health Care Use at the Local Level: A Case Study of Type 2 Diabetes Medication Use and Its Association with Demographic Change and Socioeconomic Status," *Plos One*, vol 8, n° 8, 2013.

[6]   Coly S., Charras-Garrido M., Abrial D., and Yao-Lafourcade A. F., "Spatiotemporal Disease Mapping Applied to Infectious Diseases," *Procedia Environ. Sci.*, vol. 26, pp. 32-37, 2015.

[7]   Vivas-Consuelo D., Usó-Talamantes R., Guadalajara-Olmeda N., Trillo-Mata J. L., Sancho-Mestre C., and Buigues-Pastor L., "Pharmaceutical cost management in an ambulatory setting using a risk adjustment tool.," *BMC Health Serv. Res.*, vol. 14, no. 1, p. 462, 2014.

[8]   Caballer Tarazona V., Guadalajara Olmeda N., Vivas Consuelo D., and Clemente Collado A., "Impact of Morbidity on Health Care Costs of a Department of Health through Clinical Risk Groups. Valencian Community, Spain," *Rev. Esp. Salud Publica*, vol. 90, pp. e1-e15, 2016.

In: Modeling Social Behavior and Its Applications
Editors: L. A. Jódar Sánchez et al.

ISBN: 978-1-53613-666-1
© 2018 Nova Science Publishers, Inc.

Chapter 17

THE AUTHORS OF THE OBRA NOVA, THE LITTLE GREAT WORK ON VALENCIA'S CATHEDRAL: THEIR TIME AND CRAFTING OF A VISION ABOUT TWO OF THE MOST IMPORTANT PERSONS OF SPANISH RENAISSANCE ARCHITECTURE IN VALENCIA

Vicente Blasco[1], Ángeles Mas[1],
Carlos Lerma[1],* and Enrique Gil[2]
[1]Department Architectural Constructions,
Universitat Politècnica de València, Valencia, Spain
[2]Department of Continuous Medium Mechanics and Theory
of Structures, Universitat Politècnica de València, Valencia, Spain

ABSTRACT

The Canons´ Loggia of the Cathedral of Valencia, also known as *Llotgeta dels Canonges, Obra Nova u Obra Nueva del Cabildo*, is one of the first Renaissance pieces of Valencian architecture, introduced in Spain in sixteenth century. Drew by the carpenter master Gaspar Gregori, who carried out a whole recently Renaissance language in Spain, its construction is attributed to the stonemason master Miguel Porcar, heir of gothic tradition of the most renowned local builders and aware of the stereotomy secrets and the medieval construction techniques.

* Corresponding Author Email: clerma@csa.upv.es.

1566 is the commonly attributed for these galleries' construction, but it was actually 1563 when Porcar started them. The discussion about these galleries revolves around the two recognized authors, since the history of Valencian architecture always attributes the work to Gregori when it doesn't. At least we should say that the merit is for both.

Gaspar Gregori was the most representative figure of Valencian architecture of the sixteenth century and the first in acquiring the esteem as an architect on the Vitruvian sense of the term, but his participation in this work is only for the construction of the two upper storeys and is exclusively known by means of the capitulations that the performer of the works, Miguel Porcar, signed on 17 July 1566. This previously had signed by himself (it's unknown how because he neither knew write nor read) other capitulations on 26 Juny 1563 for completing the ground floor arcades and the top cover (what now is the first floor terrace).

Gregori's incorporation to that work implied a new Renaissance language for the galleries from then. That is why the figure of Gregori is important. Nevertheless, Miguel Porcar -a simple stonemason- was the work's physical author in tracing the little building added to the Cathedral in its northwestern side and the first one in riging its stone fabrics. Therefore, according to the existing documentation, the original layouts of Obra Nova galleries of Valencia's Cathedral were a Miguel Porcar's exclusive responsibility.

Keywords: Valencia, cathedral, stonework, Spanish Renaissance

INTRODUCTION

The Canons´ Loggia of the Cathedral of Valencia, also known as *Llotgeta dels Canonges, Obra Nova u Obra Nueva del Cabildo*, is one of the first pieces of Valencian architecture of the Renaissance. Overlapped to the gothic ambulatory of the Cathedral between the Apostles´ Door and the seventeenth bridge that connects it with Helpless Virgin basilica, makes up a new façade, with a curve outline that, hiding the first chapels of the chevet close by that named Door, changed radically the architectonic appreciation of the chevet of this magnificent building.

Drew by the carpenter master Gaspar Gregori and the stonemason master Miguel Porcar, who, inspired by Serlio's treatise of architecture, translated in that time in Spain (Venice, 1537; Toledo, 1552), carried out a whole recently Renaissance language in our country introduced at that moment. Its construction is attributed to the stonemason master Miguel Porcar, heir of gothic tradition of the most renowned local builders and aware, without any doubt, of the stereotomy secrets and the medieval construction techniques.

The commonly attributed date for the construction of these galleries is1566, but in fact, the works were started by Porcar three years before, in 1563, the same year in which Wijngaerde did his famous drawings about Valencian (Figure 1) sights, in which is still possible to appreciate the gothic outline of the chevet (Blasco, 2016:7). A fresco painting located in San Vicente Ferrer chapel into the Seminary-School of Corpus Christi in Valencia. Painted between 1597 and 1605, belongs to painter Bartolomé Matarana's whole programme (Figure 2). It's the first existing graphic document about the Obra Nova of Valencia's Cathedral.

Figure 1. View of Valencia, 1563. Anthoine Van den Wijngaerde (Public domain).

Figure 2. A comparison between the Obra Nova at present (left) and in 1561, 35 years after of its construction, according to a painting by Bartolomé Matarana (right).

THE ROMAN MEASUREMENTS BY DIEGO DE SAGREDO AS INTRODUCTION OF CLASSICAL ARCHITECTURE IN SPAIN

Architecture understood as a liberal profession was introduced in Spain by Diego de Sagredo at the beginning of sixteenth century through his treatise 'Roman Measurements' (Marias&Pereda, 2000), printed and published in Toledo in 1526. The purpose of this author was to offer Spanish readers ready access to the rules of Classical Architecture to bring them up to date with Italian theories and to construct a particularly Spanish manifestation of a famous Classical locus, the Vitruvian book. The fulfillment of these aims required considerable skill on Sagredo's part, for he had to satisfy his readership with a sufficiency of local reference and subject accessibility as well as carry authority in his treatment of the Classical canon and of the body of learning developed in Renaissance Italy (Llewellyn, 1998:122-123).

Just like the Italian architectonic theory of the previous century did, that treatise established the difference between those dedicated to purely handmade activities and those considered as liberal architects, that is to say, those who worked only with the enthusiasm of the spirit and the creativity (Llopis, 2002:48-51; Llopis & Torres, 2011:65).

In those years, the spreading of the proper term *architect* was made slowly and in a progressive way. According to Fernando Marías, those great Spanish architects in the middle of sixteenth century, who introduced the authentic classicism in Spanish peninsula (Siloé, Machuca, Covarrubias, Quijano and so on) were still considered *masters* but not yet architects (Marias, 1986:69-98; Marias, 1979:175-226).

As Marías says, in the middle of sixteenth century there are in Spain two meanings of the term *architect* coexisting at the same time: on the one hand the official meaning, which was that used in juridical and legal writings referring to the engravers or sculptors. On the other hand, the term architect understood on its Vitruvian sense, which became official from 1570 when the King Felipe II of Spain reorganized the architecture in Spain and set up the purism and the strict traditionalism as official style.

As a consequence, it's in that moment when the liberal conception of the architectonic profession is recognized in a permanently way and the term architect is identified as the definition of the scholar architect, which task is purely theoretical and out of the architectonic practice on the work site, being the architectonic drawing the way of expression for his creativity. In that way, the term architect is used with almost total exclusivity to *a draughtsman architect* (Llopis, 2002:49).

THE FIGURE OF GASPAR GREGORI AND HIS ROLE
AS AN *ARCHITECT*

In Valencia, Spain, the most representative figure of Valencian architecture of the sixteenth century and the first in acquiring the esteem as an architect on the Vitruvian sense of the term was Gaspar Gregori. Even though, his figure has been traditionally associated to that of a mere carpenter because of his connection to this trade along his whole life.

He was named as *a master carpenter* on May 14th 1541 (Gómez-Ferrer, 1995:806) by an exam in front of the carpenters trade, holding later titles like mestre de la fusta del senyor Rey at the Royal Palace from 1559 and *mestre de la fusta de la casa de deputacio* from 1563 until his death in 1592.

In his youth, Gregori got a cultural education bound to the study and knowledge of the architectonic treatises, strongly influenced by the cultural environment that was being prepared on the occasion of the Royal Palace works. In the Valencian cultural scope there were some libraries magnificently equipped in those ages, like Duke of Calabria's or Marquis of Zenete's (Llopis, 2002:51).

Thus, Gregori was evolving progressively and playing a more active role in the assimilation of a new linguistic code and in the new design habits associated to it, which would flow out on the formal evolution of his work and on its important role on the Valencian architectonic medium.

After his architectonic preparation on works for Valencia's Royal Palace in the shadow of their principal architects Vidanya and Covarrubias, he will appear by that time to some singular works of that era, such as the General Hospital, the Generalitat Palace, the Casa de Armas (weapons house) and the Obra Nova of the Valencia Cathedral (Llopis 2002:51-52), his most important work of this period and that in which the control of Renaissance formal elements are more clearly appreciated.

His participation in this work for the construction of the two upper storeys is known exclusively by means of the capitulations that the performer of the works, Miguel Porcar, signed on 17 July 1566 (Cathedral of Valencia's Archive, 1566a).

Miguel Porcar had previously signed by himself (it's unknown how because he neither knew write nor read) other capitulations on 26 Juny 1563 (Cathedral of Valencia's Archive, 1566b:36) for completing the nayas (the ground floor arcades) and the top cover (what now is the first floor terrace).

Figure 3 and Figure 4 show different parts of the building and their authors.

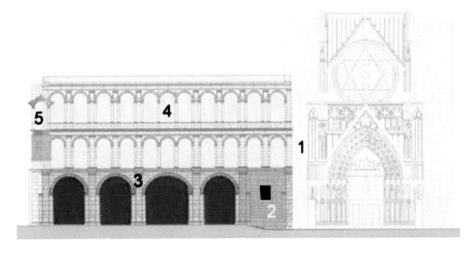

Figure 3. Parts of the building and their authors. 1: Apostles' Door; 2: Sacristy Nova's enlargement to the front (made by Porcar, before 1563); 3: Ground floor arcades (Porcar, work agreements on 1563); 4: Upper floors (Gregori y Porcar, work agreements on 1566). 5: Connection bridge to the Virgin Basilica (1660).

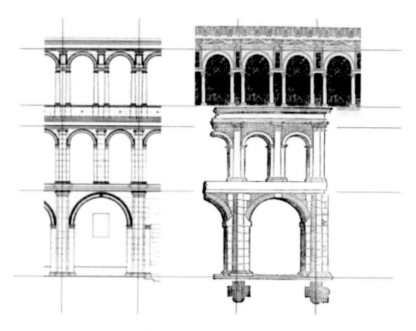

Figure 4. Comparison between a section of the Obra Nova (left) and an assembly (right) overlapping some sheets from the Treatise of Architecture of Sebastian Serlio, modifying some figures and its proportions in order to adapt them to the Obra Nova's.

All this will make Gregori a figure who would take part to a greater o lesser degree on the most important Renaissance interventions held in Valencia and would be the axis in whom all the process of the assimilation of the renaissance architecture principles in the city's surrounding area was structured in a constructive and structural side and not just formal facet.

His personality fully illustrates the introduction of the figure of the renaissance architects as well as the ways for creating the design ideas associated to them (Llopis, 2002:50).

The figure of Gregori fully symbolizes the transit between two eras: that of the medieval master educated into the professional guilds where he was qualified as a master through the experience, and that of the renaissance architect where the qualification was based on the theory knowledge, the ability for graphic ideation of buildings and some other subjects. Thus, from his beginnings as *mestre de fusta*, he became so called along the years first a *sobrestant*, then as a *mestre major*, *ingenier* and, finally, as an *arquitector* (Llopis, 2002:58).

THE IMPORTANCE OF THE TREATISES

In order to assimilate the Renaissance architecture the Architectural Treatises were crucial in all this process of conformation of the new *architect*, since all the needed knowledge for the background of an architect from a Vitruvian conception were contained in them.

The accessibility to them instituted a clear difference between masters and architects in relation to officials and labourers, since we cannot forget that the latter were largely illiterate persons (Llopis, 2002:54). This was the case of Gaspar Gregori and Miguel Porcar as is evident from the agreements for the *Obra Nova*, in which it is stated that the first one signs on behalf of the second one for not knowing write this last one (Cathedral of Valencia's Archive, 1566a). This can also be seen in the construction of the Seminary-School of Corpus Christi of Valencia (Lerma et al., 2013).

The architectonic treatises were crucial on cultural formation of sixteenth century Spanish architects. It could be said that their cultural level was in lockstep with the rest of the European architects. The good constructive practice of the architects has meant a durability and comfort of the buildings for more than four centuries, recently confronted (Gil et al. 2017, Lerma et al., 2014). The architectonic texts arrived quickly to the Iberian Peninsula where the most trained architects had the Italian texts almost at the same time they were published in their original versions, although the possession of books and their theoretical knowledge was limited to a culturally trained elite, that of the tracer architects (Llopis, 2002:54).

As for the masters, they had and used very little books, hardly a breviary, some municipal ordinances and a *Serlio's* (Marias, 1986:83), using this last one as a formal and typological compendium but without any theoretical interest.

The abundance of treatises proves the interest of the sixteenth century architects for getting a theoretical formation in a Vitruvian and Albertian (from Vitruvio and Leon Battista Alberti) sense. The treatises would be for them a way of knowledge and as formal guides for ornamental elements, application of classic, typological and constructive architectonic orders.

In Gregori's case, he was importantly influenced, as clearly seems to be, by that from Sebastiano Serlio, as it appears along the majority of his work. According to professors Bustamante and Marías, the Serlian Treatises had a huge diffusion in Spain, above all as a result of Villalpando's Spanish translation of books III and IV into Spanish edition in 1552 (Marias & Bustamante, 1986:205).

Nevertheless, it's possible that Gregori already knew previously the foils from Serlio's books without any translation, since the image about a church which appears on foil 4 from the fifth book could has served to himself as inspiration for the elliptical trace of the crossing of the General Hospital in Valencia made in 1546, because of the different width of its plan solution with Greek cross naves. That's why the solution for the crossing could not be circular but elliptical.

Professor Llopis Verdú goes even further with these hypotheses saying that another possible reference to Serlio's and to the published treatises would be the use of the oval shape on Valencian architect work, being Gregori one of the rare Valencian architects that appeals to it, such as it can be appreciated at General Hospital crossing and at the plan for the Obra Nova of Valencia's Cathedral (Llopis, 2002:55).

This hypothesis is possible in the case of the Hospital, but questionable in the case of the Obra Nova, since by the analysis of checked documents it seems that the plan traces were made by Porcar before Gregori's intervention, as displayed by work capitulations.

But for Miguel Porcar, it's almost certain that he didn't follow the letter of the treatises because of, as it's expressed in the capitulations of July 17th 1566, he didn't know how to write, supposing, therefore, he didn't know how to read either.

It's known that the constructive tradition of home stonecutters, heirs of gothic masters, made unnecessary the reading of stereotomy treatises, since they were based, after all, on medieval drawing techniques (Sanchis, 1925:23-52), and this, without any doubt, Porcar was able to do.

His knowledge stemmed from the observation of some of these drawings but, above all, from his experience and constructive intuition, as he could prove on the construction of the Obra Nova, which had a particular stereotomy because of its curved outline and, therefore, a lot of difficulties on physical construction.

THE TRACES OF MIGUEL PORCAR

The importance of Gregori on the so called Obra Nova of Valencia's Cathedral was because of his incorporation to that work implied that from that moment the Obra Nova embodies a clearly new renaissance language.

We have established previously that Miguel Porcar, a simple stonemason, was the material author of the works of the Obra Nova of the Cathedral of Valencia, the first in tracing the traces of the little building added to the Cathedral in its northwestern side and the first in rising its stone fabrics.

We cannot forget that in those years of the middle of sixteenth century, the constructive tradition, in most cases, still was that from medieval gothic fashions and customs.

In fact, the master builder who begins both the traces and the construction of these galleries, the Valencian *pedrapiquer* (stonecutter) Miguel Porcar, Cathedral master stonemason in those years (Gómez-Ferrer, 1995:805), was a disciple of Juan Bautista Corbera (Navarro, 2003:79), an active stonemason in Valencia who can be considered as a figure of the transition between a totally assumed architecture in Valencia and another which was starting to introduce some elements which would condition the change of both spatial organization and structural in buildings. In the forties of that century he was working in some reparation works of the *Valencia's Lonja*, made by master Pere Compte, and in 1565 is documented his work making an arch in *Bailía* house where he was working from 1550 (Gómez-Ferrer, 1995:353-358).

The importance of Porcar as a master builder is evident for the fact of both being known and documented that the collaboration between Porcar and Gregori in the *Obra Nova* wouldn't be the only one, since subsequently, and among others, they worked together around the Council House, the *Casa de Armas* (weapon store) and in some recognitions and exams of other works (Gómez-Ferrer, 1995:353).

The fact of Porcar didn't Know to write, something common in that time between those dedicated to the material part of a construction, doesn't mean he didn't know how to trace or draw. In fact it is known that he had certain capacity as tracer for some specifics elements, for it is known that already in 1548 he had constructed the chapel gate of the Consulate *conforme a una trasa que aquell ha donat* (according to a trace given by him), which makes us think about that he not only was dedicated to the material execution in his craft but also it is likely that, although he didn't know to write, as is mentioned in the Notary Public Joan Alamany *Llibre de Provisions* (the Provisions Book) on 17 July 1566, he had a somewhat greater background.

Sanchis Sivera (1925:23-52), as the greatest knowledgeable of Valencia's Cathedral, says, for reaching the title for being a master builder, a need of great theoretical knowledge and specially practical ones were required. And among the remits afforded to Porcar when he was named as the Cathedral master stonemason appeared that of attending and taking a closer look to all works that were executed in this building and also *opera predicta traçare et ordinare*, in other words, draw and order the planned work. Consequently, the traces fulfillment was a part of his duties, even only it were for certain items (Gómez-Ferrer, 1995:354).

According to the existing documentation, as it can be seen in notary acts, the original layouts of Obra Nova galleries of Valencia's Cathedral were a Miguel Porcar's exclusive responsibility.

THE KNOWLEDGE ACQUIRED BY THE STONECUTTER MASTER PORCAR

In 1545, stonecutter Miguel Porcar signed an agreement with the town of Valencia to lay down paving stones on two of the shipyards' warehouses, most likely to prepare them better for their use as wheat deposits. That paving was expanded again in 1565, also by Miguel Porcar.

That was only one of Porcar's activities. But it's known that in the age of the great medieval constructions, and Valencia Cathedral was certainly one of them, there were professionals who planned the works, those called architects or master builders, preparatory sketches, drawings and models were made, each craft had its workshop, and the workrooms, as they are today, might show an amazing activity, requiring big scaffolds, cranes and some other auxiliary means.

Besides, and frequently, the most prestigious master builders in Valencia (between them those of the Cathedral) were, at the same time, the most identified as water leveling masters. A very qualified body of specialists in the hydraulic balance, the so called _Livelladors_ (levelers), is documented in Valencia. It's like the knowledge about geometry given by a master's degree for the construction of a cathedral were adequate to solve whatever problem about leveling and hydraulics or vice versa.

That is the case of Pere Compte –with whom Miguel Porcar worked on the works of the Lonja- as well as of many of his contemporaries, for whom the work as levelers was not an anecdote on their professional lives but a substantial part, important and specific of the _mestre pedrapiquer_ (stonemason master) (Zaragozá, 2007:10).

The Valencian master builders, with category as architects, who were able to trace the countless constructions built over fourteenth, fifteenth and sixteenth centuries in Valencia, came from two significant crafts from medieval society: the _pedrapiquers_ (stonecutters or stonemasons) and the _obrers de vila_ (masons or bricklayers). It is documented in Valencia that from the last quarter of fifteenth century, the stonemasons needed pass an exam, regulated in great detail on their own craft ordinances, in order to get the master's degree that enabled them for the architectonic design exercise (Navarro, 2008).

Therefore, we should assume that if the job of Cathedral stonecutter was granted to Miguel Porcar, who in addition to his duties had to make some traces, it was because he had to overcome some type of exam which empowered him to make such functions, since the cathedral's chapterhouse took great care and precautions for going ahead to the designation of its _operarius sedis Valentie_ or master builder, who was subject to certain tests and conditions which were consigned in a notary act (Sanchis, 1933:14).

CONCLUSION

One of the first works of the Valencian Renaissance was the _Obra Nova_ of the Cathedral of Valencia ever since the liberal conception of Architecture was introduced in Spain by Diego de Sagredo at the beginning of the sixteenth century through his treatise _Medidas del Romano_ (Roman measurements).

Gaspar Gregori, the most representative figure of Valencian architecture of the sixteenth century and the first in acquiring the esteem as an architect on the Vitruvian sense of the term was one of its authors. Gregori was evolving progressively and playing a more active role in the assimilation of a new linguistic code and in the new design habits associated to it, which would flow out on the formal evolution of his work and on its important role on the Valencian architectonic medium.

As a consequence, when he incorporates to the works of the *Obra Nova* three years after Miguel Porcar had initiated its traces and works, he introduced the Renaissance formal elements which, from that moment, would be the beginning of the assimilation process of the Renaissance architecture principles in the city's surrounding area.

Gregori is a very important historical figure from this point of view, but in the case of the *Obra Nova* he was not the only figure. Before him, Miguel Porcar was the other figure for this work. According to the existing documentation, as it can be seen in notary acts, the original layouts of Obra Nova galleries of Valencia's Cathedral were a Miguel Porcar's exclusive responsibility.

Unlike Gregori, for Porcar, heir of the constructive tradition of home stonecutters and connoisseur of medieval drawing techniques, it was unnecessary the reading of stereotomy treatises. His knowledge stemmed from the observation of some of these drawings but, above all, from his experience and constructive intuition, as he could prove on the construction of the Obra Nova, which had a particular stereotomy because of its curved outline and, therefore, a lot of difficulties on physical construction.

REFERENCES

Blasco García, V. (2016). *La construcción de la Obra Nova de la Catedral de Valencia. Un ejercicio de impostación y transformaciones renacentistas en torno a la girola gótica.* [The construction of the Nova Work of the Cathedral of Valencia. An exercise of imposition and Renaissance transformations around the Gothic ambulatory.] PhD thesis. Doi:10.4995/Thesis/10251/76165.

Cathedral of Valencia's Archive. (1566). *Libre de Provisions del notario Joan Alamany*, [Book of Provisions of Notary Public Juan Alemany,] fecha 17 de julio 1566. Vol. 3640, control number 3.738, pag. CCCLXXJ. Valencia.

Cathedral of Valencia's Archive. (1566). *Legajo* [File] 36. Valencia.

Gil, E., Lerma, C., Vercher, J., Mas, Á. (2017). Methodology for Thermal Behaviour Assessment of Homogeneous Façades in Heritage Buildings. *Journal of Sensors,* 2017. Doi:10.1155/2017/3280691.

Gómez-Ferrer, M. (1995). *Arquitectura y arquitectos en la Valencia del S. XVI. El Hospital General y sus artífices.* [Architecture and architects in the Valencia of the XVI century. The General Hospital and its architects.] PhD Thesis. Valencia.

Lerma, C., Mas, Á., Blasco, V. (2013). Analysis procedure of a previous planning organization: The area of the seminary school of Corpus Christi in Valencia, Spain. *International Journal of Architectural Heritage*, 7 (2), 135-152. Doi:10.1080/15583058.2011.624252.

Lerma, C., Mas, Á., Gil, E., Vercher, J., Peñalver, MJ. (2014). Pathology of building materials in historic buildings. Relationship between laboratory testing and infrared thermography. *Materiales de Construcción* 64 (313), 009. Doi:10.3989/mc.2013.06612.

Llewellyn, N. (1998). 'Hungry and desperate for knowledge': Diego de Sagredo's Spanish point of view. Paper Palaces: *The Rise of the Renaissance Architectural Treatise.* New Haven, CT: Yale University Press, c1998.

Llopis Verdú, J. (2002). Gaspar Gregori y la introducción de la metodología proyectual renacentista en Valencia. [Gaspar Gregori and the introduction of Renaissance project methodology in Valencia.] *Revista EGA* nº 7.

Llopis Verdú, J., Torres Barrachino, A. M. (2011). Tratadística e imagen arquitectónica en el siglo XVI en Valencia. [Tratadistics and architectural image in the 16th century in Valencia.] *EGA* Vol. 16, No. 18.

Marias, F. (1986). *La Arquitectura del Renacimiento en Toledo* [The Renaissance Architecture in Toledo] *(1541-1631).* Instituto Provincial de investigaciones y estudios toledanos. Toledo.

Marias, F. (1979). El problema del arquitecto en la España del siglo XVI. [The problem of the architect in sixteenth-century Spain.] Academia, nº 48.

Marias, F., Bustamante, A. (1986). *El Escorial y la cultura arquitectónica de su tiempo.* [El Escorial and the architectural culture of its time.] El Escorial en la Biblioteca Nacional. Madrid.

Marias, F., Pereda, F. (2000). *Medidas del Romano, Diego de Sagredo*, [Measures of the Roman, Diego de Sagredo] Toledo 1526, Toledo.

Navarro Fajardo, J. C. (2003). Las trazas de la catedral de Valencia. Hipótesis de su ichnographia [The traces of the cathedral of Valencia. Hypothesis of his ichnographia], *Journal EGA,* 8.

Navarro Fajardo, J. C. (2008). Mestres. lapicidas v obrers de vila en el antiguo Reino de Valencia. Artífices de la arquitectura gótica. [Mestres lapicidas v obrers de vila in the ancient Kingdom of Valencia. Artisans of Gothic architecture.] *Journal EGA,* 13.

Sanchis Sivera, J. (1933). Arquitectos y escultores de la Catedral de Valencia, [Architects and sculptors of the Cathedral of Valencia] *Valencian Art Archive*, Valencia.

Sanchis Sivera, J. (1925). Maestros de obras y lápidas valencianos en la Edad Media. [Masters of Valencian works and tombstones in the Middle Ages.] *Archive of Valencian Art*, 11, Valencia.

Zaragozá Catalán, A. (2007). *Catálogo de la exposición Pere Compte y Matteo Carnilivari, dos maestros del gótico mediterráneo* [Catalog of the exhibition Pere Compte and Matteo Carnilivari, two masters of the Mediterranean Gothic]. Valencia.

In: Modeling Social Behavior and Its Applications
Editors: L. A. Jódar Sánchez et al.

ISBN: 978-1-53613-666-1
© 2018 Nova Science Publishers, Inc.

Chapter 18

CONTROLLING THE DYNAMIC IMPACT OF HUMANS IN ARCHAEOLOGICAL SITES FOR PREVENTIVE CONSERVATION

Paloma Merello Giménez [1],, Fernando J. García-Diego[2]
and Claudia Scatigno[3]*
[1]Department of Accounting, University of Valencia, Valencia, Spain
[2]Department of Applied Physics, Universitat Politècnica de València, Valencia, Spain
[3]Department of Physics, University of Rome "Tor Vergata," Rome, Italy

ABSTRACT

Preventive conservation of an archaeological site is based on the control of the microclimatic conditions to prevent damage to the cultural heritage before it occurs and minimize the cost of future interventions. The upset of the thermo-hygrometric equilibrium is one of the main causes of deterioration. The monitoring of thermo-hygrometric conditions of Casa di Diana (Ostia Antica, Italy) is carried out using a system of temperature and relative humidity sensors with high frequency of monitoring. As an innovation, the human impact (visitors) on the thermal balance is evaluated using non-parametric tests on the residuals of a regression model, controlling the effect of the outdoors climate and its annual dynamic. In addition, this is a dynamic study since the effect of the visits is tested over time. The results show a significant effect of a tourist visit on the hourly variation of temperature and a possible thermal drift of up to 2 hours. The relative humidity is constant and close to saturation; therefore, its analysis is discarded as no effect of the visits on the upset of the hygrometric balance is expected.

* Corresponding Author address: Email: paloma.merello@uv.es.

Keywords: human impact, temperature, relative humidity, thermo-hygrometric balance, continuous monitoring, preventive conservation; tourist visits

INTRODUCTION

Preventive conservation of a cultural or archaeological site is understood as the whole control process of the deterioration factors. The aim of preventive conservation is to prevent damage to the cultural heritage (CH) and minimize future interventions (Camuffo, D., 2013). In this vein, preventive conservation has an important impact reducing the cost of the future conservation measures (Kontozova-Deutsch et al, 2011).

Thermo-hygrometric parameters affect chemical reactions and appear as some of the most influential factors on the conservation of a CH site (Fernández-Navajas et al., 2013).

Microclimatic monitoring studies have been conducted in different closed and open CH sites, such as churches (Camuffo et al., 2002; Corgnati, S.P. & Filippi, M., 2006; Legnér, M., 2011), museums (Camuffo, D., Sturaro, G. & Valentino, A., 1999; Tabunschikov, Y. & Brodatch, M., 2004; García-Diego, F.-J. & Zarzo, M., 2010; Zarzo, M., Fernández-Navajas, A. & García-Diego, F.-J., 2011) and archaeological sites (Maekawa, S., Lambert, F. & Meyer, J., 1995; Merello, P., García-Diego, F.-J. & Zarzo, M., 2012; Scatigno et al., 2016; Scatigno et al., 2016).

CH has survived for many centuries in conditions that must be considered risky but stable (equilibrium). Abrupt changes of microclimate parameters interrupting these equilibrium conditions induce damage to the materials until a new equilibrium is reached (Visco, et al., 2017).

The visits to an archaeological site may cause large deviations from the usual conditions (Camuffo et al., 2001) as humans can alter with their presence or behavior the aforementioned parameters, affecting the conservation. In the past, most of the microclimates have been planned only for the well-being of visitors disregarding that conservation requires a constant climate (Camuffo et al., 2001). An interesting debate between the prevalence of preventive conservation and human comfort arose and, hopefully, in recent decades the conservation of the heritage site has been prioritized.

In the literature, many authors have studied the impact of visitors in tourist sites with protection interest such as Geoparks and other geological sites (Walpole, M. J., Goodwin, H. J., & Ward, K. G., 2001; Wang et al., 2010; Guo, W., & Chung, S., 2017; Buckley, R., Zhong, L., & Ma, X., 2017), museums (Camuffo et al., 2001) and cultural and archaeological sites (García-Hernández, M., de la Calle-Vaquero & M., Yubero, C., 2017; Visco et al., 2017; Sanchez-Moral et al., 2005; Scatigno et al., 2016).

The *Casa di Diana,* Region I, Insula III, is a Roman building (130 CE) located in Ostia Antica, at 23 km from the center of Rome. The building, comprised of *tabernae* and *cenacula*, presents a particular microclimate, especially in two inter-communicating rooms (*Mithraeum* and *pre-Mithraeum*). The principal building materials are brick and pozzolanic mortar aligned with *opus caementicium* technique (Scatigno, C., et al., 2016; Scatigno, C., et al., 2017). The two rooms are characterized by different heights due to the presence at the sides of *podium* (Scatigno et al., 2016). The ventilation is natural and comes from several openings (no artificial ventilation systems are installed). The rooms are covered and protected against the rain by a roof, but small areas are directly exposed to sunlight and air due to the openings (Scatigno et al., 2016). The microclimate of *Casa di Diana* is similar to a *hypogeum*, despite being structurally comparable to a semi-confined environment (Scatigno et al., 2016; Scatigno et al., 2016).

Furthermore, guided tours with booking take place in *Casa di Diana* one or two days a week, normally at 10:30 a.m., with a mean duration of 30 minutes (only 10 minutes in the *Mithraeum's rooms*).

Hypogea environments are characterized by a great stability (constant humidity and temperature) (Scatigno et al., 2016) and the abundance of nutrients providing a suitable niche for phototrophic microorganisms when combined with artificial illumination (Sanchez-Moral et al., 2005; Scatigno et al., 2016). In *hypogea* environments, visitors can be considered as a possible upset of the equilibrium conditions.

The aim of this paper is to determine the impact of the touristic visits in the microclimate balance of *Casa de Diana*; as well as determine the dynamic effect of this impact until a new balance is reached. As far as we know, this is the first time that a dynamic quantitative study is carried out with the aim of determining the influence of visitors on the upset of the thermo-hygrometric equilibrium in an archaeological site.

The paper is organized as follows. The first section deals with the introduction. The second section presents the monitoring system and the sample. Section three deals with the characterization of *Casa de Diana* and some statistical analyses. Finally, the main conclusions are presented.

MATERIAL AND METHODS

Monitoring System

The monitoring system consist of probes that contain a temperature (T) and a relative humidity (RH) sensor. Each probe contains an 8-pin small-outline integrated circuit (SOIC), model DS2438 (Maxim Integrated Products, Inc., Sunnyvale, CA, USA) that incorporates a temperature sensor with an accuracy of $\pm$ 2 °C, as well as an analogue-to-digital voltage converter which measures the output voltage of a relative humidity sensor (HIH-4000, Honeywell International, Inc., Minneapolis, MN, USA).

The RH sensors, with an accuracy of $\pm$ 3.5%, were calibrated in the laboratory with a saturated solution of salt (García-Diego, F. J., & Zarzo, M., 2010; Merello, P., García-

Diego, F. J., & Zarzo, M., 2012). The T and RH sensors have high repeatability between measures (García-Diego, F. J., & Zarzo, M., 2010; Merello, P., García-Diego, F. J., & Zarzo, M., 2012).

Three electric wires come out from each probe; one wire for + 5 V DC power supply, one for ground and another for data transfer. As specified by the manufacturer, the output voltage of a HIH-4000 sensor is proportional to voltage supply. The exact value of the voltage supply was measured for each RH sensor once the system was installed. The calibration curves of each sensor were applied.

Sensors were connected in parallel to a microcontroller recording the measurements in digital. Recorded data were downloaded to a pen drive and stored in Burrito software (Fernández-Navajas et al., 2013).

A total of 29 probes were installed, 28 inside the *Mithraeum* and *pre-Mithraeum* of *Casa di Diana,* and an additional one on the sill of a window as control of the outdoors climate (Figure 1).

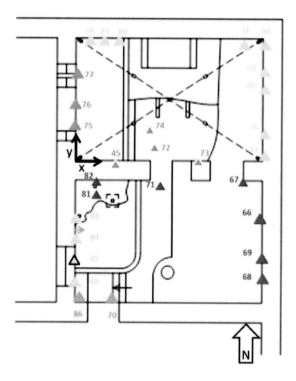

Figure 1. Sensors location (numbered triangles).

The location of each sensor (coordinates yz) is given in Table 1. Coordinate y indicates the vertical distance to the pedestrian level; coordinate z indicates the distance to the wall surface for two sensors (#72, #73). The other sensors are placed along the wall.

Table 1. Sensors description and coordinated allocation

	Sensors N.	y (cm)	z (cm)	Reference system	Sensors N.	y (cm)	z (cm)
blue	45	102	0	green	70	217	0
	72	0	94		86	136	0
	73	80	116	yellow	83	90	0
	74	140	0		84	120	0
pink	46	192	0		85	204	0
	47	89	0		88	169	0
	48	142	0	red	66	70	0
	49	304	0		68	154	0
fuchsia	75	163	0		69	280	0
	76	302	0	violet	67	164	0
	77	93	0		71	106	0
azure	50	146	0		81	-12	0
	51	201	0		82	80	0
	78	139	0				
	79	148	0				
	80	197	0				

The Data Set

The monitoring campaign was started on 29th June 2014 and finished on 21st May 2015. The records of March were completely missing. In order to avoid possible abnormal measurements, data after 31st January 2015 were discarded for the analyses.

The system records data with a frequency of 60 data points per hour (1 data point per minute). In this study, we have a data base of 15,451,200 data, organized in a data matrix of 266,400 rows (185 days × 24 h × 60 min) and 58 columns (29 sensors T + 29 sensors RH). Note that, data of August 2014 was disregarded due to the data of outdoors sensor (#85) was missing. On the other hand, sensor RH #77 was completely discarded due to instrument anomalies during the entire campaign. For some analyses, the hourly average was calculated obtaining a sample of 257,520 observations (4,440 rows x 58 columns).

RESULTS AND DISCUSSION

Exploratory Analysis of Thermo-Hygrometric Conditions

Balance is understood as the stability of microclimatic conditions. The deviations from the balance conditions may cause deterioration (Visco et al., 2017). The hourly variations of the thermo-hygrometric parameters can be considered as a proxy of the upset of the microclimatic equilibrium. Thus, our approach is based on analyzing data with substantial hourly variation non attributable, in principle, to the architectural characteristics of the site.

Principal Component Analyses (PCA) are performed on the original data in order to characterize the archaeological site. The dataset was previously auto-scaled and models with two principal components are selected. The components explain 100% of the total variance of T (Figure 2a) and 89% of the total variance of RH (Figure 2b).

In our approach, the aim is selecting data not heavily influenced by the architectural characteristics of the site. Regarding temperature (Figure 2a), a group of 8 sensors (#68, #81- #88) that were situated between the south-west *pre-Mithraeum* wall and the north *pre-Mithraeum* wall (Figure 1 – yellow and orange triangles) were discarded for the future analyses. These sensors present a very variable behavior, different from the rest of the sensors, as a result of their location in a more ventilated area (near a window and the main entrance). All other sensors (#45- #80) have a similar behavior and will be considered in our analyses.

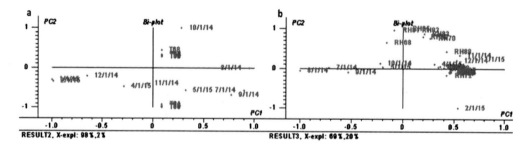

Figure 2. PCA Bi-plot (Scores-Loadings). a) Temperature PC1-PC2; b) Relative Humidity PC1-PC2.

Regarding RH (Figure 2b), the exploratory analyses have shown that *Casa di Diana* has a stable RH. The largest variations occur in temperature and during autumn-winter, when RH is close to saturation (97-99%).

According to the characterization, the hourly variation (HV) of temperature is selected as variable of interest for the forthcoming analyses.

In order to understand the thermo-hygrometric behavior during the year, Box & Whisker plots of the HV of temperature are represented per months (Figure 3). The months from October to January are selected for the subsequent analyses as they present the largest HV.

Note that, a priori we were interested in selecting a set of sensors with similar temperature avoiding that the differences between them are attributable to their positioning. However, in the case of HV, we are interested in selecting the months with larger hourly variability in order to easily detect significant differences attributable to tourist visits.

ASSESSING THE DYNAMIC IMPACT OF VISITS IN THE THERMAL BALANCE

As aforementioned, the hourly variation (HV) of temperature is selected as variable of interest. It is intended to observe variations in the temperature that, in principle, are not derived from the architectural characteristics of the site; therefore, data of sensors #45-#80, excluding sensor #68, are considered. We remove from the sample these observations with missing data for the outdoors sensor (#85). In addition, the RH data is disregarded since it is almost constant during the whole monitoring campaign and no effect of visits could be detected.

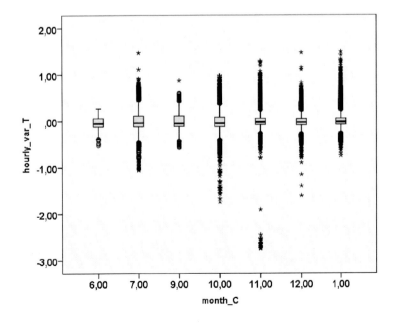

Figure 3. Box & Whisker plots of HV of temperature per months.

Significant correlation (r-Pearson = 0.423, p-value = 0.000) between the HV of the inner sensors and the HV of the outdoors sensor is found. In order to control the hourly variation attributable to specific climate conditions of a day or a year, a multiple linear regression analysis is performed considering as dependent variable *HV of temperature* and as independent variables *HV_85* (outdoors), the *months* (dummy variables, taking January as reference) and their interactions. The subsequent analyses are performed on the regression residuals. The stepwise regression model has a R^2 of 55.4%. The model is significant with p-value < 0.001 and the coefficients of the significant variables appear in Table 2.

Table 2. Estimated coefficients of the independent variables
(first multiple linear regression model)

parameter	coefficient	sig.	parameter	coefficient	sig.
var_85	0.596	0.000	Var85*OCT	-0.538	0.000
October	-0.012	0.000	Var85*NOV	0.091	0.000
December	-0.004	0.002			

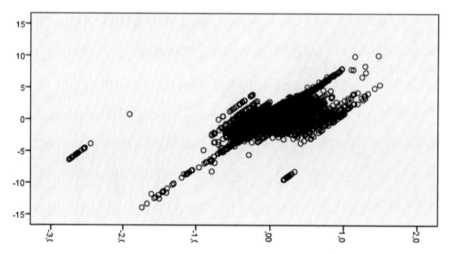

Figure 4. Scatter plot of the standardized residuals (vertical axis) according to the dependent variable (horizontal axis).

The residuals do not follow a normal distribution. In order to determine the significant effect of the visits on the HV of temperature, non-parametric tests are applied.

The 6 categories of the categorical variable *visit* are considered independent samples and analyses of Kruskal-Wallis are performed. Variable *visit* takes the following values; value 0 when there is no visit that day and time, value 1 when there is a visit that day and time, value 2 when there has been a visit 1 hour before, value 3 when there has been a visit 2 hours before, value 4 when there has been a visit 3 hours before and value 5 when there has been a visit 4 hours before.

Table 3. Ranges and number of observations (Kruskal-Wallis test)

	visit	N	Average Range
	0	44520	22736.35
	1	315	32657.12
	2	315	35435.47
Residuals	3	315	35391.53
	4	315	27166.15
	5	315	28636.51
	Total	46095	

Table 4. Table of frequencies (Test of the median)

		Visit					
		0	1	2	3	4	5
Residuals	> Median	21949	222	247	252	189	188
	<= Median	22571	93	68	63	126	127
	> Median	49.30%	70.50%	78.40%	80.00%	60.00%	59.70%
	<= Median	50.70%	29.50%	21.60%	20.00%	40.00%	40.30%

Kruskal-Wallis test allows us to decide if the hypothesis that the 6 independent samples come from the same population (or from identical populations with the same median) can be accepted. Our variable satisfies the necessary assumptions of being continuous and measured on an ordinal scale.

Table 3 shows the number of cases and the average ranges for the 6 categories. The average ranges are obtained dividing the sum of the ranks of each category by the number of cases in the category.

The null hypothesis of the test is rejected (P-value < 0.001); therefore, significant differences are found in the residuals between the categories of the variable *visit* (Chi-square = 818.454).

The test of the median is also significant (P-value < 0.001). The table of frequencies (Table 4) shows that 70.5%, 78.4% and 80% of the residuals take values higher than the median when the variable *visit* = 1,2,3, respectively.

Paired U Mann-Whitney tests are performed to determine the differences between categories of the variable *visit*. Bonferroni modification of the level of significance (0.05/3 = 0.017) is applied. Table 5 deals with the results of the tests.

Under the alternative hypothesis of the test, the values of one sample tend to exceed the values of the other. In our case, the null hypothesis is accepted (both groups follow the same distribution) only when comparing the samples for *visit* = 1 and *visit* = 4, *visit* = 1 and *visit* = 5, and *visit* = 4 and *visit* = 5.

P. Merello Giménez, F. J. García-Diego and C. Scatigno

Table 5. Results of Paired U Mann-Whitney tests. The asymptotic significance appears between brackets. Legend: R means residuals, HVi is the HV of temperature of the inner sensors, HVo is the HV of temperature of the outdoors sensor

	VISIT					
VISIT	0	1	2	3	4	5
0		2865043.50	1245501.50	955337.50	3077876.00	
		(0.000)	(0.000)	(0.000)	(0.000)	
1			30778.00	23798.00	49590.50	48747.50
			(0.000)	(0.000)	(0.992)	(0.705)
2				42136.50	30609.00	26184.00
				(0.001)	(0.000)	(0.000)
3					20888.00	12722.00
					(0.000)	(0.000)
4						49176.00
						(0.848)
MEDIAN (R)	0.003	0.100	0.118	0.110	0.022	0.024
AVERAGE (R)	-0.001	0.135	0.179	0.143	0.034	0.044
MEDIAN (HVi)	-0.019	0.129	0.259	0.300	0.140	0.149
AVERAGE (HVi)	-0.007	0.161	0.280	0.318	0.152	0.132
MEDIAN (HVo)	-0.049	0.110	0.349	0.420	0.230	0.259
AVERAGE (HVo)	-0.009	0.163	0.381	0.451	0.311	0.236

Note that when a residual is positive and different from zero, this implies that HV of temperature is not explained by the climatic conditions of the day and month, and it may be attributable to the visits and/or other variables not considered (solar radiation or ventilation).

Regarding results in Table 5, the median of the residuals presents substantially higher values for *visit* = 1, 2, 3, which coincides with the median test (Table 4). It seems that there is a thermal drift of up to 2 hours due to the effect of visitors. However, the median of the residuals is similar for *visit* = 4, 5. Therefore, we may discard an effect of visitors on the upset of the thermal balance 3 and 4 hours after the visit takes place.

Conclusion

The literature supports the idea that the main cause of damage of the CH is the upset of the microclimatic balance. For the first time, the effect of tourist visits on the upset of the microclimatic equilibrium is assessed, as well as its dynamic behavior.

Casa di Diana has constant hygrometric conditions close to saturation during the monitoring campaign; therefore, relative humidity data are discarded for the analyses since they are not affected by the tourist visits.

Prior exploratory analyses allowed selecting sensors with a similar pattern of temperature in order to avoid differences between sensors attributable to their positioning. Regarding the hourly variation of temperature, we select the months with larger variability (from October to January) in the interest of easily detecting significant differences attributable to tourist visits.

As an innovation, the human impact on the thermal balance is evaluated using non-parametric tests on the residuals of a regression model, avoiding confusion effects with the outdoors climate and its annual dynamics.

The results reveal a significant effect of the tourist visits on the hourly variation of temperature. In addition, a thermal drift of up to 2 hours is detected and, in principle, we may discard an effect 3 and 4 hours after the visit takes place. These results are useful for planning future monitoring campaigns as well as for the design of preventive conservation measures.

Acknowledgments

The authors would like to thank the staff of the archaeological area of Ostia Antica. This work is partially supported by the projects HAR2013-47895-C2-1-P and HAR2013-47895-C2-2-P from MINECO.

References

Arnold, A., & Zehnder, K. (1991). Monitoring wall paintings affected by soluble salts. *The conservation of wall paintings*, *1*, 103-35.

Buckley, R., Zhong, L., & Ma, X. (2017). Visitors to protected areas in China. *Biological Conservation*, *209*, 83-88.

Camuffo, D. (2013). *Microclimate for cultural heritage: conservation, restoration, and maintenance of indoor and outdoor monuments*. Elsevier.

Camuffo, D., Bernardi, A., Sturaro, G., & Valentino, A. (2002). The microclimate inside the Pollaiolo and Botticelli rooms in the Uffizi Gallery, Florence. *Journal of Cultural Heritage*, *3*(2), 155-161.

Camuffo, D., Sturaro, G., & Valentino, A. (1999). Thermodynamic exchanges between the external boundary layer and the indoor microclimate at the Basilica of Santa Maria Maggiore, Rome, Italy: the problem of conservation of ancient works of art. *Boundary-Layer Meteorology*, *92*(2), 243-262.

Camuffo, D., Van Grieken, R., Busse, H. J., Sturaro, G., Valentino, A., Bernardi, A., Shooter, D., Gysels, K., Deutsch, F., Wieser, M., Kim, O. & Ulrych, U., (2001). Environmental monitoring in four European museums. *Atmospheric Environment*, *35*, S127-S140.

Cardarelli E., De Donno G., Oliveti I. & Scatigno C. (2018). Three-dimensional reconstruction of a masonry building through electrical and seismic tomography validated by biological analyses. *Near Surface Geophysics*, 16(1).

Corgnati, S. P., & Filippi, M. (2010). Assessment of thermo-hygrometric quality in museums: Method and in-field application to the "Duccio di Buoninsegna" exhibition at Santa Maria della Scala (Siena, Italy). *Journal of Cultural Heritage*, *11*(3), 345-349.

Fernández-Navajas, Á., Merello, P., Beltrán, P., & García-Diego, F. J. (2013). Multivariate thermo-hygrometric characterisation of the archaeological site of plaza de l'Almoina (Valencia, Spain) for preventive conservation. *Sensors*, *13*(8), 9729-9746.

García-Diego, F. J., & Zarzo, M. (2010). Microclimate monitoring by multivariate statistical control: The renaissance frescoes of the Cathedral of Valencia (Spain). *Journal of Cultural Heritage*, *11*(3), 339-344.

García-Hernández, M., de la Calle-Vaquero & M., Yubero, C. (2017). Cultural heritage and urban tourism: Historic city centres under pressure. *Sustainability*, *9*(8), 1346.

Guo, W., & Chung, S. (2017). Using Tourism Carrying Capacity to Strengthen UNESCO Global Geopark Management in Hong Kong. *Geoheritage*, 1-13.

Honeywell. HIH-4000 *Series Integrated Circuit Humidity Sensor Datasheet*. Available online: http://www.farnell.com/datasheets/ 1685535.pdf (accessed on 15 December 2017).

Kontozova-Deutsch, V., Cardell, C., Urosevic, M., Ruiz-Agudo, E., Deutsch, F., & Van Grieken, R. (2011). Characterization of indoor and outdoor atmospheric pollutants impacting architectural monuments: the case of San Jerónimo Monastery (Granada, Spain). *Environmental Earth Sciences*, *63*(7-8), 1433-1445.

La Gennusa, M., Rizzo, G., Scaccianoce, G., & Nicoletti, F. (2005). Control of indoor environments in heritage buildings: experimental measurements in an old Italian museum and proposal of a methodology. *Journal of Cultural Heritage*, *6*(2), 147-155.

Legnér, M. (2011). On the Early History of Museum Environment Control-Nationalmuseum and Gripsholm Castle in Sweden, c. 1866-1932. *Studies in Conservation*, *56*(2), 125-137.

Maekawa, S., Lambert, F., & Meyer, J. (1995). Environmental monitoring at Tiwanaku. *MRS Online Proceedings Library Archive*, *352*, 885–892.

Maxim Integrated Products. *DS2438 Smart Battery Monitor Datasheet*. Available online: https://datasheets.maximintegrated.com/en/ds/ DS2438.pdf (accessed on 15 December 2017).

Merello, P., García-Diego, F. J., & Zarzo, M. (2012). Microclimate monitoring of Ariadne's house (Pompeii, Italy) for preventive conservation of fresco paintings. *Chemistry Central Journal*, *6*(1), 145.

Sanchez-Moral, S., Luque, L., Cuezva, S., Soler, V., Benavente, D., Laiz, L., Gonzalez, J. M., & Saiz-Jimenez, C. (2005). Deterioration of building materials in Roman catacombs: the influence of visitors. *Science of the Total Environment*, *349*(1), 260-276.

Scatigno, C., Gaudenzi, S., Sammartino, M. P., & Visco, G. (2016). A microclimate study on hypogea environments of ancient roman building. *Science of the Total Environment*, *566*, 298-305.

Scatigno, C., Moricca, C., Tortolini, C., & Favero, G. (2016). The influence of environmental parameters in the biocolonization of the Mithraeum in the roman masonry of casa di Diana (Ostia Antica, Italy). *Environmental Science and Pollution Research*, *23*(13), 13403-13412.

Scatigno, C., Prieto-Taboada, N., Martinez, M. P., Conte, A. M., García-Diego, F. J., & Madariaga, J. M. (2016). Analitycal techniques for the characterisation of historical building materials: case study "Casa di Diana" Mithraeum (Archeological site in Ostia Antica, Italy). *Advances in Materials Science Research*, 31.

Scatigno, C., Prieto-Taboada, N., García-Florentino, C., Fdez-Ortiz de Vallejuelo, S., Maguregui, M. & Madariaga, J. M. (2017). Combination of in situ specyroscopy and chemometric techniques to discriminate different types of Roman bricks and the influence of microclimate environment. *Environmental Science and Pollution Research*.

Tabunschikov, Y., & Brodatch, M. (2004). Indoor air climate requirements for Russian churches and cathedrals. *Indoor Air*, *14*(s7), 168-174.

Visco, G., Plattner, S. H., Fortini, P., & Sammartino, M. (2017). A multivariate approach for a comparison of big data matrices. Case study: thermo-hygrometric monitoring inside the Carcer Tullianum (Rome) in the absence and in the presence of visitors. *Environmental Science and Pollution Research*, 1-15.

Walpole, M. J., Goodwin, H. J., & Ward, K. G. (2001). Pricing policy for tourism in protected areas: lessons from Komodo National Park, Indonesia. *Conservation Biology*, *15*(1), 218-227.

Wang, W., Ma, Y., Ma, X., Wu, F., Ma, X., An, L., & Feng, H. (2010). Seasonal variations of airborne bacteria in the Mogao Grottoes, Dunhuang, China. *International Biodeterioration & Biodegradation, 64*(4), 309-315.

Zarzo, M., Fernández-Navajas, A., & García-Diego, F. J. (2011). Long-term monitoring of fresco paintings in the Cathedral of Valencia (Spain) through humidity and temperature sensors in various locations for preventive conservation. *Sensors, 11*(9), 8685-8710.

In: Modeling Social Behavior and Its Applications   ISBN: 978-1-53613-666-1
Editors: L. A. Jódar Sánchez et al.   © 2018 Nova Science Publishers, Inc.

Chapter 19

AUTOMATIC PREDICTION OF THE COMMERCIAL QUALITY OF SLATE SLABS USING A MATHEMATICAL MODEL

Carla Iglesias[1,], Javier Martínez[2], Javier Taboada[1]*
and Eduardo Giráldez[1]
[1]Department of Environmental Engineering. University of Vigo, Spain
[2]Centro Universitario de la Defensa de Marín. Marín, Pontevedra, Spain

ABSTRACT

Slate is a natural material whose impermeability, fissibility and resistance to weathering makes it a valuable natural resource for construction purposes. As a natural geological material, it may be affected by certain singularities that alter its mechanical and aesthetic properties. These singularities have traditionally been assessed manually by an expert, who classifies each slate according to predefined commercial grades.

The purpose of our research was to build a model capable of classifying slate slab quality from an analysis of imaging data captured by a computer vision system. A sample of 70 slabs was used whose commercial quality was graded by 2 human experts. The computer vision system acquired the range, grayscale and RGB image data for each slab, then applied algorithms to obtain a vector of characteristics. These characteristics were used to predict quality, whether primary or secondary commercial quality (grade 1 or 2) or reject quality (grade 3).

This classification problem was tackled using decision trees, multilayer perceptron neural networks and support vector machines. The best results were obtained using the decision trees, whereas the other 2 techniques proved incapable of reproducing classification criteria. This fact points to the linear separability of the classes in this classification problem.

---

[*] Corresponding author: carlaiglesias@uvigo.es.

Keywords: decision trees, multilayer perceptron, support vector machines, slate quality classification

INTRODUCTION

Natural resources, exploited through mining techniques, play a fundamental role in modern society in providing basic raw materials to the industrial sector. Slate is a natural material that has traditionally been used in construction, given that it is highly resistant to degradation due to weathering, is impermeable and has low thermal conductivity. These characteristics make it particularly suitable for roofing.

For ornamental rock like slate, as happens with other industrial materials such as wood, ceramics, textiles and ornamental rocks (granite, marble and slate), physical appearance (aesthetic value) is a key factor in saleability terms. This property has traditionally been evaluated visually by human experts, although in recent years attempts have been made to objectively quantify properties so that a human expert can assign a certain quality or grade to the material.

In the case of slate, although slabs have traditionally been produced manually, most stages in the slab-making process are nowadays automated, with plants using machinery to reduce the amount of manual labour involved. One of the final stages in the slate slab production process is inspection and classification of slate slabs according to commercial grades, a task that continues to be done manually, given the lack of automated systems. Thus, human experts analyse each slab visually, determine if it is suitable for commercialization and assign it a grade.

This human visual analysis of the physical appearance of slate is a tedious task that is highly subjective and so not generally replicable. In a globally competitive global marketplace, reliable and effective product quality evaluation and control is key to maintaining high standards and ensuring the success of a company. Automatic classification based on computer vision (and artificial intelligence) techniques — combining software and hardware tools in order to obtain, process and analyse information obtained by digital cameras — are thus beginning to be used in various industrial sectors as a means to ensuring higher quality standards, better reproducibility and more standard products [1, 2].

Computer vision systems analyse images of a material in order to characterize its physical appearance, taking into account factors pertinent to each specific material or application. There are many applications of this kind of computer vision systems in the industry, including inspection and classification systems applied to natural resources. Various automatic systems have been developed in recent years to inspect the colour, texture and natural defects of wood [3, 4]. Automatic classification systems have also been developed for ceramic products, aimed at evaluating defects in the final product and defining commercial categories [5, 6]. As for ornamental rocks, a number of studies have developed vision systems for application to marble [7, 8] and granite [9-11].

With regard to slate, few studies to date deal with the classification of natural slate slabs using computer vision systems.

The aim of this study was to construct an automatic slate slab classification model — suitable for an industrial setting — that is robust in performance and improves on previous prototypes in terms of its portability and ability to analyse defects. This automatic classification system, based on combining computer vision techniques and artificial intelligence algorithms, analyses images of slate slabs and extracts useful information that enable commercial grades to be assigned. This research builds on a previously developed prototype [12] that captures images of the slate slabs using a different vision system (without colour information) and applies a directed acyclic graph-support vector machine (DAG-SVM) algorithm — a multiclassification algorithm based on SVM binary classifiers with a one-versus-all approach that was presented at a Mathematical Modelling in Engineering and Human Behaviour conference in 2013(Valencia, Spain). Essentially, a set of slabs is first examined by 2 human experts, who inspect defects and, applying their own criteria, assign slabs a grade. Images are then taken of the slabs and analysed with a computer vision system, resulting in a vector of slab characteristics.

In this research we constructed a classification model for slabs that was fed with the resulting characteristic vector and then analysed using the following supervised automatic learning techniques: decision trees, artificial neural networks and support vector machines.

METHODOLOGY

Computer Vision System

Our automatic grading system for slate slabs is depicted in Figure 1. The laboratory prototype simulates a slate slab production line that transports slabs on roller belts. The belt moves the slab to a position illuminated with white LED and laser lighting located under a SICK ColorRanger E50 camera. When the photocells detect the slab the vision system captures information on monochrome and colour (RGB) components, scatter and 3D range.

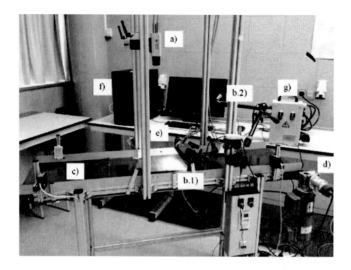

Figure 1. Laboratory prototype of the automatic slate slab classification system. The automated inspection system consists of the following elements:

(a) Camera: SICK ColorRanger E50.

(b) Illumination: (b.1) CCS white LED barlight that provides direct illumination for colour and monochrome image acquisition, and (b.2) laser to provide structured light in a 1-line pattern in order to gather 3D information through laser triangulation.

(c) Conveyor belt to transport the slabs to the vision system setup.

(d) Encoder connected to both the conveyor belt and the camera to ensure that object proportions are not influenced by changes in conveyor speed.

(e) Photoswitches connected to the camera to act as an enabling signal.

(f) Software to process the data captured by the camera.

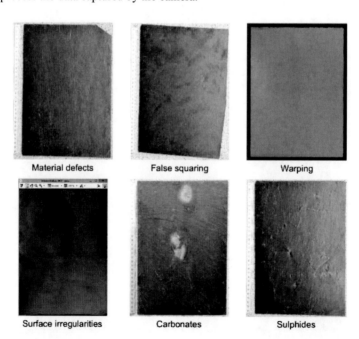

Figure 2. Slate defects.

Table 1. Details of variables defined for each kind of slab singularity

Singularity	Variable	Units	Description
Material defects	RatiosMD*$\in \mathbb{R}^4$	Dimensionless	Ratio between real and theoretical areas
	$(+)$RectangMD*$\in \mathbb{R}^4$	Dimensionless	Rectangularity factor
False squaring	AngleFE$\in \mathbb{R}^4$	Degree	Corner angle divergence from 90°
	$(+)$RectangFE*	Dimensionless	Rectangularity factor
Warping	AngleW$\in \mathbb{R}^{10}$	Pixel intensity	Difference between corner mean range values and centre mean range values
Surface defects	DevS	Pixel intensity	Deviation in pixel values
	NumEdges*$\in \mathbb{R}^4$	Dimensionless	Number of edges
	MaxAmplEdg*$\in \mathbb{R}^4$	Pixel intensity	Maximum amplitude of edges
	MeanAmplEdg*$\in \mathbb{R}^4$	Pixel intensity	Mean amplitude of edges
	VarAmplEdg*$\in \mathbb{R}^4$	Pixel intensity	Variance in amplitude of edges
	$(+)$MeanDistEdg*$\in \mathbb{R}^4$	Pixel	Mean distance between edges
Carbonates	MAreaCBW**$\in \mathbb{R}^3$	$Pixel^2$	Mean area of regions of interest (greyscale image)
	MCircCBW**$\in \mathbb{R}^3$	Dimensionless	Mean circularity of regions of interest (greyscale image)
Singularity	Variable	Units	Description
	$(+)$MRoundCBW**$\in \mathbb{R}^3$	Dimensionless	Mean roundness of regions of interest (greyscale image)
	MAreaCRGB**$\in \mathbb{R}^3$	$Pixel^2$	Mean area of regions of interest (colour image)
	MCircCRGB**$\in \mathbb{R}^3$	Dimensionless	Mean circularity of regions of interest (colour image)
	$(+)$MRoundCRGB**$\in \mathbb{R}^3$	Dimensionless	Mean roundness of regions of interest (colour image)
Sulphides	MAreaS**$\in \mathbb{R}^3$	$Pixel^2$	Mean area of regions of interest (colour image)
	MCircS**$\in \mathbb{R}^3$	Dimensionless	Mean circularity of regions of interest (colour image)
	$(+)$MRoundS**$\in \mathbb{R}^3$	Dimensionless	Mean roundness of regions of interest (colour image)

This information is uploaded to a computer for analysis using vision software. The captured images of the slate slabs are pre-processed and then analysed for the presence of 6 kinds of defects (Table 1). The aesthetic and dimensional defects evaluated are those determined by the UNE-EN 12326-1: 2015 standard, which establishes requirements for roofing slate slabs. Based on these requirements and the characteristics of the variety of slate studied, the presence of the following individual petrological and tectonic defects is considered: carbonates (or flowerlike staining), sulphides and various kinds of surface defects (kink-bands, knots, flakiness, etc). Since the final geometry of the slabs must also be checked before being commercialized, so material defects, false squaring and warping are also considered (Figure 2).

The outcome of slab images evaluated using the codes developed for the vision software is a vector of characteristics consisting of 71 variables: 53 basic variables, denoted vi; and 18 auxiliary variables, denoted wi (Table 1).

The results obtained are used to assign a commercial grade to each slate slab according to the particular characteristics of the slab and the requirements of a particular market. Expert judgement is therefore required to distinguish between grade 1 (no defects), grade 2 (only aesthetic defects) and reject grade 3 (defects that render the slate unsuitable for sale). The expert criteria are simulated by mathematical techniques, as will be explained below.

Sample Description

The sample was composed of 70 slate slabs evaluated by 2 experts (Experts 1 and 2), who evaluated the presence of the 6 defects considered and assigned a commercial grade according to their own criteria.

Table 2. Sampled slate slabs classified by 2 experts according to defects and commercial grade

		Expert 1	Expert 2
Commercial grade	1 (primary)	4	7
	2 (secondary)	6	11
	3 (reject)	60	52
	Total	70	70
Defect	False squaring	1	1
	Warping	1	0
	Material defects	2	5
	Surface irregularities	25	41
	Carbonates	28	24
	Sulphides	20	11

Table 3. Confusion matrix resulting from a comparison of the criteria of the 2 experts

		Grade as per Expert 2			
		1	2	3	
Grade as per Expert 1	1	3	1	0	4
	2	1	4	1	6
	3	3	6	51	60
		7	11	52	70

Table 2 summarizes information regarding the sampled slabs and their defects. Note that, for several of the slabs, the experts identified more than 1 type of defect, and also that the experts, knowledgeable both regarding this material and its market, did not have the same criteria, as is evident from the disparities in their assessments.

The grades assigned by each of the experts were cross-tabulated (Table 3), resulting in 58 coincidences and 12 discrepancies (a 17% error rate). This divergence demonstrates the difficulty of modelling decision criteria, since not even the 2 expert humans could classify the same slab in the same way.

From the confusion matrix, we defined the 3 types of errors that were used to compare the results of the different classification techniques, whether as either of the 2 commercial grades (grades 1 or 2) or as the reject grade (grade 3). Thus, defined as positive is the detection of a defective slab as grade 3, and defined as negative is the detection of a defective slab as grades 1 or 2. The 3 kinds of error, ranging from the most serious to the least serious error, are as follows:

1. A false positive refers to a slab being assigned reject grade 3 when it is, in fact, commercial grade 1 or 2. This is the most serious error, since it involves material that is suitable for sale being discarded, with the consequent economic loss.
2. A false negative refers to a slab being assigned commercial grade 1 or 2 when it is, in fact, a reject grade. This is a less serious error, as avoiding false positives is prioritized over avoiding false negatives in optimizing the classification system.
3. A neutral error refers to a commercial grade slab being assigned the wrong commercial grade. This is the least serious error, as, although a slab is correctly evaluated as having saleable quality, it is graded wrongly (as grade 1 when it should have been 2 or vice versa).

Analysis of the Vector of Characteristics. Principal Component Analysis

In the construction of automatic learning models, a crucial aspect is the definition of input variables so that they are as representative as possible of the data to be modelled. The number of variables is not as important as the information they contribute, as was found elsewhere [13].

After the images of the slabs were evaluated according to the codes, a total of 71 variables (53 basic and 18 auxiliary) were found to characterize the slabs. For the variables to contribute as much information as possible to the automatic learning model, a first step was to eliminate those whose amplitude was zero.

Even so, the number of available variables remained high at 65 variables (49 basic and 16 auxiliary). This posed difficulties in terms of studying the relationships and the probable correlations between variables, as redundant information would result.

To solve this problem, we performed principal component analysis (PCA) on initially defined input sets for both the basic variables and for the full set of basic and auxiliary variables. The input variables were standardized using the z-score to eliminate the effect of different units of measurement and the resulting matrix of correlations was used in the PCA.

Mathematical Techniques

Our problem was a classification problem, since the response was 1 of 3 grades that represent the quality of slate slabs. The codes used were grade 1 for primary commercial quality, grade 2 for secondary commercial quality and grade 3 for reject quality.

The following supervised learning techniques were applied: decision trees, multilayer perceptron (MLP) neural networks and support vector machines (SVMs).

Decision trees, called also classification and regression trees or identification trees, are one of the most widely used supervised learning models, as they have the advantage of being easy to understand and to represent graphically [14]. These models are constructed by top-down induction of decision trees (TDIDT); thus, an input observation x is classified through successive binary decisions throughout the tree, with each node divided into 2 branches on the basis of a decision criterion. Several algorithms can be used, including classical ones such as ID3 [15], C4.5 [16] or, as used here, CART [17]. Also, since these are applied to a classification problem, when measuring the model error, the Gini index and entropy measures can be used to evaluate node diversity.

Artificial neural networks are based on the biological-mathematical analogy between brain neurons and model neurons [18]. The network architecture is characterized by the layered distribution of neurons in an input layer, one or more hidden layers and an output layer. Considering the functional model of the network, we focused on a feed-forward network (each layer is connected only in the forward direction) represented as an acyclic graph with the corresponding activation functions and weights. A particular case of feed-forward neural networks is the multilayer perceptron (MLP), where each node is a perceptron [19] and where a back-propagation algorithm is typically used [20]. This kind of algorithm adjusts the weights of the network during the training process. We used a Gaussian activation function and completed network definition by means of a cross-validation process [21].

Finally, SVMs, based on the concept of the optimum separating hyperplane [22], have, in recent years, attracted growing interest for pattern recognition applications, given their globally optimum nature, prediction capacity, parsimony and flexibility [23]. SVMs are based on binary classifications, so multiclass problems are addressed by constructing binary classifiers and confronting the classes one-against-one or one-versus-all [24, 25]. Separating hyperplanes, however, have 2 major weaknesses: the need for linear separability of the sample and their linear nature. To overcome these weaknesses, we used the kernel trick (which transforms the input space into a large dimension space of characteristics) and the soft margin algorithm (which controls the influence of misclassified observations).

Trained Model Configuration

Using automatic learning techniques, 8 different mathematical models were constructed to simulate expert criteria and to predict commercial grades from the vector of slate characteristics.

The configuration of these models was analysed to ensure not only the most suitable mathematical technique, but also the best input variables. A total of 4 input sets were used, namely Input A, Input B, Input PCA-A and Input PCA-B (Table 1).

Input A was composed of the basic variables and Input B was composed of the complete database (both the basic and auxiliary variables). After eliminating the zero amplitude variables, the inputs were as follows: for Input A, the 53 initial variables reduced to 49, and for Input B, the initial 71 variables reduced to 65.

Further models were constructed with the variables resulting from the PCA study, namely, Input PCA-A resulting from the principal components of the initial set A, and Input PCA-B resulting from the principal components of the initial set B.

Table 4. Configurations of the grade prediction models: inputs and outputs

	Input A	Input B	Input PCA-A	Input PCA-B
Expert 1 criteria	Config. A.1	Config. B.1	Config. PCA-A.1	Config. PCA-B.1
Expert 2 criteria	Config. A.2	Config. B.2	Config. PCA-A.2	Config. PCA-B.2

The model outputs reflect slab grades, with 2 different outputs: grades assigned according to Expert 1 and grades assigned according to Expert 2 criteria. Table 4 shows the configurations of the 8 models.

RESULTS AND DISCUSSION

Principal Component Analysis

Analysis of the principal components of the 49 basic variables revealed the information to be widely distributed among all of them. Analysing the initial variance explained by each principal component, it was observed that although the first 5 explained a larger percentage of variance, they explained just 57% of the total. To explain 80%, it was necessary to take the first 12 components. Finally, taking principal components that explained more than 2% of variance, we found that the first 13 explained 83.3% of the total variance.

Following an analogous procedure, PCA was applied to the full set of basic and auxiliary variables. In this case, the first 8 principal components together explained around 68% of the total variance, while the other components explained percentages below 3%. It was necessary to take the first 17 components explaining more than 1.5% of variance to explain 87.6% of the total variance.

On the basis of those 13 and 17 principal components, we built a new database to train the automatic learning models, obtaining Input PCA-A and Input PCA-B, respectively.

Decision Tree Model Results

Table 5 summarizes the error rates obtained for the 8 models.

Table 5. Error rates and mean absolute error (MAE) rates obtained for the decision tree models implemented with the 8 defined configurations

		Output	
		Expert 1	Expert 2
Input	A	Error rate = 0.057 MAE = 0.100	Error rate = 0.100 MAE = 0.129
	B	Error rate = 0.057 MAE = 0.100	Error rate = 0.100 MAE = 0.129
	PCA-A	Error rate = 0.100 MAE = 0.114	Error rate = 0.086 MAE = 0.114
	PCA-B	Error rate = 0.100 MAE = 0.114	Error rate = 0.086 MAE = 0.100

When simulating Expert 1 criteria, the trees constructed using Input A and Input B were very similar (Model A.1 and Model B.1 in Figure 3), consisting, as they did, of 2 levels and 4 terminal nodes representing the 3 slate slab grades. The most influential variable was local surface defects, established as the first decision criterion.

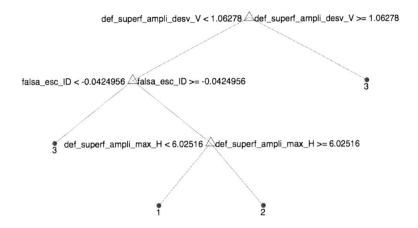

Figure 3. Decision tree corresponding to Input A and Expert 1 output criteria.

Table 6. Confusion matrices for optimal decision tree models for configurations A.1 and A.2

		Predicted grade					
		Expert 1			Expert 2		
		1	2	3	1	2	3
Real grade	1	4	0	0	4	1	2
	2	1	5	0	0	7	4
	3	3	0	57	0	0	52

As for the simulation of Expert 2 criteria, the trees constructed with Input A and Input B (configurations A.2 and B.2) were, again, similar to each other and also to the previous trees, with 2 levels and 4 terminal nodes representing the 3 slate slab grades and, again, with local surface defects as the first decision criterion. Table 6 shows the confusion matrices for the trees corresponding to configurations A.1 and A.2.

The tree corresponding to the PCA-A.1 configuration (Figure 4) was simpler than the previous trees, with 1 level and 3 terminal nodes that did not reflect grade 2. In this case, the first principal component, representing slab squaring, was the first decision criterion. The tree corresponding to the PCA-A.2 configuration (Figure 5) had 2 levels and 6 terminal nodes distributed homogeneously in the different branches. All 3 grades were represented and the first principal component was, again, the first decision criterion. The tree corresponding to the PCA-B.1 configuration was very similar to that corresponding to the PCA-A.1 configuration: it had 1 level and 3 terminal nodes that excluded grade 2 and, again, the first principal component was the first decision criterion. Finally, the tree corresponding to the PCA-B.2 configuration had 3 levels and 3 terminal nodes reflecting the 3 grades and, yet again, the first principal component was the first decision criterion.

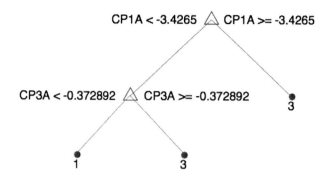

Figure 4. Decision tree corresponding to Input PCA-A and Expert 1 output criteria.

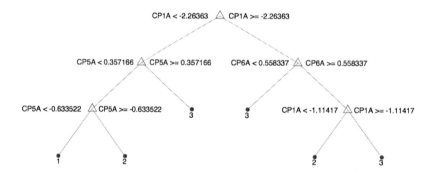

Figure 5. Decision tree corresponding to Input PCA-A and Expert 2 output criteria.

MLP Model Results

Table 7 summarizes the results for the MLP model for the 4 input sets and 2 output criteria described above.

The networks were constructed by dividing the database into 3 sets and implementing a cross-validation process in such a way that all of them were used as training and test sets.

As this was a classification problem, the number of observations in each class limited the number of sets into which the initial database could be divided for model construction purposes: thus, the maximum number of sets that could be defined for this problem was 3 (k-fold = 3, 3-fold).

The predictions were evaluated using the resulting confusion matrices. An average confusion matrix was calculated from the confusion matrices obtained for each of the 3 test sets, with values rounded to the nearest integer. Analogously, the MAE was again the average of the 3 mean absolute errors for each confusion matrix. By way of an example, Table 8 shows the confusion matrices corresponding to Input PCA-A.

Table 7. Error rates and mean absolute error (MAE) rates obtained for the MLP models implemented with the 8 defined configurations

		Output	
		Expert 1	Expert 2
Input	A	Training error rate = 0.143 Test error rate = 0.142 MAE = 0.199 (37 neurons)	Training error rate = 0.256 Test error rate = 0.254 MAE = 0.353 (25 neurons)
	B	Training error rate = 0.143 Test error rate = 0.142 MAE = 0.199 (35 neurons)	Training error rate = 0.181 Test error rate = 0.254 MAE = 0.340 (20 neurons)
	PCA-A	Training error rate = 0.035 Test error rate = 0.156 MAE = 0.186 (2 neurons)	Training error rate = 0.226 Test error rate = 0.254 MAE = 0.353 (10 neurons)
	PCA-B	Training error rate = 0.071 Test error rate =0.171 MAE = 0.257 (4 neurons)	Training error rate = 0.234 Test error rate = 0.254 MAE = 0.353 (22 neurons)

Table 8. Average confusion matrices for the optimal neural networks obtained for configurations PCA-A.1 and PCA-A.2

		Predicted grade					
		Expert 1			Expert 2		
		1	2	3	1	2	3
Real grade	1	0	0	1	0	0	2
	2	0	1	1	0	0	4
	3	0	0	20	0	0	17

SVM MODEL RESULTS

The SVM models were implemented in a similar way to the neural networks, using the 8 different configurations and applying a cross-validation process to the 3 sets. Table 9 summarizes the best results obtained for each configuration.

As with the neural networks, the confusion matrices were averages (with values rounded to the nearest integer) of the confusion matrices obtained for the 3 test sets. The MAE was again the average of the 3 MAEs for each confusion matrix. Example results are shown for the confusion matrices for the SVM models constructed with Input A (Table 10) and Input PCA-B (Table 11).

Table 9. Error rates and mean absolute error (MAE) rates obtained for the SVM models implemented with the 8 defined configurations

		Output	
		Expert 1	Expert 2
Input	A	Training error rate = 0 Test error rate = 0.142 MAE = 0.198 (C = 10, sigma = 10)	Training error rate = 0 Test error rate =0.196 MAE = 0.221 (C = 10, sigma = 10)
	B	Training error rate = 0 Test error rate = 0.142 MAE = 0.199 (C=1, sigma=1000)	Training error rate = 0 Test error rate =0.211 MAE = 0.237 (C = 10, sigma = 10)
	PCA-A	Training error rate = 0 Test error rate = 0.142 MAE = 0.199 (C = 1, sigma = 100)	Training error rate = 0.127 Test error rate =0.224 MAE = 0.265 (C = 1, sigma = 1)
	PCA-B	Training error rate = 0 Test error rate = 0.142 MAE = 0.199 (C = 1, sigma = 10)	Training error rate = 0 Test error rate = 0.254 MAE = 0.353 (C = 1, sigma = 10)

DISCUSSION

From the PCA it can be concluded that the 6 types of defects accurately reflect slab grades, since all 6 were prominently represented in the principal components that explained higher percentages of variance. Those percentages also indicate that the information, in general terms, was widely distributed among all variables.

As for the decision tree models, the same results were obtained for both Input A (basic variables) and Input B (basic and auxiliary variables), which would indicate that the auxiliary variables did not contribute additional useful information for model construction.

Those initial models simulated the criteria of both experts well, with low error rates (5.7% for Expert 1 and 10.0% for Expert 2). The main difference was in the classification errors. Thus, in simulating Expert 1 criteria, there were 4 errors (3 false negatives, 1 neutral error and no false positive), whereas a less desirable situation resulted from the simulation of Expert 2 criteria, with 7 errors (1 neutral error, 6 false positives and no false negative), given the higher comparative number of false positives.

However, looking at the resulting trees, in simulating Expert 1, decision-making was based only on local surface defects and false squaring, whereas in simulating Expert 2, decision-making was based on local surface defects and warping. There was thus a failure to take into account other important defects, such as the presence of carbonates or sulphides, when making predictions.

Table 10. Confusion matrices for the optimal SVM models obtained for configurations A.1 and A.2

		Predicted grade					
		Expert 1			Expert 2		
		1	2	3	1	2	3
Real grade	1	0	0	1	1	1	1
	2	0	1	1	1	2	1
	3	0	1	19	0	2	16

Table 11. Confusion matrices for the optimal SVM models obtained for configurations PCA-B.1 and PCA-B.2

		Predicted grade					
		Expert 1			Expert 2		
		1	2	3	1	2	3
Real grade	1	0	0	1	0	0	2
	2	0	0	2	0	0	4
	3	0	0	20	0	0	17

Analysing the decision tree results together with the PCA inputs, in simulating Expert 1 criteria, insufficient information was fed to ensure that grade 2 was discerned, given that all observations were classified as either grade 1 or 3. Grade 3 was almost always predicted correctly, and in general, accuracy rates were very high for those 4 configurations (PCA-A.1, PCA-A.2, PCA-B.1, PCA-B.2).

The results obtained for the 8 decision tree models were generally similar. The most notable differences were in the type of error, whether false positives, false negatives or neutral errors. Considering false positives to be the least desirable kind of error, and prioritizing the lowest possible error rate, the model constructed with Input A and Expert 1 criteria yielded the best results for this approach.

As for the neural networks, notable was the obvious difficulty in modelling the experts' criteria, and especially that of Expert 2, as evidenced by the errors and confusion matrices. Furthermore, analysing the average confusion matrices, it could be observed that half of the models were incapable of acquiring the necessary knowledge to assign grades 1 and 2, hence all the observations were classified as grade 3.

In the remaining cases, a general tendency to assign grade 3 to observations was again observed, although some grades 1 and 2 were also identified. The model reflecting the PCA-A.1 configuration yielded the best results (the lowest error and MAE rates), although, like the others, it had difficulties assigning grades other than the reject grade.

Finally, the situation for the SVM models was very similar to that of the neural networks. The SVM models had difficulties in learning the experts' criteria for assigning the 3 grades and reproducing the variability of the outputs, tending to classify observations as grade 3 to minimize error. This was especially evident regarding Expert

1, who classified 60 of the 70 slabs as grade 3; consequently, the SVM models constructed to simulate Expert 1 systematically assigned grade 3 to slabs.

The model configured according to Input A.1 seemed to be best at discerning the 3 grades (it had the lowest number classification errors) and was, therefore, the best of the 8 implemented models.

CONCLUSION

This research focused on modelling human expert judgement in evaluating slate slabs for quality and assigning them specific grades (commercial or reject). This evaluation process is currently done manually, with the resulting lack of objectivity and replicability.

The objective of this study was to construct an automatic classification model that was robust and adaptable to the characteristics of a given slate deposit and market and, ultimately, capable of applying objective and reproducible criteria to commercial quality classifications. This model works with data produced by a computer vision system that captures and analyses images of the slabs.

A database was built with the characteristics of the slabs and a classification model was constructed using machine learning techniques, which after an initial training stage, classified slabs according to quality grades on the basis of the analysed images.

Constructing a model for classification according to objective criteria is a complex matter, as highlighted by the evaluations of the 2 human experts in our study, who did not coincide in their grading (whether between the 2 commercial grades or between reject and non-reject grades).

The automated learning models implemented were decision trees, MLP neural networks and SVMs. In the latter 2 cases, there was a generalized tendency to assign the reject grade (the most frequent grade in the sample), which reflects an inability to reproduce the criteria of the experts in terms of differentiating between the 3 possible grades. The decision trees, in contrast, performed well, with low overall error rates and MAEs close to zero.

Image analysis algorithms and classification techniques are applicable to the problem of assigning grades to slate slabs, as indicated by the fact that we were able to successfully identify both the most appropriate variables for inclusion in the vector of slate slab characteristics and the classification technique that best adapts to this kind of problem.

ACKNOWLEDGMENTS

This work was supported by the Spanish Ministry of Education, Culture and Sport (grant number FPU 12/02283).

REFERENCES

[1] González, E; Bianconi, F; Álvarez, MX; Saetta, SA. Automatic characterization of the visual appearance of industrial materials through colour and texture analysis: An overview of methods and applications, *Adv. Opt. Technol.*, (2013), 1–11. doi:10.1155/2013/ 503541.

[2] Karimi, MH; Asemani, D. Surface defect detection in tiling Industries using digital image processing methods: Analysis and evaluation, *ISA Trans.*, 53, (2014), 834–844. doi:10.1016/j.isatra. 2013.11.015.

[3] Ruz, GA; Estevez, PA; Ramirez, PA. Automated visual inspection system for wood defect classification using computational intelligence techniques, *Int. J. Syst. Sci.*, 40, (2009), 163–172. doi:10.1080/00207720802630685.

[4] Bianconi, F; Fernández, A; González, E; Saetta, SA. Performance analysis of colour descriptors for parquet sorting, *Expert Syst. Appl.*, 40, (2013), 1636–1644.

[5] Keser, T; Hocenski, Z; Hocenskp, V. Intelligent machine vision system for automated quality control in ceramic tiles industry, *Strojarstvo.*, 52, (2010).

[6] Smith, ML; Stamp, RJ. Automated inspection of textured ceramic tiles, *Comput. Ind.*, 43, (2000), 73–82. doi:10.1016/S0166-3615(00)00052-X.

[7] Akkoyun, O. An evaluation of image processing methods applied to marble quality classification, in: ICCTD 2010 - 2010 2nd Int. *Conf. Comput. Technol. Dev. Proc.*, 2010, pp. 158–162. doi:10.1109/ICCTD.2010.5646128.

[8] Gökay, MK; Gundogdu, IB. Color identification of some Turkish marbles, *Constr. Build. Mater.*, 22, (2008), 1342–1349. doi:10.1016/j.conbuildmat.2007.04.016.

[9] Bianconi, F; González, E; Fernández, A; Saetta, SA. Automatic classification of granite tiles through colour and texture features, *Expert Syst. Appl.*, 39, (2012), 11212–11218. doi:10.1016/ j.eswa.2012.03.052.

[10] Álvarez, MJ; González, E; Bianconi, F; Armesto, J; Fernández, A. Colour and texture features for image retrieval in granite industry, *DYNA.*, 77, (2010), 121–130.

[11] López, M; Martínez, J; Matías, JM; Taboada, J; Vilán, JA. Functional classification of ornamental stone using machine learning techniques, *J. Comput. Appl. Math.*, 234, (2010), 1338–1345. doi:10.1016/ j.cam.2010.01.054.

[12] Martínez, J; Iglesias, C; Matías, JM; Taboada, J; Araújo, M. Solving the slate tile classification problem using a DAGSVM multiclassification algorithm based on

SVM binary classifiers with a one-versus-all approach, *Appl. Math. Comput.*, 230, (2014), 464–472. doi:10.1016/j.amc.2013.12.087.

[13] Anjos, O; Iglesias, C; Peres, F; Martínez, J; García, Á; Taboada, J. Neural networks applied to discriminate botanical origin of honeys, *Food Chem.*, 175, (2015), 128–136. doi:10.1016/j.foodchem. 2014.11.121.

[14] Bishop, CM. *Pattern Recognition and Machine Learning*, Springer-Verlag New York, New York, 2006.

[15] Quinlan, JR. Induction on decision trees, *Mach. Learn.*, 1, (1986), 81–106.

[16] Quinlan, JR. C4.5: *Programs for machine learning*, Morgan Kaufmann, 1993.

[17] Breiman, L; Friedman, J; Stone, CJ; Olshen, RA. *Classification and regression trees*, Wadsworth Inc., Belmont, 1984.

[18] McCulloch, WS; Pitts, W. A logical calculus of the ideas immanent in nervous activity, *Bull. Math. Biophys.*, 5, (1943), 115–133.

[19] Rosenblatt, F. The perceptron: a probabilistic model for information storage and organization in the brain., *Psychol. Rev.*, 65, (1958), 386–408. doi:10.1037/h0042519.

[20] Bishop, CM. *Neural Networks for Pattern Recognition*, Oxford University Press, New York, 1995.

[21] Stone, M. Cross-validatory choice and assessment of statistical predictions, J. R. Stat. Soc. Ser. *B-Statistical Methodol.*, 36, (1974), 111–133.

[22] Cortes, C; Vapnik, V. Support-vector networks, *Mach. Learn.*, 20, (1995), 273–297. doi:10.1007/BF00994018.

[23] Burges, CJC. A tutorial on support vector machines for pattern recognition, *Data Min. Knowl. Discov.* 2, (1998), 121–167.

[24] Hsu, CW; Lin, CJ. A comparison of methods for multiclass support vector machines, IEEE Trans. *Neural Networks.*, 13, (2002), 415–425. doi:10.1109/72.991427.

[25] Lorena, AC; De Carvalho, ACPLF; Gama, JMP. A review on the combination of binary classifiers in multiclass problems, *Artif. Intell. Rev.*, 30, (2008), 19–37. doi:10.1007/s10462-009-9114-9.

ABOUT THE EDITORS

Lucas A. Jódar Sánchez, PhD

Professor (Full)
Instituto Universitario de Matemática Multidisciplinar,
Universitat Politècnica de València, Spain
Email: ljodar@imm.upv.es

Dr. Lucas A. Jódar Sánchez graduated and earned a doctor in Mathematical Sciences at the University of Valencia in 1978 and 1982, respectively. Since 1991 he has been a full University Professor in Applied Mathematics. He was head of the Department of Applied Mathematics of the Universitat Politècnica de València, from 1992-2002. He is head of the University Institute of Research in Cross-disciplinary Mathematics since its foundation in 2004. He holds five six-year periods of research and has directed 30 doctoral theses. He is co-author of 425 research articles. He has been in charge of competitive research projects since 1988. He just finished to be in charge of the Spanish team within the European Project entitled STRIKE which is based on the use of computational methods in finance. He is editor in several international journals specialised in topics such as Modelling and Numerical Methods.

Elena de la Poza Plaza, PhD

Assistant Professor
Departamento de Economía y Ciencias Sociales,
Universtitat Politècnica de València, Spain

Dr. Elena de la Poza Plaza holds a PhD in Assets Valuation from the UPV. During and after receiving her PhD degree, she spent research periods at the University of North

Carolina, University of Tennessee, University of Padova and University of Panama. She taught courses at Washington State University, but also research workshops at the University of Michigan, Technical University of Ostrava (Czech Republic) and Faculty of Economic Sciences of Warsaw University of Life Sciences, (Poland). Also, she has served as a reviewer for international scientific journals. Her research is focused on modeling individuals and organizations behavior, but also on economic valuation of assets of investment such as real estate, fine arts and healthcare. Currently, Dr. de la Poza takes part as a researcher in several European projects.

Paloma Merello Giménez, PhD
Assistant Professor
Department of Accounting, Universitat de València, Spain

Dr. Paloma Merello Giménez is graduated in Business Administration and has a PhD in Business Administration and PhD in Statistics by the Polytechnic University of Valencia in 2010, 2013 and 2015, respectively. Assistant Professor of Accounting in the University of Valencia since 2015. She is co-author of more than 20 research articles and holds a six-year period of research. She has been member of six competitive research projects since 2010, as well as member of the Organizing Committee of the 40th Congress of the European Accounting Association with more than 1500 attendees and Program committee chair of the 4th International Conference on Higher Education Advances (HEAd'18). Her research interests are the mathematical modeling of economic (Leontief models), social behaviors (such as workaholism or buying compulsion), financial information and accounting, as well as the analysis of physical parameters for the preventive conservation of Cultural Heritage.

Luis Acedo Rodríguez, PhD
Research Assistant
Instituto Universitario de Matemática Multidisciplinar,
Universitat Politècnica de València, Spain

Dr. Luis Acedo Rodríguez received his graduate degree and his PhD in fundamental physics at the University of Extremadura in Badajoz, Spain. He has been visiting scientist at the Universities of Utrecht and Mexico. From 1998 to 2006 he was teaching assistant in Physics and Mathematics at the Universities of Extremadura and Salamanca. His current research interests are interdisciplinary: including mathematical modelling of infectious diseases, epidemiology, networks and gravitational physics. He has published more than 80 refereed journal papers and book chapters and he has been co-organizer of ten international conferences on mathematical modelling as well as being the guest editor of several special issues by internationally-recognized publishers. He has also participated on research projects for the modelization of meningitis propagation and control and research contracts with the pharmaceutical industry.

INDEX

incomes, 26, 28, 153, 166, 167, 169
inflation, 150, 157, 158, 159
inflation targeting, 157, 159
interest rate, 112, 113, 157, 158, 159, 197, 201, 202, 203

J

Japan, 157, 158, 160, 175
job, 1, 2, 5, 6, 7, 8, 9, 10, 11, 53, 81, 83, 212, 236

K

Kahneman, Daniel, 155, 156, 160
kinds of management, 125, 126, 127, 129, 140, 145

L

leadership styles, 41, 43, 44, 45, 51
leases, ix, 105, 106, 107, 108, 109, 115, 118, 120, 121, 122, 123
leisure time, 1, 4, 6, 8
leverage, 105, 107, 118, 119, 121, 129
liabilities, 87, 88, 89, 92, 93, 100, 105, 106, 107, 109, 112, 113, 114, 115, 116, 117, 118, 119, 121, 129, 150
linear regression models, 221
liquidity, 95, 97, 105, 107, 118, 125, 127, 133, 134, 136, 137, 138, 145, 146, 147, 194
liquidity on transactions, 125, 127, 133, 134, 145
listed companies, 105, 106, 115, 116, 128, 146
Lucas, Robert, 156

M

management behaviour, vi, 125, 126, 127, 145
market, v, 26, 37, 46, 78, 87, 88, 91, 92, 94, 95, 98, 101, 122, 128, 129, 133, 139, 141, 145, 146, 152, 154, 156, 159, 164, 165, 166, 167, 168, 169, 174, 182, 193, 194, 196, 197, 207, 258, 259, 268
Marshall, Alfred, 153
method, vi, ix, 3, 29, 30, 31, 62, 69, 70, 78, 82, 83, 88, 106, 109, 113, 114, 115, 116, 121, 156, 163, 164, 167, 168, 169, 174, 193, 195, 197, 198, 199, 201, 203, 205, 207, 209, 250
method of creating organizational culture, 82
microclimate balance, 241

Mill, John Stuart, 153, 161, 164, 165, 167, 170, 171, 172, 173, 174
models, v, ix, 1, 10, 11, 12, 23, 29, 41, 42, 43, 47, 48, 52, 53, 57, 58, 59, 61, 62, 64, 70, 89, 106, 111, 115, 126, 128, 149, 150, 152, 154, 157, 158, 159, 163, 164, 165, 166, 167, 170, 172, 173, 174, 182, 186, 187, 192, 220, 235, 244, 259, 260, 261, 262, 263, 265, 266, 267, 268, 272
monetary policy, vi, ix, 26, 27, 149, 150, 151, 154, 156, 157, 158, 159, 160, 161, 162
monetary-policy rate, 158
multilayer perceptron, 253, 254, 260
multiple linear regression, 3, 246
multiple regression, 7
multivariate regression analysis, 2, 165
Muth, J. F., 156, 159, 161

N

national debt, 87
natural resources, 254
natural sciences, 151, 153
net equity, 172
net result, 163, 172, 173, 174
nominal rigidities, 158
non-parametric tests, 239, 246, 249
number of employees, 139, 141, 172, 174, 180
number of shares, 172
NUTS 2, 24, 29, 32, 33, 34, 35, 36
NUTS 2 regions, 24, 29, 32, 33, 34, 35, 36

O

online influence, vi, 177, 178, 180, 181, 182, 183
operating income, 172
operating leases, vi, 105, 106, 107, 108, 109, 110, 113, 114, 116, 117, 118, 120, 121, 122
optimal management, 125, 127, 134, 138, 139, 140, 141, 145
organizational culture, 69, 70, 71, 74, 75, 76, 77, 78, 79, 81, 82, 83, 84, 85, 86
organizational learning, v, 69, 70, 72, 73, 74, 75, 77, 78, 79, 80, 81, 83, 84, 85, 86
organizational learning processes, 69, 72, 73
outsider(s), 13, 15